Rule-Making Rules

Stefano Bartolini argues that, despite the growth of a large theoretical literature about institutions and institutionalism over the last thirty years, the specific nature of political institutions has been relatively neglected. Political institutions have been subsumed into the broader problems of the emergence, persistence, change and functions of all types of institutions. The author defines political institutions strictly as norms and rules of 'conferral', to be distinguished from norms/rules of 'conduct' and of 'recognition'. They are those norms and rules that empower rulers, set limits to the capacity to ensure behavioural compliance, and define the proper means for achieving such compliance. This book draws logical and empirical consequences from this understanding, to distinguish different types of norms/rules, and to specify the peculiarities of those norms/rules that are 'political'. The book will appeal to researchers of political institutions in comparative politics, and in political science and political sociology more broadly.

Stefano Bartolini is Emeritus Professor, Department of Political and Social Sciences, European University Institute, Florence, Italy. He has previously published several books, including *Identity, Competition, and Electoral Availability* (1990), *The Class Cleavage* (2000), *Restructuring Europe* (2005) and *The Political* (2018).

Rule-Making Rules

An Analytical Framework for Political Institutions

STEFANO BARTOLINI
European University Institute

CAMBRIDGE
UNIVERSITY PRESS

CAMBRIDGE
UNIVERSITY PRESS

University Printing House, Cambridge CB2 8BS, United Kingdom

One Liberty Plaza, 20th Floor, New York, NY 10006, USA

477 Williamstown Road, Port Melbourne, VIC 3207, Australia

314–321, 3rd Floor, Plot 3, Splendor Forum, Jasola District Centre,
New Delhi – 110025, India

103 Penang Road, #05–06/07, Visioncrest Commercial, Singapore 238467

Cambridge University Press is part of the University of Cambridge.

It furthers the University's mission by disseminating knowledge in the pursuit of
education, learning, and research at the highest international levels of excellence.

www.cambridge.org
Information on this title: www.cambridge.org/9781009206273
DOI: 10.1017/9781009206303

© Stefano Bartolini 2022

First published 2022

A catalogue record for this publication is available from the British Library.

ISBN 978-1-009-20627-3 Hardback

To Ginevra and Lapo

"Salomon saith, There is no new thing upon the earth. So that as Plato had an imagination, That all knowledge was but remembrance; so Solomon giveth his sentence, That all novelty is but oblivion."

Francis Bacon, Essays, Civil and Moral, *LVIII*

Contents

Figures

Tables

Acknowledgements

This book was drafted within the pandemic bubble caused by the severe acute respiratory syndrome coronavirus 2 (SARS-CoV-2), the effects of which were particularly profound and lengthy in my country, Italy, from February 2020 to May 2021. As a result of this, no part of this work has been circulated or published before in any form. I owe a special debt of gratitude to Alexander Trechsel, who insisted on inviting me to the University of Lucerne in 2018 to give a talk on the core ideas of this work. He made me tentatively put these ideas down in writing for the first time. I am indebted to the students who endured my last doctoral seminars devoted to the topic in the years 2017–18 and 2018–19 at the European University Institute. The notes that I drew from their seminar papers, comments, criticisms and requests for explanations have helped to clarify and make explicit my thinking on many points. I acknowledge the support of all the colleagues and friends who read the manuscript or parts of it, offering comments and criticisms. Among them, a special mention is due to Anton Hemerijck, Adrienne Heritier, Hanspeter Kriesi, Leonardo Morlino, Johan Olsen, Gianfranco Pasquino and the readers of Cambridge University Press. Finally, once again I thank David Barnes for the final touch of his English editing.

Introduction
Institutions and Political Science

While the term 'institution' means different things to different people, a rather uncontroversial point is that institutions are constraints that operate on the possibilities of human action. In any concrete instance, the existence of institutions means that certain kinds of human conduct are no longer optional but in some sense required and compelling.

Institutions operate indirectly on the individual. They are not direct requests for compliance coming from another actor, and neither are they agreements reached by actors themselves. They do not originate from a personalised other but from an impersonal norm/rule, which is faceless in most cases or for which a face is simply the carrier of the impersonal norm. They are humanmade but dehumanised requests and can usually be evaluated in terms of their universality and duration in time.

In this work, institutions are understood as norms and rules. This lexicographic definition is neither new nor accepted without exceptions. On the one hand, there is no novelty in considering norms and rules to be institutions. On the other hand, many schools and scholars disagree with the perspective of understanding institutions as deontic or normative facts. Sometimes institutions are conceptualised as behavioural regularities, game forms, organisations or broad cultural and moral templates that provide the frame of meaning guiding human action. There are, therefore, *different ways of understanding institutions*.

These different understandings apply to *different types of institutions*. A variety of phenomena live together under the roof of the 'institution' concept: systems of meaning, customs and conventions, social norms, role expectations, administrative standard operating procedures and routines, codified 'private' rules, state regulations, organisations, constitutions and regimes.

Finally, *different types of theories* derive from these different understandings and different types of institutions. Genetic theories are concerned with how institutions come about – through spontaneous and self-evolving adaptation or by intentional design. Functional theories discuss what purpose institutions serve: to foster cooperation, to overcome opportunisms, to improve economic performance and so on. They are often associated with theories of institutional efficiency, understanding institutions as the most suitable answer to specific problems. Other theories discuss how stable institutions are, how they evolve and change, and what they deliver. This book discusses the extent to which different *types of understandings* and different *types of theories* relate to different *types of institutions* and should not be generalised outside their original ambits.

One type of institution is called 'political'. To the extent that political science attributes a theoretical role to the concept of 'institution', which it shares with many other disciplines, it inherits the theoretical and definitional problems that make this concept one of the most controversial of human sciences. Therefore, political science must face these problems sensitively. For this reason, before engaging in a discussion on the particularity of political institutions – the core object of this volume – it is necessary to review the entire semantic field of the term 'institution', to discuss the dimensions of institutional analysis, the different types of institutions and their specific features and problems.

To understand what commonly understood key 'political institutions' are, we may check textbooks and specialised works, which usually provide listings such as human rights, constitutions, state formats, executives, legislatures, judiciaries, election systems, democracy, the rule of law. There is disagreement about missing, redundant or unnecessary items. In perusing the literature further, one encounters additional bedfellows. Party systems, parties, trade unions and more generally interest organisations are often considered political institutions, as are regimes such as 'democracy' and 'presidentialism', cleavages and the standard operating procedures of administrative bureaucracies. The range extends further to include public policies and political economies. The list of 'which' grows and with it grows the complexity, and perplexity too.

Perhaps trying to answer the 'which' question is not the right strategy. Which political institutions exist logically depends on 'what' political institutions are. If we fail to agree on the 'what', we are unlikely to concur on the 'which'. However, analytical elaborations and theoretical definitions of the concept of 'political institutions' are rare and often concise. The compound term 'political institutions' may refer to things that belong to the genus of 'institutions' and at the same time to the species of the political. Contrarywise, political institutions may refer to things that belong to the genus of the political and to the species of institutions. Either way, between 'institutions' and 'the political' there must be an intersection area, which implies that there are institutions that do not belong to the realm of the political and political realities that do not belong to the realm of institutions. The issue is to specify the properties of this intersection area. Whether the 'institutional' or the 'political' element prevails in what we call a 'political institution' is an issue that identifies the constitutive ambiguity of the term and of its analysis, and it is an additional core of this work.

In line with the understanding of all institutions, political institutions are also norms and rules. In particular, political institutions are those norms and rules that empower the rulership, set limits on the monopolistic capacity to produce and distribute behavioural compliance and define the 'proper' means for achieving such compliance. As said, there is no novelty in understanding institutions as normative facts. The point is to draw all the logical and empirical consequences from this understanding, to distinguish clearly among different types of norms/rules and to specify the particularities of those norms/rules that we define as 'political'.

This work reviews contributions from neighbouring disciplines and in particular from sociology and economics. Its aim, however, is to offer an analytical underpinning and a more solid theoretical background to that tradition of political institution studies which is autochthonous to the discipline of politics. This rests on the works of scholars such as Carl Friedrich, Ferdinand Hermens, Herman and Samuel Finer, Juan Linz, Maurice Duverger, Giovanni Sartori, Arend Lijphart, Matthew Shugart, John Carey and the many others in the tradition that Guy Peters has defined with the label 'empirical institutionalism'.[1] These scholars are usually not included in neo-institutionalist approaches, which criticise them for being excessively descriptive, too legalistic and insufficiently theoretical.

The criticism is probably deserved. Empirical institutionalists have been busy with political institutions since Aristotle's comparative

---

[1]   Peters, B. G. (1999), *Institutional Theory in Political Science: The 'New Institutionalism'*, London, Pinter.

analysis of Greek city-state constitutions. Concerned with the analysis of concrete historical political institutions, this tradition has participated less intensely in the new theoretical effervescence of the field, and this is witnessed by the paucity of contributions explicitly addressing the particular nature of political institutions. While not entirely without theoretical thickness, their conceptual elaboration of institutions has been less abstract and more limited to geo-historical environments than those elaborated by organisational sociology and the rationalistic tradition deriving from neo-institutional economics.

However, rather than filling this gap and theoretical lag in empirical institutionalist research, recent analyses tend to swallow political institutions in the mushrooming debates about neo-institutionalisms deeply influenced by the neighbouring disciplines of organisational sociology and institutional economics. Inevitably, the latter pay less attention to the particularities of political institutions and their specificity has remained somewhat in the shade. Moreover, the attenuated reference to the descriptive-legalistic definition of political institutions in these more abstract approaches makes an analytical discussion of the concept more impelling.

My impression is that at the theoretical level 'political institutions' have been phagocytised into the broader problems of the emergence, persistence, change and functions of all types of institutions, from cultural templates to customs and conventions, from social norms to administrative cultures and role expectations, and from property rights to organisational forms. The mixing of all sorts of institutions together and the difficulty in clearly distinguishing 'political institutions' from other kinds of institutions has attributed to them problems that do not pertain to them and resulted in a failure to discuss problems that are typically their own.

Political institutions are currently seen in very different lights. In one version, they are assimilated to institutions that dispense criteria for appropriate conduct and attributions of meanings. In a different perspective, they are analysed as bulwarks of individual rights and protection from government in a theoretical framework that refers to modern liberal democracies and their defence of liberties. An additional image sees political institutions as regulators of individuals' and groups' egotistic drives in view of achieving self-enforcing equilibria that foster cooperation and help to overcome social dilemmas. In yet another framework, they are identified with the organisational forms of political society. In this light, they are often viewed as forms of organisational symbolism, as ritual and ceremonial components that outweigh other dimensions to the point of subsuming any other type of institutional return. Finally, they are regarded as forms of government, as instruments of sharing or concentrating the coercive power of the political. These different views probably ask too much of political institutions. It is likely that such widely diverging frameworks result from the application of the properties of other kinds of institutions to political institutions.

Amalgamating different types of institutions and stretching the concept of political institutions leave us with a blurred concept of institution. It is difficult to advance generalisations, be they behavioural or functional, about the nature, generation, change, functions, efficiency and effects of institutions that range from funeral conventions to Chinese lotus feet to institutional regimes. It is hard to develop theories for institutions created by autonomous interacting actors as opposed to institutions extended beyond their life, self-sustaining institutions, externally enforced institutions, institutions inherited and marginally changeable, and institutions devised by other institutions. Encompassing definitions make it even harder to define what an institution is and is not. This wealth of approaches, understandings and types of institutions leaves an impression of disorder pervading the field that looks like a jumble of poorly connected concepts. The point is that, in the absence of an analytical treatment of the core concept, general definitions and theories lack denotation; that is, they poorly identify the objects and phenomena to which they specifically apply and those to which they do not.

The risk exists that the appeal of pan-institutionalist paradigms rests on an excessive conceptual stretching and a corresponding vagueness and ambiguity. If so, pan-institutionalism could face the same fate as previous approaches, such as the group, functionalist, structural and system approach. Their conceptual stretching prompted a success and a spreading that covered too broad a variety of objects and phenomena. Eventually, they began to fade away and left room for rediscoveries and returns. In political science we cannot afford for the concept of 'political institution' to risk such a fate.

There is a need for analytical clarification of the semantic field, distinguishing different types of institutions, different dimensions of each type of institution and related different mechanisms of generation and change. This is what this book is about. It tries to set political institutions aside from other kinds of social, administrative and economic institutions. It focusses on the particularities of political institutions, arguing that they deserve special treatment rather than assimilation. The book has, therefore, a primary analytical goal. I try to provide a general analytical framework to systematise different theories, to check their logical consistency and completeness and to offer a few insights of my own on how the field can be reconceptualised. The level of disagreement about the terminology and taxonomy of the institutional forms proposed here should be compensated by the advantages of specifying which institutions can be explained better by which approach and which problems are typical of certain institutions but not of others. The result will doubtless be controversial and contested, yet I do believe that a step in the direction outlined in this volume is helpful if it opens a reflection necessary to order the wealth of research.

As I have argued above, to face the particularity of 'institutions' that are labelled 'political', one needs to clarify the field of the institutional and to combine it with the field of the political. For this reason, the book unfolds in two parts. Part I includes three chapters dealing with institutions in general. Chapter 1 discusses the available evidence on the origin of institutions understood as norms and rules that have ordered the cooperative life of our pre-human ancestors and of humans. Chapter 2 deals with the way in which social sciences have interpreted the nature of this accumulated normative endowment that characterised the living together of our ancestors and *Homo sapiens* and probably decided our success. Chapter 3 derives from this review a number of dimensions essential for institutional analysis, discusses a typology of institutions based on these dimensions and elaborates on the crucial distinction between 'norms' and 'rules'.

Part II is devoted to 'political institutions' and their specificity. It includes four chapters. Chapter 4 proposes a precise definition of the nature of political institutions. Chapter 5 introduces the concept of 'political institutes' as clusters of micro-rules and norms that preside over the solution to a functional political problem. Chapter 6 analyses the macro-political institutions of territories, constitutions and regimes seen as specific combinations of political institutes. Finally, Chapter 7 reviews the specificities of political institutions and what sets them apart from other types of social or economic institutions. The contents of each chapter and their connections are more extensively discussed at the introductions to the two Parts.

In approaching a topic as vast as that of institutions and political institutions, spanning through the disciplines of history, economics, law, sociology and political science, I am bound to specify the boundaries I impose on myself in this endeavour. What the book is *not* about can be defined in two points. First, this book does not deal with specific historical political institutions, and the concrete examples discussed in the text are illustrative of the analytical points. Second, this study is not normative either, and does not engage in an axiological evaluation of different institutional designs, or in institutional engineering discussions. It is a book best described as an analytical political theory of institutions. However, the analytical clarification is foundational for any precise analysis of the impact of concrete institutions and for any normative evaluation of them.

PART I

On Institutions

Before engaging in a discussion of the particularity of political institutions – the core object of this volume – it is necessary to clarify the semantic field of the term 'institution'. This requires, first of all, dealing with the origin of normative orientations, the institutional phenomenology understood as the normative endowment of humankind. In the times of Hobbes, Locke, Montesquieu and Rousseau, political philosophers resorted to a thought experiment or philosophical fiction describing humans at a time when none of these normative orientations existed, before society and government of any sort: the state of nature. From this, rationalistic accounts were constructed of how organised social and political life could develop. This tradition survives in contemporary rationalistic approaches to the emergence of institutions. It sees normative endowment as resulting from repeated interactions among independent, autonomous and cognitively developed humans struggling to overcome an innate difficulty in cooperating. Special conditions then allow them to establish norms and rules through agreements that they hope not to regret at a later stage.

In the past, the philosophical fiction of the state of nature permitted bridging the ignorance of the time. It rested on the idea that the universe of life forms was 'created' and existed by divine action and was not the result of long-term biological and social evolution. It leaned on the unawareness that humans were only a recent offspring of long-evolving primates, of the family *Homininae*, of the genus *Homo* and of the species *sapiens*. A hundred and fifty years of evolutionary science research have filled the knowledge gap, clarifying that the *sapiens* were not the first and were not alone in developing normative orientations. We owe a lot to our ancestors, and we share a lot with them.

In Chapter 1 I discuss the available evidence in evolutionary biology, psychology, palaeontology, anthropology and neuroscience on the origins of *Homo sapiens*' normative orientations. I review plausible interpretations of the evolutionary emergence of these normative orientations in the histories of humankind and of its predecessors. This normative endowment was probably our best-fitting quality, explaining our capacity to emerge as the most effective predator on Earth. It is likely that, without a long-evolved disposition to cooperation, humans would never have achieved a stage of civilisation in which it is possible to ask the question of how cooperation is possible. The chapter also reviews the evidence on whether early political institutions derived from preceding different types of institutions or co-evolved with them.

The next step is to review the way in which social sciences have interpreted the nature of this accumulated normative patrimony that characterised our ancestors and *Homo sapiens* living together and probably decided our success. Chapter 2 deals with this. There is no paucity of definitions of the concept of 'institution', and often they are somewhat over-encompassing. The chapter discusses several approaches and elaborates on the implications of each. The conclusion is that what constitutes an institution is not generalisable and depends largely on the researcher, the object of research and the research question. Different conceptions of institution serve vastly different research programmes and different types of situations. However, too often, different approaches extend their specific understandings of institution to the whole world of institutions, presenting themselves as general theories of institution. This generates inconsistencies when the approach and its theoretical results are applied outside the original scope and extended to the entire universe of institutions. Discussion of the different approaches helps to identify the core properties each highlights and to reconstruct the semantic field of the concept of institution. I focus on the main characterising elements of different understandings.

Chapter 3 first discusses separately and in an analytical way the main properties of the institutions identified by the different approaches reviewed in Chapter 2. The property space of the term 'institution' is unpacked in the following set of analytical properties: stability, normativity, sanctionability, enforcement, layering, intentionality, endogeneity and efficiency. In the second part of the chapter, I propose a typology of different institutions based on the values these properties have. This exercise allows inherent and constitutive difficulties in institutional analysis to emerge. It is necessary to take a clear stand on these problems and to try to disentangle the definitional maze. The chapter concludes by discussing the fundamental difference between 'norms' and 'rules' and suggests a line along which this can be established.

1 | *The Origins of Institutions*

'During entire aeons a man's lot was identical with that of the group, of the tribe he belonged to and outside of which he could not survive. The tribe, for its part, was able to survive and defend itself only through its cohesion. Whence the extreme force of the inward coercion exerted by the rules that organised and guaranteed such cohesion.'[1] In this chapter I synthesise evidence from all the evolutionary sciences into a plausible interpretation of the evolutionary emergence of this force of cohesion in the histories of humankind and its predecessors.

The origin of institutions is lost in the mists of time. From the beginning of the genus *Homo*, about 2.5 million years ago, until about 3,000 years BCE, the normative patrimony was made up of orally transmitted norms. We have few insights into how the very early systems of elementary norms began to be articulated into complex and interconnected institutions, and there is limited archaeological and anthropological evidence of this process. Undoubtedly, symbolic thinking and feelings about sanctified places, prophecies and ethics relating humanity to supernatural, transcendental or spiritual elements played an important early role. By the time our ancestors painted the Cave of Altamira (in modern Cantabria) about 13–18,000 years ago, their world vision was already dominated by symbols and related norms. The mysterious circular and T-shaped anthropomorphic pillars of Gobekli Tepe, built between 10,000 and 11,600 years ago in the core area of the Fertile Crescent near the city of Urfa (perhaps the Ur of Genesis?), the most ancient monumental architecture in the history of humankind, were a site of worship for the hunter-gatherer. They required more than 100 years and enormous resources to be built and point to a symbolic patrimony, temples, figures and sophisticated set of

---

[1] Monod, J. (1971), *Chance and Necessity: An Essay on the Natural Philosophy of Modern Biology*, New York, Alfred A. Knopf, p. 166.

norms.[2] When humans began to domesticate cereals and cattle in the Fertile Crescent about 6–7,000 years BCE, the normative dimension of their social life complexified in connection with the new demands of sedentary life and the organisational problems of agriculture and breeding. When recorded history emerged thanks to the invention of writing around the fourth millennium BCE, we find a world densely populated by a variety of institutions, most of which were taken for granted.

Since then, we have evidence of the early attempts at codification of this accumulated normative world, mostly in Mesopotamia and Asia Minor.[3] Some of the collections achieved a wide audience throughout Mesopotamia for centuries; others were scribal exercises limited to a local school centre. The best known of these codes are, in chronological order, the Code of Urukagina (2380–2360 BCE); the Sumerian Code of Ur-Nammu (c.2100–2050 BCE); the Babylonian Code of Hammurabi (c.1760 BCE); the Laws of Eshnunna (c.1930 BCE); the Code of the Nesilim (c.1650–1500 BCE); the Law of Moses (fourteenth century BCE); the Assyrian Laws (c.1075 BCE); the Draconian Constitution (seventh century BCE); the Twelve Tables of Roman Law (450 BCE); the Edicts of Ashoka of Buddhist law (269–236 BCE); and the Law of Manu (c.200 BCE).[4] Greek civilisation, which was so crucial for the Western cultural tradition, codified less than expected, and its norms, most often ritual, emanate from many different sources.[5] Next to these ancient codified rules we find textually encoded norms that derive from various sources: sacred books, handbooks of rules and regulations, foundations of organisations (for

---

[2] Gobekli Tepe was discovered and excavated at the beginning of the 1960s. Attendance at these edifices ended about 10,000 years ago with their voluntary burial, as if the actors had decided to conclude a specific experience. See Schmidt, K. (2006), *Sie bauten die ersten Tempel. Das rätselhafte Heiligtum der Steinzeitjäger*, Munich, C. H. Beck.

[3] Roth, M. T. (1995), *Law Collection from Mesopotamia and Asia Minor*, Atlanta, GA, Scholar Press. The law collections in this volume are compilations varying in legal and literary sophistication recorded by scribes in the schools and royal centres of ancient Mesopotamia and Asia Minor from the end of the third millennium to the middle of the first millennium BCE.

[4] These are the most important and best known. The list is incomplete.

[5] A large project aims to collect all Greek norms: The Collection of Greek Ritual Norms (CGRN) project, directed by Vinciane Pirenne-Delforge. See Carbon, J.-M., S. Peels and V. Pirenne-Delforge (2018), *Collection of Greek Ritual Norms*, 2 vols, Paris, Editions de Boccard.

instance, bureaucracies) and rules for applying technologies in a given setting.

These ancient rules have common features. They share a religious origin, Deuteronomy being the most conspicuous example;[6] they encourage people to sacrifice their selfish interests for the good of the broader group; and they share a rather universal moral grammar, prohibiting inflicting costs on the innocent, taking more than a fair share of resources and contributing less than other members of the group. They all include rules of conduct (how to organise a sacrifice or the prohibition of marriages between women and their stepsons), together with definitions of the roles and authorities in charge of defending, implementing and interpreting these norms/rules. In this early production, we already find the problem of a divergence between written and often codified rules and less formal norms. In short, they already address the whole problem of institutional analysis.

There is also limited knowledge of the origins of political institutions. We know little about how the centralised Egyptian pharaonic political structure evolved from what previous arrangements and through which means; how the passage from loose structures among allied tribes, gens, lines of descent – the Jewish tribes, the Greek *oikos*, the Roman gens or similar – slowly evolved into centralised kingdoms. The vast empire that the Mexica discovered in the fourteenth century in the valley of the city of Teotihuacán was constituted at the beginning of the Common Era and rapidly collapsed five centuries later. This civilisation is rich in archaeological remains, but without a name, without writing and without history. Archaeologists debate whether its political institutions were those of a powerful and centralised monarchical state or those of a mercantile decentralised structure based on shifting alliances among prominent trading families.[7]

[6] Mille, P. D. (2011, reprint), *Deuteronomy*, Westminster, John Knox Press.
[7] For the thesis of a mercantile decentralised political structure, see Sugiyama, S. (2005), *Human Sacrifice, Militarism and Rulership: Materialization of State Ideology at the Feathered Serpent Pyramid, Teotihuacan*, Cambridge, Cambridge University Press. For the powerful kingdom thesis, see Manzanilla, L. R. (2009), 'Corporate life in apartment and barrio compounds at Teotihuacan, central Mexico', in Manzanilla, L. R. and C. Chapdelaine (eds.), *Domestic Life in Prehispanic Capitals: A Study of Specialization, Hierarchy, and Ethnicity*, Ann Arbor, University of Michigan Museum of Anthropology, pp. 21–42.

In short, even leaving aside our ancestor hominids,[8] the genus *Homo* has accumulated 2.5 million years of 'norms' and only a few millennia of (partial) 'rules'. Therefore, to discuss the origins of early institutions, we need to chart the indirect evidence that archaeology, evolutionary paleoethology, anthropology, psychology, and neuro and brain sciences offer us.

1.1 Hunting and Early Normative Orientation

The *Homo* and chimpanzee evolutionary lines separated between 7 and 8 million years ago, the exact date being the subject of debate.[9] About 3 million years ago the vast forests in which our ancestors could easily find fruit, leaves and other vegetables began to recede, leaving room for open grasslands. In these, finding food became difficult and risky, and hominids had to adapt. One line (the robust australopithecines) adapted by developing massive jaws and teeth suited to grinding herbs and other hard foods. The line which was to be our own followed a different path about 2.6 million years ago: it enlarged its diet from an exclusively vegetarian one to one using animal fats and proteins. For a long time both approaches seemed valid adaptations, but about 1 million years ago the australopithecines became extinct. Scientists have no agreed explanation for this extinction. It seems, nevertheless, that the solution of searching for sustenance in other animals provided an advantage.

Paleo-anthropological research shows that several species of hominids lived on Earth at the same time over the last 4 million years. Even our recent history of the last 100,000 years is characterised by this co-evolution of several *Homo* species: the Neanderthals, the Denisovans, the Floresiensis and the Erectus (or Ergaster), the first species to leave Africa and populate South East Asia and Europe.

Progress in hunting depended on key elements in our evolution. Several physical transformations distinguishing us from our nearest

---

[8] The use of the term 'hominid' has varied over time. The original meaning referred only to humans (*Homo*) and their closest extinct relatives. This restrictive meaning is now indicated by the term 'hominin', which comprises all members of the human clade after the split from the chimpanzees.

[9] The most recent research tends to locate the separation at 10–12 million years ago. See Katoh, S. et al. (2016), 'New geological and paleontological age constraint for the gorilla–human lineage split', *Nature*, 530: 215–18, doi: 10.1038/nature16510.

great ape relatives – the capacity to run long distances, an extra-large brain, arms suited to throwing objects long distances because of the flexibility of the shoulder joint – developed as a function of our specialisation as hunters. They also possibly influenced the emergence of material culture in the form of primitive stone tools about 2.4–2.6 million years ago before the emergence of the genus *Homo*. These hominids preyed rather than eating abandoned carcasses or stealing prey from other carnivores.[10] Their type of hunting targeted big mammals by stalking and waiting for them in appropriate places where they were expected to rally.[11] For about 2 million years, hunting dominated the life of the genus *Homo*.[12]

The impact of the shift to a carnivorous diet can hardly be underestimated. Better food quality implied brain accretion, which in turn fostered new techniques for hunting, further generating better food quality and brain growth. Between 200,000 and 2 million years ago, the *Homo* brain grew from the average 600 cubic centimetres of the first *Homo* to the average 1,300 cubic centimetres of *Homo sapiens*. The explanation for the rapid development of the brain preferred by evolutionary psychologists – detected in at least three independent offspring lines of *Homo*: the *neanderthalensis* in Europe, the *erectus* in Asia and the *sapiens* in Africa – takes the name 'gene–culture co-evolution'. It involves strong positive feedback between innovations in the spheres of biology and culture: a bigger brain, more intelligence, better tools and better adaptation to the environment.

With the growing size of the brain and the need to feed a larger population, hominids began to develop strategies for capturing their prey, and these hunting circumstances exercised a strong selective

---

[10] I rely on Ferraro, J. V. et al. (2013), 'Earliest archaeological evidence of persistent hominin carnivory', *PLoS ONE*, 8, 4: article N.162164; Bunn, H. T. and A. N. Gurtov (2014), 'Prey mortality profiles indicate that early Pleistocene Homo at Olduvai was an ambush predator', *Quaternary International*, 322/323, 16: February; Wong, K. (2014), 'L'ascesa del predatore umano', *Le Scienze*, 554: 54–9.

[11] See Lee, R. B., I. DeVore, L. Sherwood Washburn and C. S. Lancaster (1968), 'The evolution of hunting', in Lee, R. B. and DeVore, I. (eds.), *Man the Hunter*, New York, Aldine Publishing Company, ch. 32.

[12] The controversial book by Ardrey, R. (1976), *The Hunting Hypothesis*, London, William Collins Sons & Co., popularised the impact of hunting on human development. The controversy was not about the importance of the hunting step but the author's deductions deriving from it on violence and human nature.

pressure towards cooperation. Any component of a group of hunters unable to work in a team on complex hunting strategies would be excluded from subsequent hunting expeditions and would face a bleak future. Being side-tracked by the individual search for a rabbit, rather than the collective effort to hunt a mammoth, was very risky.

Venatorial life not only requires a division of labour, but it is also made possible by the use of weapons and is completely different from hunting by other mammals. Hunting voluminous prey and storing and sharing the resulting supply of meat led to a growing social organisation and division of labour. From the beginning, females gathered and males hunted. Food was then shared not only among relatives but also among unrelated members of the same group.[13] Everybody helped everybody else. Mothers helped each other to find food and to raise their children; fathers helped each other to hunt, to build shelter, to defend resources and so on.[14] This cooperation required cognitive skills. To cooperate effectively, it is necessary to guess what another person is thinking, to communicate with some language, to reason, to suppress your own immediate needs, to plan activities and to limit in-group aggressiveness. Internal conflicts must be resolved before a band of hunters gets underway. From this arose attention to equality and reciprocity. 'In the very collaborative world of the hunter-gatherer, to refuse to share and a lack of propensity to cooperate could make the difference between life and death.'[15]

Experimental research has revealed the special human capacity to engage with others to achieve or attain a common goal through a 'shared intentionality'.[16] Mutual understanding of what was needed to reach a result set the basis for the beginning of social interactions and a culture based on cooperation. The development of cognitive skills permitted the use of new practices of hunting, fishing and harvesting plants that transformed into *social conventions*. A system of social

[13] Stiner, M. C. et al. (2009), 'Cooperative hunting and meat sharing 400–200 kya at Qesem Cave, Israel', *Proceedings of the Natural Academy of Sciences*, 106, 32: 13207–12.

[14] Schipman, P. (2014), 'How do you kill 86 mammoths?', *Quaternary International*, 30: 1–9.

[15] Lieberman, D. E. (2014), *The Story of the Human Body: Evolution, Health and Diseases*, London, Penguin, p.85.

[16] Tomasello, M. (2014), *A Natural History of Human Thinking*, Cambridge, MA, Harvard University Press.

norms requires everyone to be aware of the values shared by the group, of the group mentality. Social norms then led to moral principles, which eventually constituted the foundations of an institutional structure for respect for the group's norms of coexistence.

Hunting was also related to other crucial developments. The key innovation of non-seasonal sexual receptivity of females is probably linked to the bipolarity resulting from the division of labour concerning hunting. The male role of caterer, the bipolar society partially segregated from the sexual point of view and the female role of defender of the home area are unknown to vegetarian primates. A monogamic tendency and extended social ties were further elements in our development. Scientists do not agree on when humans became monogamic, but three factors are considered crucial: (1) spatial separation, with females making it difficult for males to find and keep a mate; (2) threats to the life of children, requiring double protection; and (3) the role of the male and his contribution to parental care.[17]

In particular, the cost of raising children was so high that it eventually required a collective effort including parents but also allogeneic parenting. A *Homo erectus* female needed 3,000–4,500 calories a day during nursing and post-weaning. The exorbitant quantity of 12 million calories is necessary for a child to become an adult – twice as many as are needed by chimpanzees. No child could survive in the absence of high levels of investment and patience among the adults of the group.[18] The quantity of time and energy that females and males needed to invest in their offspring had important consequences for the social behaviour of our species. This style of allogeneic parenting required cognitive capacities for cooperation and communication, altruism and reciprocity. The couple helped to develop social ties and family ties from both parents, widening family links and bonds across generations. *Homos* became hyper-social primates, embedded in community networks, with isolation and a lack of social support being crucial risk factors.[19] In short, about 1.5 million years ago the capacity

---

[17] Chapais, B. (2013), 'Monogamy, strongly bonded groups and the evolution of human social structure', *Evolutionary Anthropology*, 22: 52–65.

[18] I draw the information in this section from Lieberman, *The Story of the Human Body*, pp. 62, 64–5, 86, 93, 111.

[19] Smith, H. J. (2005), *Parenting for Primates*, Cambridge, MA, Harvard University Press; Kappeler, P. M. and J. Silk (eds.) (2010), *Mind the Gap: Tracing the Origins of Human Universals*, Frankfurt, Springer.

to carry food in the hand, feeding in a biped posture, the concealment of external signals of female ovulation and the creation of couple bonds brought about family bonds that extended to the relatives of both parents and an expansion of the social circle.[20]

Even the special value attached to territory as a 'defended area' could be related to hunting at a time in which territory became scarce and the various groups came into more frequent and closer contact. From the evolutionary point of view, it is logical that if the territory has a survival value, then one will be territorial; otherwise not. In our passage from forest to savannah, the need for an exclusive hunting territory may have increased, although, given the immensity of the early African spaces, social groups rarely came into contact. Mutual avoidance was perhaps enough. In any case, territoriality always involves the same features: isolation in a private reservation, intolerance of neighbours, attention to boundaries and resistance to invasion. Perhaps *Homo* is a territorial genus, but it is not proven that territoriality is genetically embedded.[21]

Some of these cooperative behaviours are also typical of other non-kinship-linked primates.[22] They are based on reciprocity and motivated by 'empathy', a feature of all mammals that implies that we identify with others in moments of pain or need.[23] Primates, and particularly great apes, help each other even in cases of significant losses (e.g. they adopt orphans and defend mates from leopards). These tendencies probably evolved starting with the maternal care required for all mammals and were later enlarged to other relationships. However, the behavioural combination of eating meat, sharing and cooperating with strangers, fabricating instruments and preparing food is specific to hominids and *Homos*. The way in which hominid communities allow foreigners to cross their territory, share food, exchange goods and gifts, and coalesce against a common enemy is an uncommon behaviour among other primates. Hominids were able to establish complex hierarchical structures for the realisation of

---

[20] Lovejoy, C. O. (2009), 'Reexamining human origins in light of *Ardipithecus ramidus*', *Science*, 326: 74–8.

[21] Wilson defines territoriality as a set of behaviours evolved independently (and occasionally lost and evolved again) during relatively short evolutionary periods to meet specific environmental needs; Wilson, H. E. O. (1975), *Sociobiology*, Cambridge, MA, Harvard University Press.

[22] De Waal, F. (2005), *Our Inner Ape*, New York, Penguin Books.

[23] This thesis is argued in De Waal, F. (2010), *The Age of Empathy: Nature's Lessons for a Kinder Society*, Portland, OR, Broadway Books.

projects, while cooperation among most animals does not seem to be coordinated from above but is auto-organised.

1.2 *Homo sapiens* and Symbolic Cognition

The roots of our species, *Homo sapiens*, can be traced back to Africa between 200,000 and 300,000 years ago. A subgroup of *Homo sapiens* dispersed outside Africa between 80,000 and 100,000 years ago. Modern humans appeared for the first time in the Middle East, Europe, Asia, New Guinea and Australia between 40,000 and 80,000 years ago. Archaeological evidence suggests that we managed to cross the Bering Strait and began to colonise the Americas between 15,000 and 30,000 years ago.[24] *Sapiens* hunter-gatherers lived in small groups, possibly twenty-five to fifty people, seven to eight families, in areas of approximately 250–500 square kilometres. It is estimated that our brains evolved to deal with about 100–130 people, about the number that a typical hunter-gatherer would have encountered in their life. Given their small size, these groups must have been strongly egalitarian. The sharing and exchange of food was 'a daily activity fully institutionalised'.[25]

In about 170,000 years, *Homo sapiens* evolved in Africa and colonised all parts of the world with the exclusion of Antarctica. Wherever *Homo sapiens* diffused, all other archaic *Homos* disappeared: the Neanderthals, the Denisovans, the hobbits of Flores and the many descendants of *Homo erectus*. Ours is the only human species that survived on the planet. Notwithstanding our slowness, physical weakness and absence of the formidable teeth and claws of other carnivores, humans have brought to extinction all other big predators and have been the most effective and lethal predators on Earth for a long time. Our special ability to cooperate is the only credible answer to how this was possible. We were too small and vulnerable to dominate. The scientific evidence so far accumulated

---

[24] Oppenheimer, S. (2003), *The Real Eve*, New York, Carroll & Graft, pp. 70–1. This is a study of migration based on the world distribution of mitochondrial DNA. The predominant trip direction was from the Horn of Africa through the Yemen Strait to the Arabian coast and then to India and Indonesia. This migration took about 10,000 years.

[25] Tharakan, G. (2007), 'The Maduga and Kurumba of Kerala, South India, and the social organisation of the hunting and gathering', *Journal of Ecological Anthropology*, 11: 12–13.

suggests that *sapiens* developed with a mixed set of predispositions. These included a natural egoism that presided over individual survival combined with a necessary and evolutionarily fitting tendency to in-group cooperation and aggressive predispositions in out-group relationships.

A capacity for *symbolic cognition* developed quite late, no more than 100,000 years ago. The first objects which are clearly symbolic were discovered in South Africa and date to 77,000 years ago. About 50,000 years ago the *Homo sapiens* of the Upper Palaeolithic engaged in making bone tools, fishing tools, flutes and so on, building more complex settlements and developing manufactured goods that did not have a direct practical use and that we may define as artistic or symbolic. This represented a turning point in the invention of culture; that is, in the capacity and inclination to innovate through 'culture'.

Cultural creativity is a force which is stronger, more exuberant and faster than biological evolution. In the last 600 generations at most, *Homo sapiens* invented agriculture, sheep farming, writing, the city, inanimate energy sources, antibiotics, computers and the Internet. In this period, human genetic endowment has not changed.[26] The scope of cultural evolution has become incommensurable with that of biological evolution. A unique advantage has resulted from the acquisition of an exclusively human characteristic, the highest symbolic activity: language. Unfortunately, there is no source of evidence that can help to identify this crucial passage, but evolutionary biologists are sceptical about the claim that syntactic knowledge is transmitted in the human genome.[27] Although natural selection never stops, in the last millennia it had only local and limited effects on human biology. Undoubtedly, cultural developments have helped human beings to go beyond the slow pace of natural selection.

[26] Tomasello, *A Natural History of Human Thinking*, p. 168.
[27] There is ongoing debate over whether our ability to use language was an evolutionary process and the skill is passed down genetically or, on the contrary, it is a cultural achievement entirely due to learning on the basis of general but not language-specific skills. See Tomasello, M. (2003), *Constructing a Language: A Usage-Based Theory of Language Acquisition*, Cambridge, MA, Harvard University Press. Another hotly debated issue is whether the biological contribution includes capacities specific to language acquisition, referred to as universal grammar, as Noam Chomsky has argued: Chomsky, N. (1965), *Aspects of the Theory of Syntax*, Boston, MA, MIT Press.

1.3 Agriculture

Hunting and gathering subsistence, small populations and dispersed resources meant that relatively few people could be aggregated together in any time and place. The improvement of the climate at the onset of the Holocene was followed by the beginning of plant-intensive resource exploitation, and increasing agricultural subsistence meant a rising population.[28] About 12,000 years ago, some groups of individuals began to establish standing communities. In the course of a few millennia, villages developed from small boroughs of a few houses in the Natufian to Neolithic villages with fifty houses to become, about 7,000 years ago, villages with 1,000 inhabitants or more. Five thousand years ago, some villages exploded into true cities such as Ur and Nohenjo with tens of thousands of inhabitants. Why this happened is not clear. Perhaps climate change and an increasing population made gathering and hunting difficult. There is no comprehensive and agreed explanation for why these developments were so late, so rapid, so decisive and so irreversible.

The area in which cereals and livestock were first domesticated in the Neolithic is a region in south-east Turkey between the upper courses of the rivers Tigris and Euphrates, in the central area of the Fertile Crescent. The slopes of the Karaka Dag offered fields of wild Gramineae and an abundant fauna. The domestication of einkorn wheat (*Tricum monococcum*) was probably the first, about 10,000 years ago.[29] Then sheep, goats, pigs and at least one of the four genetic lines of the current cattle were domesticated.[30] The 'Neolithic

---

[28] Richieston, P. J. and R. Boyd (2001), *Institutional Evolution in the Holocene: The Rise of Complex Societies*, in Runciman, W. G. (ed.), *The Origins of Human Social Institutions*, Proceedings of The British Academy, New York, Oxford University Press, pp. 198–234, 216.

[29] This result was achieved by genotyping the DNA of a group of wild diploid einkorn wheats. Durum wheat and spelt come from the same region. Abbo, S. et al. (2006), 'The ripples of "The Big (Agricultural) Bang": the spread of the early wheat cultivation', *Genome*, 49: 861–3; Salamini, F. et al. (2002), 'Genetics and geography of wild cereals domestication in the Near East', *Nature Reviews Genetics*, 3: 429–41; Bar, Y. O. (2002), *The Natufian Culture and the Early Neolithic: Social and Economic Trends in Southwest Asia*, in Bellwood, P. and C. Renfrew (eds.), *Examining the Farming/Language Dispersal Hypothesis*, Cambridge, McDonald Institute for Archeological Research, pp. 113–26.

[30] Zeder, M. A. (2007), 'The neolithic macro (re)evolution: macroevolutionary theory and the study of culture change', *Journal of Archeological Research*, 17: 611–63.

revolution'[31] affected agriculture, a sedentary lifestyle, social stratification generated by an agricultural food surplus from which oppression and slavery perhaps emerged, and the development of civilian and priestly rituals. In a few millennia, the increase in the number of peasants determined the expulsion or extermination of the hunter-gatherers.

Denser societies made possible by agriculture realised considerable returns by exploiting the potential for cooperation and the division of labour, but this also required the development of appropriate and more complex institutions. In fact, the trajectory of institutional evolution is similar. States evolved first in the Mesopotamia area about 5,500 years ago, and in many other areas at a later stage, perhaps ten or more times in various parts of the world. This area was also where monotheist religions emerged.

The sedentary lifestyle was not due exclusively to agriculture. In Asia Minor, climate change and a decrease in big prey stimulated and preceded the social novelties of the Neolithic. Sedentary villages were already present in the early Natufian, about 24,000 years ago. During the period of cold known as the 'Younger Dryas' (12,800–11,600 years ago), the pre-agricultural villages of Mureybit and Abu were already sedentary, although they did not practise agriculture. Stone instruments to grind wild cereals can be dated to 24,000 years ago and about 13,000 years ago were present in the entire Fertile Crescent. It is likely that agriculture and a sedentary lifestyle were not immediately seen as superior in the eyes of the hunter-gatherers. Scholars use the term 'frailisation' to describe the conditions of the population of the agricultural Neolithic, who, compared with the population of hunter-gatherers, were worse off and subject to more illnesses and bone deformations due to higher workloads.

From an anthropological point of view, the shortness of the period during which these momentous changes took place implies evolution by jumps rather than at a gradual pace. After hundreds of thousand years of subsistence linked to hunting and gathering, the advent of the late Neolithic brought about elements of economy, urban planning and social and ideological action in communities and confederations. Favourable climatic changes have been documented. However, other

---

[31] The term was popularised by Cole, S. (1970), *The Neolithic Revolution*, London, Trustees of the British Museum.

contingent factors must have triggered, in a few thousand years, a process that repeated itself in north and south China, sub-Saharan Africa, the eastern United States, central Mexico and the south-central Andes.

1.4 Reciprocal Altruism

Neo-Darwinian evolutionary biology has gone beyond mere egotism, suggesting the 'inclusive fitness' theory.[32] Altruistic and cooperative behaviours can develop if they contribute to the fitness not only of the individual themselves but also that of related individuals, taking as a reference point the capacity of a gene to duplicate itself, therefore making the object of fitness not the single individual but genes.[33] However, the inclusive fitness idea only explains cooperation among related individuals, while the evidence suggests that humans and their predecessors already cooperated in large numbers and in large numbers of unrelated individuals. Let us, therefore, discuss other evolutionary mechanisms that may be invoked to interpret these rapid and colossal changes in our social life.

A second mechanism introduced to explain the emergence of cooperation is 'reciprocal altruism'. Reciprocal altruists are 'conditional cooperators' who cooperate with cooperators and refuse to do so with non-cooperators, opportunists and cheaters: 'given the universal and nearly daily practice of reciprocal altruism among humans today, it is reasonable to assume that it has been an important factor in recent human evolution and that underlying emotional dispositions affecting altruistic behaviour have important genetic components'.[34]

Reciprocal altruism requires a few conditions. Humans must be able to recognise other individuals as reciprocators or non-reciprocators. For this, they must interact frequently to check reciprocation credentials, with frequent reversals of donors and recipients, and must remember past interactions with other group members. Chronic

---

[32] Hamilton, W. D. (1964b), 'Genetic evolution of social behaviour', II, *Journal of Theoretical Biology*, 7: 17–52; Williams, G. C. (1966), *Adaptation and Natural Selection*, Princeton, NJ, Princeton University Press.

[33] From which comes the gene-centred view of Dawkins, R. (1976), *The Selfish Gene*, Oxford, Oxford University Press.

[34] Trivers, R. L. (1971), 'The evolution of reciprocal altruism', *Quarterly Review of Biology*, 46, 35–57: 48.

cheaters can maintain their strategy only by frequent changes of location, meeting and cheating a series of grudgers susceptible to one-off deception. The mechanisms for detecting cheats are primarily emotional. Emotions are a pan-cultural involuntary and invasive limbic system override shaped by natural selection which adjusts our behaviour in social situations. They animate, focus and modify neural activity in ways that lead us to choose certain responses over other possible responses to the stream of information we constantly receive.[35] Emotions move us to behave in ways that enhanced our distant ancestors' reproductive fitness by 'overriding neocortical decisions suggesting alternatives (i.e. cheating); such alternatives may have been more rational in the short term, but ultimately reduced fitness'.[36]

Because reproductive success is the principal reason for the existence of all sexually reproducing organisms, the emotions accompanying the acquisition or loss of resources that facilitate this goal became the basis for detecting cheats. We feel contentment and joy when we acquire resources, sad and frustrated when we do not, envy when others have more and anger when others try to take them away from us. When we cooperate with others to obtain resources, we experience a sense of friendship and obligation that enhances future cooperation. We feel angry when we cooperate and others cheat, and the cheater also feels anxiety and guilt. The emotions accompanying cooperation are rewarding and those accompanying defection are displeasing. Emotions thus work to keep our temptations in check by overriding rational calculations of immediate gain.

Despite these evolved emotions, the desire to punish that they generate and the grudging strategy followed by most human beings, the continued presence of chronic cheaters among us indicates that our ability to detect and punish them is less than perfect. Because cheating in some circumstances confers fitness benefits, it is unlikely that natural selection can eliminate it.[37] Cooperators undergo evolutionary tuning of their senses for detecting cheats and cheats evolve mechanisms that serve to hide their true intentions. The size of a group in which cooperation is based on reciprocal altruism is limited by memory and knowledge of other people's behaviour. This is true even in modern societies.

---

[35] Wilson, *Sociobiology*, p. 851.
[36] Walsh, A. (2000), 'Evolutionary psychology and the origins of Justice', *Justice Quarterly*, 17: 841–64, 851.
[37] Ibid., pp. 851–2.

Small groups maintain a stronger capacity for emotional solidarity that makes free riding considerably harder and punishment through discontinued cooperation easier. Therefore, 'inclusive fitness' and 'reciprocal altruism' do not add up to a satisfactory explanation of the human capacity for large-scale cooperation in town-size and larger settlements, which remains a puzzle.

1.5 Punishment and Strong Reciprocity

To fill the gap between forms of reciprocal altruism and the normative requirements for cooperation in large-scale societies, *stronger reciprocity* is needed.[38] Experimental evidence suggests that humans are conditional cooperators and also willing to bear costs to punish unfair behaviour. The willingness to punish is a constant in humans. In small groups, punishment is easy as it is the same thing as non-cooperation and bears no or minimal additional costs. To be excluded from common rituals and the common distribution of food resources is already a punishment leading to physical suffering, lower reproduction capacity and even death. It took a long time for the option to develop for an individual expelled from his/her own community to be able to survive by being accepted and hosted in a different community. In the new community, however, the same problem of ostracism of opportunists had to be faced. Strong reciprocators have a disposition to incur costs to punish the violation of social norms. Potential punishment discourages the individuals who try to cheat the system of cooperation. In this case, the advantages of free riding diminish rapidly. There is some disagreement about when the human disposition for strong reciprocity and altruistic punishment emerged.[39]

If reciprocal altruism generates positive emotions that reinforce cooperation, negative emotions accompany being cheated: '[a] taste

---

[38] See Gintis, H. (2000), 'Strong reciprocity and human sociability', *Journal of Theoretical Biology*, 43: 169–79; Dubreuil, B. (2008), 'Strong reciprocity and the emergence of large-scale societies', *Philosophy of the Social Sciences*, 38: 192–210.

[39] Some research locates the emergence of strong reciprocity at the time of the speciation of *Homo ergaster, erectus* and maybe *habilis* more than 2 million years ago. Other scholars locate this development in the last half of the Pleistocene (about 800,000 years ago) in connection with the rapid cephalisation of *Homo heidelbergensis, neanderthalensis* and *sapiens*. Dubreuil, 'Strong reciprocity and the emergence of large-scale societies', pp. 196–7.

of revenge is the other side of the coin of reciprocity'.[40] Victims are angry and hurt at being treated unfairly and feel frustration and confusion at losing the expectation of predictability. The sum of these evolved emotions amounts to 'moral outrage'. Without moral outrage, there would be no motivation to react against those who violate the norms of reciprocity, cheats would have thrived in our ancestral environment and we might have evolved as conscienceless psychopaths. From the evolutionary point of view, it is no use feeling angry and hurt when victimised if these feelings do not generate behaviour designed to prevent their recurrence. Such negative feelings are assuaged by punishing violators. Punishment signals the restoration of fairness and predictability. Punishment must be inflicted collectively; it must be a lynching because the essential element is not the punishment itself but the fact of gathering united in the punishment. In this act, the community not only punishes but also recognises itself as a community and recuperates its sense of orientation.[41] In this case, the role of punishing goes against a rationalistic parading of individual sanctioning.

Therefore, the explanation of cooperation on a large scale is linked to the development of more complex institutions for punishment that make control of the cost and efficiency of punishment possible.[42] Such institutional control requires punishment to not be mere revenge, which can degenerate into a cycle of blood feuds. The urgency for vengeance is not adaptive in social groups much larger than the hunter-gatherer band.[43] The struggle to contain 'revenge'[44] has been conducted at the highest level of moral and civic awareness in each stage of the development of civilisation. This effort is expectable in view of the persistent state of tension between uncontrollable vengeance as a destroyer and controlled vengeance as a component of justice. Moral outrage responses are universally guided by evolved mental mechanisms, but the way in which we respond to wrongdoers is shaped by culture.

In some circumstances, a measure of forgiveness helps to overcome the destructive effects of a pure tit-for-tat strategy and avoids losing

---

[40] Walsh, 'Evolutionary psychology and the origins of justice', p. 853.
[41] Girard, R. (1972), *La Violence et le Sacré*, Paris, Grassett (English translation: *Violence and the Sacred*, Baltimore, MD, Johns Hopkins University Press, 1977).
[42] Dubreuil, 'Strong reciprocity and the emergence of large-scale societies', p. 203.
[43] Walsh, 'Evolutionary psychology and the origins of justice', p. 855.
[44] Jacoby, S. (1985), *Wild Justice: The Evolution of Revenge*, London, William Collins.

valuable cooperation over an accidental cheating event, in which cases punishment can be disintegrative rather than reintegrative. Forgiveness is contingent on the wrong not being too egregious, payment or restitution, apologies, assurances and so on. If the urge to punish has become inherent in human nature and it serves an expiatory function, we can also temper it with sympathy. Culture may engage the emotions that temper punishment with mercy but it also allows vengeful passions to turn wild. Culture may help us go from repressive to restitutive justice, based more on deterrence.

Therefore, to go along the path of strong reciprocation, institutions are necessary to *facilitate punishment, lower the individual costs of punishing rule-breakers* and, at the same time, *discipline revenge.* As cheating is vital for the evolution of cooperation, so deviance is necessary for social solidarity (a synonym for cooperation). The rituals of punishment reaffirm the justness of the social norm.[45]

In conclusion, simple tit-for-tat reciprocity is effective for generating cooperative behaviour in small groups; tit-for-tat modified by punishment is effective against defectors in large groups. Strong reciprocation is the more robust candidate to explain the unique level and patterns of cooperation among humans. The overwhelming anthropological evidence of violence being used and legitimated against rule-breakers also seems to confirm this. Both punishers and non-punishers benefit from the punishment of non-cooperators because the whole group benefits by changing cheating into cooperation. But even if punishment is institutionalised, and its cost is therefore reduced, why should some members of a group punish non-cooperators for the benefit of other members? How does this act increase the punishers' fitness?

1.6 From Strong Reciprocity to Morality

Punishment and revenge are not enough to establish the normative universe. The problem of human morality is more complex than that of cooperation based on inclusive fitness, conditional reciprocation or even strong reciprocation. Human morality consists of a sense of responsibility that humans feel for non-relative others. For individuals interdependent in the search for daily sustenance, the choice of

---

[45] Spitzer, S. (1975), 'Punishment and social organization: a study of Durkheim's theory of penal evolution', *Law & Society Review*, 9: 613–38.

companions was essential. Individuals unable to cooperate at the cognitive level (the capacity to understand common objectives or to communicate efficiently with others) were not chosen as companions and had more difficulties in finding food and reproducing. Individuals socially and morally non-cooperative in their interactions with others were left out and alone and their reproductive chances were reduced. If the environment in which behaviours must be fitting is cooperative, then a selection emerged favouring individuals who were more competent, motivated and skilled in cooperation. Their better reproductive capacities slowly made them prevail within the group's population.

These same results can derive from a group selection capacity rather than exclusively from individual genetic selection. Individuals who live in an interdependent and cooperative social group have an interest in caring about the well-being of others.[46] If somebody depended on somebody else, it made sense to help them whenever necessary so that they could be in good shape for the next cooperation. The strong motivation to cooperate led to experiencing sympathy and helping new or already acquired companions. Given that the survival of the individual depended on others considering him or her a good mate, individuals began to worry about how others perceived them. We became oversensitive to the opinions of others.

Laboratory research reveals that human beings involved in cooperation tend to treat others not only with sympathy but also as mates worth equal consideration, with a sense of equity based on the understanding of an equivalence between themselves and others.[47] Mates understood that they could take whatever role they wished in the cooperation, and this helped the development of a sort of 'common mental field' that defined the best way for people to perform their roles.[48] These expectations are 'impartial' in the sense that they specify what each abstract companion has to do to behave correctly. When selecting mates for a cooperative effort, humans wanted to have an individual able to perform an expected role, and those who deviated from what was expected would find it difficult to acquire mates and

---

[46] See Tomasello, M. (2018), 'L'origine della moralità', *Le Scienze*, November, pp. 66–71.

[47] These results derive from experimental game theory, neural region activation research and studies concerning other emotions such as shame and guilt.

[48] Tomasello, 'L'origine della moralità'.

would eventually develop a sense of guilt. In this way, a morality emerged based on the idea that the 'we' was even more important than the 'I'. In cooperation to defend the group from external threats, these moral prerequisites and the expected performances were even more important. Groups of individuals better equipped with these orientations tended to prevail over groups without them.

Learning to conform was the basis of cumulative cultural evolution. Behavioural studies on three-year-old children show that the fundamental psychological characteristic of individuals adapted to cultural life is the group mentality in which they learn and adopt the cognitive perspective of the whole group.[49] Common goals and the cultural unity of the group help to create an 'objective' perspective; that is, a perspective which is not 'mine' but 'our', of the entire group. Human morality developed the characteristics of an objective form of 'right' and 'wrong'. Of course, individuals could choose to act not according to morality and shared aims, locating themselves outside the values and practices shared by the group, and eventually this could lead to their exclusion from it.[50]

Such an agent-neutral grasp of social norms develops very early in human ontogeny. Children often spontaneously protest against, criticise and teach wrongdoers even in pretend games and scenarios. Recent research also suggests that children pick up social norms quickly, easily and in a systematic and flexible way, and that they learn them from more competent members of their culture. Finally, children make quick inferences from single-action observations about the general normative structure of a type of action. Children swiftly learn about novel norms, follow such norms, enforce them in others in an agent-neutral way, understand some of their essential logical properties and reason about them systematically.

Different disciplines from child development to linguistics offer empirical evidence that human beings are born with a moral grammar hard-wired in their neural circuits.[51] The literature on early

---

[49]   See Schmidt, M. F. H. et al. (2012), 'Young children enforce social norms', *Current Directions in Psychological Science*, 21: 232–6.

[50]   See Tomasello, M. (2016), *A Natural History of Human Morality*, Cambridge, MA, Harvard University Press.

[51]   See Monroe, K. R., A. Martin and P. Ghosh (2009), 'Politics and an innate moral sense: scientific evidence for an old theory?', *Political Research Quarterly*, 62: 614–34.

cognition[52] suggests that social cognition is not only based on learning and understanding but also incorporates a normative stance. It could not have been any other way if we consider that probably for 6–8 million years our best evolutionary assets were 'cooperative' skills and capacities.

Conventional social norms share several features:

(1) *Normative force and generality*: they stand as standards of correctness and appropriateness. They are agent-neutral in the sense that they are applied to any participant in equivalent circumstances. Such norms can figure as reasons for acting and also as a basis for evaluation and criticism of others' acts.

(2) *Context sensitivity*: most of these social norms apply only to specific social contexts in which their validity prescribes what is appropriate. Children understand that a behaviour is a mistake if performed in the context of a game, but it is perfectly appropriate outside the game context.

(3) *Conventionality*: they exist because of shared assignment and acceptance; they are brought about by the shared intentionality of a community.

The crucial point is that the evolution of morality takes place not only in the field of natural selection but also in that of social selection. Behavioural genetics focusses on the extent to which differences among individuals can be related to their genetic patrimony. Evolutionary psychology focusses on the universal features shared by the members of our species. Evolutionary psychologists are aware that there are genes underlying human traits because we all share a uniform human genotype, but they tend to explain behavioural differences among individuals in environmental, not genetic, terms. Geneticists will not find a justice gene or a cooperation gene somewhere among our chromosomes, much as they will not find an egoistic gene. Genes are strands of DNA that code the acid sequence of a protein or the base sequence of an RNA molecule. They do not code for any kind of behaviour, feeling or emotion, particularly not one as complex as a sense of justice. The protein products of gene activity such as enzymes and hormones (including neurotransmitters) have much to do with how we behave and feel but they do not *cause* us to behave or

---

[52] See Rakoczy, H. and M. F. H. Schmidt (2013), 'The early ontogeny of social norms', *Child Development Perspectives*, 7: 17–21.

feel a certain way; they facilitate our behaviour and our feelings. These substances produce tendencies or dispositions to respond to the environment in one way or another.[53]

Gene–culture evolution is an important and adaptive way of achieving and maintaining within-group conformity and cooperation (thus enabling processes of genetic and cultural group selection). Norm psychology also enables the diachronic stability necessary for cumulative cultural evolution. Although some form of social expectation exists in non-human primates, no other species shows signs of following social norms and enforcing them in agent-neutral ways on others.

This interpretation is valid for any type of theory of human action: those that see social norms as explanations of behaviours without considering intentional stance information; those that see intentional stance information as influencing the normative evaluation of actions; and those that see the normative evaluation of an action as affecting its intentional interpretation.[54]

1.7 Complex Normative Structures and Early Political Institutions

Hunting and gathering societies in the ethnographic record always have tribal-scale institutions. In a successive phase, bigger social groups faced new challenges or tasks for their survival and attainment of their goals. This generated needs and interests that became conflicting for a confined community. These conflicts were potentially dangerous for

---

[53] Recently, a number of politics scholars have argued the contrary; that is, that there is a genetic determination of political attitudes. Political behaviour, including political ideologies, pre-dispositions towards liberalism and conservatism, and voting participation, is seen as genetically inheritable. These researchers usually study twins' attitudes. See Alford, J. R., C. L. Funk and J. R. Hibbing (2005), 'Are political orientations genetically transmitted?', *American Political Science Review*, 99: 153–67; Dawes, C. T. and J. H. Fawler (2009), 'Partisanship, voting, and the dopamine D receptor gene', *Journal of Politics*, 71: 1157–71; Fawler, J. H., L. A. Baker and C. T. Dawes (2008), 'Genetic variation in political participation', *American Political Science Review*, 102: 233–48; Fawler, J. H. and C. T. Dawes (2008), 'Two genes predict voter turnout', *Journal of Politics* 70: 579–94; Alford, J. R. and J. R. Hibbing (2004), 'The origin of politics: an evolutionary theory of political behavior', *Perspectives on Politics*, 2, 4: 707–23.

[54] See Granovetter, M. (1985), 'Economic action and social structure: the problem of embeddedness', *American Journal of Sociology*, 91: 481–510.

the group. More complex normative structures made possible a preventative channelling of behaviour and expectations; the possibility of resolution of conflicts; the setting up of organs for the direction of the group; and the setting up of specific procedures to generate imperative measures.

The timetable of this institutional development can be summarised as follows:

(1) The establishment of multi-male/female communities operating a small-scale fission–fusion system[55] held together by male residence and kinship dates to common ancestors of chimpanzees and hominins about 5 million years ago.

(2) The development of a more expanded fission–fusion system and the following spatially segregated communities that were held together by social relationships at a distance, and perhaps even including more exclusive male–female bonds, can be dated to about 2 million years ago and to *Homo ergaster*.

(3) While the oldest social institutions were maintained largely by physical mechanisms, the development of greater capacity for symbolic communication produced a greater variation in the institutional systems in the population that was ancestral to the Neanderthals and modern humans around 300,000 years ago.

(4) The development of larger, more ethnically identified communities with wider socially recognised networks occurred sporadically among the early modern human populations, but they developed extensively in the later Pleistocene hunter-gatherer populations between 100,000 and 20,000 years ago.

(5) A further step is the development of institutions related to aggressive/cooperative inter-group relationships, which were more likely to promote hierarchies. This change is clearly associated with changes at the end of the Pleistocene, although it may have developed sporadically before. These institutions

---

[55] A fission–fusion society is one in which the size and composition of the social group change as time passes and animals or hominins move throughout the environment, merge into a group (fusion) – for example, sleeping in one place – or split (fission) – for example, foraging in small groups during the day. For species that live in fission–fusion societies, group composition is a dynamic property; see Aureli, F. et al. (2008). 'Fission-fusion dynamic', *Current Anthropology*, 49: 627–54.

included egalitarian counter-balances preventing people from appropriating disproportionate shares of food; more formal political leadership including chieftainship; marriage in the form of contracts between families; kinship systems regulating social relationships between families; and monogamy and polygamy.[56] Humans' Pleistocene evolutionary experience did not prepare us to tolerate more than minimal command and control institutions and neither were we prepared to tolerate much inequality.[57] The punishment of deviant behaviour and norm violation effective within the family and kinship structures constituted by itself a principle of stratification based on subordination, age, grade or other stratarchical principles defining who has the duty to punish. In subsequent group-societies defined as trans-egalitarian, both private property and institutionalised hierarchies exist based on economic factors but in an attenuated form. Equality among families is often prized and excessive ostentation is regarded as unbecoming, but in fact inequalities are visible in banquets, funeral rituals and burials, and the worship of the dead and ancestors. Therefore, it is likely that some inequalities developed before agriculture and anthropologists tend to locate this at about 15,000 years ago.

(6) Then, agriculture brought about sedentary life, the possibility of exclusive land control, its hereditary transmission and the development of socio-economic inequalities. This was the beginning of highly stratified societies with pronounced productivity, high population density, economic competition and status differences.[58] The creation of village-size settlements related to increasing social differentiation and internal ranking. Hierarchical authority emerged, leaders acquired great power to coerce other citizens and people in high positions of command and control acquired a disproportionate

---

[56] Foley, A. R. (2001), 'Evolutionary perspectives on the origins of human social institutions', in Runciman, *The Origins of Human Social Institutions*, pp. 192–3.

[57] Richieston and Boyd, *Institutional Evolution in the Holocene*, p. 207.

[58] On the emergence of inequality and social stratification I rely on the evidence discussed in Hayden, B. (2011), 'Feasting and social dynamics in the Epipaleolithic of the Fertile Crescent', in Aranda Jimenez, G., S. Monton-Subias and M. Sanchez Romero (eds.), *Guess Who's Coming to Dinner: Feasting Rituals in Prehistoric Societies of Europe and the Near East*, Oxford, Oxbow Books, pp. 30–63; and the special section on good transmission and inequalities in pre-modern societies in *Current Anthropology*, 51: 7–126.

share of society's rewards. The creation of cities and settlements of tens of thousands of people introduced the 'centralisation of power' and a differentiation between the centre and the periphery.[59] At this stage there was an institutional objectification of the punishment function, at least for those offences that concerned the whole group of society. This is a process of delegation of the duty to sanction from personalised authorities to functionally specific roles through institutions.

Command and control institutions have always existed. What was new after the Neolithic revolution was their complexification and differentiation. At the new larger scale, command and control institutions had to prevent selfish temptations to expropriate advantages, nepotisms, cabals of reciprocators, organised predatory bands and classes or castes with special access to means of coercion. Further institutions developed to tame coercion and its use for narrow advantage. Some institutions balanced this situation by somehow policing the police so that they could act to the advantage of larger interests, to a certain degree at least.

The creation of political hierarchies is probably linked to the need for large-scale societies to control the rising costs and complexity of punishment.[60] The emergence of complex, specialised and differentiated institutions for the punishment of opportunistic behaviour could be the consequence of new general cognitive resources allowing *Homo sapiens* to fully represent the point of view of others. Human species prior to *Homo sapiens* were probably not able to share the duty of punishment even if the populations of *Homo ergaster*, *erectus* and *neanderthalensis* could already be composed of strong reciprocators, which explains why they were unable to live beyond small-size bands.

However, the early development of political hierarchies and of institutions of command and control should not be seen exclusively in the light of the in-group control of opportunist and deviant behaviours in enlarged groups. The *internal dimension* of enforcement problems – fostering cooperation, limiting free riding, punishing non-reciprocators and so on – could be solved satisfactorily by customary and social

[59] Earle, T. K. (1997), *How Chiefs Came to Power: The Political Economy of Prehistory*, Stanford, CA, Stanford University Press.
[60] Dubreuil, 'Strong reciprocity and the emergence of large-scale societies', p. 205.

norms. Moreover, these internal problems of the group were unlikely to overcome the fears and costs associated with the setting of stronger political authority in egalitarian groups. The monopolisation of political authority was an enforcement improvement for the traditional norms regulating internal life and disputes, but this was not its main functional reason.

Anthropology and primatology studies suggest that although we may have a deeply rooted instinct to exert power over others, we also have a strong aversion to abuses of power, along with some natural tendencies to punish people who commit such abuses. This belief was strong, and males who turned into selfish bullies, or tried to boss others around, were treated brutally as moral deviants. Despite these strong egalitarian beliefs, hunter-gatherers faced bullies or self-aggrandising political upstarts and had to be vigilant against inequality. Otherwise, they would soon have turned hierarchical, as in fact they did in the phase of sedentary life and agriculture. However, strong resistances to authority existed within the group that could only be overcome by even stronger threats to physical integrity. The 'monopolisation' of political authority took place not (only) to curb and punish in-group opportunism but primarily to effectively survive as a group in a violent world.

Although it is well known that animals can kill members of their own species, within the world of vertebrates there are no instances of the large, deliberate, organised massacres possible among humans. However, the tendency towards violence as an inherited genetic feature is contested. For most scientists, human nature may embrace motives that lead to aggression but also motives like empathy, self-control and reason, which, in the right circumstances, can outweigh the aggressive impulses.[61] Because of the absence of long-range weapons, it seems that war, in the sense we understand it today, was impracticable until about 40,000 years ago. Studies that consider both ethnographic and genetic data conclude that the people of the *sapiens* who left Africa were carriers of a culture that was both violent and inclined to war. This is witnessed not only by violent behaviours but also by the presence of certain traditions (such as competitive sports, ritual fights and wrestling games) that are usually associated with violent cultures. The

---

[61] See the discussion of the issue in Pinker, S. (2011), *The Better Angels of Our Nature*, New York, Viking.

evidence of the innate aggressiveness of humans remains uncertain but, for that concerning the early 'out of Africa', it is more convincing.[62]

The relationship between *Homo sapiens, Cro-Magnon* and *neanderthal* is a good test case. The latter two species coexisted for about 60,000 years in the Levant and perhaps for longer around modern-day France. We share elements of DNA with the Neanderthals.[63] It is argued that the *Cro-Magnon* were the cause of the Neanderthals' extinction. About 15,000 years ago at the end of the last glaciation, the *Cro-Magnon* also disappeared. The artifices of the caves of Altamira and Lascaux left room for new populations coming from the highlands of modern-day Anatolia, Iraq and Iran. Were they responsible for this quick extinction of the previous species? There is no concluding evidence, although these extinctions increase the doubt concerning the peaceful orientation of modern *Homo sapiens.*

It seems that our daily life within groups tends to be quiet and non-aggressive, while we are extremely aggressive towards other groups. The explanation is that we are a domesticated species; we are dogs, not wolves. We have auto-domesticated in the sense that to live together we began to select lower aggressiveness traits and to eliminate those who used violence to their advantage within the group and did not conform to the norms and rules of the group. The paradox is that our in-group docile and cooperative nature has evolved thanks to our past capacity to be out-group organised murderers.[64] After all, to be an organised murderer, one needs a high level of in-group cooperation. Next to egalitarian internal drives, *Homo* evidences aggressiveness in inter-group relations superior to that of other primates. As far as out-group relationships were concerned, we were not selfish but instead aggressive and orientated to the physical annihilation of the adversary.

Scholars disagree on whether war and mass killing are an evolutionary tendency of humans to eliminate competitors or a phenomenon

---

[62] Moreno, E. (2011), 'The society of our "Out of Africa Ancestors" (I): the migrant warriors that colonized the world', *Communicative and Integrative Biology*, 4: 1–9. The study also concludes that many other hunters and gatherers, such as the African Bushmen and Pygmies, among the most ancient genetic ancestors, were clearly non-violent cultures.

[63] Green, R. E., J. Krause, A. W. Briggs et al. (2010). 'A draft sequence of the Neandertal genome', *Science*, 328, 5979: 710–22.

[64] This thesis is documented in Wrangham, R. (2019), *The Goodness Paradox: The Strange Relationship Between Virtue and Violence in Human Evolution*, New York, Pantheon Books.

that only emerged in recent millennia, when changes in social and environmental conditions offered both the logistics and motivations for mass killing. One line of research argues that there are almost always archaeological proofs of bellicose episodes, and that to attribute about 25 per cent of all deaths to wars could be a conservative estimation.[65] A different line insists that, although humans have an obvious capacity to wage war, the instinct to identify and kill adversaries is not ingrained in their brains. Only the increase in size and complexity of human groups and the development of agriculture saw the emergence of lethal attacks.[66] If the question of the natural aggressiveness of humans remains controversial, the idea that intense violence and a high number of victims characterised the prehistoric period is widely shared: 'Most ethnographically reported chiefdoms seem to be involved in constant warfare.'[67]

Anthropologists and archaeologists disagree and hesitate to attribute the development of political institutions to the constitutive role of warfare and physical insecurity. The reason is that war activities are less documented than bureaucratic developments.[68] It is, however, likely that local hierarchies were under constant threat of being ousted by alternative ones, and that subjects were under constant threat of being conquered, killed and dispossessed in a lost war. Groups without an efficient defence/aggression command would fail to deploy the defence mechanisms that could ensure their survival when facing groups which had such institutions. The primordial development of a monopolistic provider of behavioural compliance was a fitting solution for group survival, providing evolutionary advantages in a situation of inter-group violence.

---

[65] LeBlanc, S. A. with K. E. Register (2003), *Constant Battles: The Myth of the Peaceful, Noble Savage*, London, St Martin's Press.

[66] Mead, M. (1990 [1940]), *War Is Only an Invention – Not a Biological Necessity*, in *The Dolphin Reader*, 2nd edition, Boston, MA, Houghton Mifflin Company, pp. 415–21.

[67] Wright, H. (1977), 'Recent research on the origin of the state', *Annual Review of Anthropology*, 6: 379–97, 381–2.

[68] Archeologists use four types of evidence to ascertain war activities: (1) art works on the walls of caves showing people at war; (2) evidence of armaments; (3) ruins of defensive settlements; (4) skeleton remains and signs of wounds (although it is often difficult to say if they come from war or simply local violence). See Ferguson, B. (2018), 'Perché combattiamo?', *Le Scienze*, 603, November, pp. 72–7.

In conclusion, the process of 'monopolisation' of political authority was greatly facilitated by the need for effectively surviving as a group in a violent world. Fundamental political predicaments which are unmanageable theoretically and impossible to solve on a rationalistic cooperation basis are easier to overcome in the face of the colossal stakes of inter-groups conflicts. Political institutions emerged very early and did not derive from the customary and social ones that served the function of internal disciplining and punishment (I shall return to this point in Chapter 7).

Therefore, in the development of political institutions, we should distinguish four distinct mechanisms: (1) internal punishment; (2) external survival; (3) protection from rulers; and (4) defence against private predation.

(1) The first political institutions for the life of a group must have been rules about the *punishment of internal opportunists*. These mechanisms required minimal institutional development in the form of customary norms and enforcement was easy (withdrawal of cooperation, expulsion from the group, exile, ostracism).

(2) Pre-human and human groups developed effective norms/rules *to ensure the external security and survival* of the group itself. Defence/offence needs were an important push towards the acceptance of the increasing capacities and powers of rulers. Effective leadership in times of harsh confrontation was a necessity that required selection rules.

(3) A third institutional development regarded institutions for the internal *protection of the ruled from the rulers* when the role of the latter and the instruments of rulership at their disposal developed to such an extent that they could generate risks of predation. Both institutions punishing opportunists and institutions offering effective defence from external threats can be abused by those who administer them, particularly when the size of the group grows and when reciprocation mechanisms and credentials are no longer based on face-to-face relations.

(4) The fourth mechanism concerns *protection against private predatory activities of other individuals and groups*, particularly at a stage in which pronounced inequalities emerge in the enlarged society. Protection of the members from the consequences of the internal asymmetries of resources becomes crucial. As much as one

fears that rulership pursues its own goals without consideration of the interests and preferences of subjects, one also fears that other groups may influence it to their disadvantage.

These four different drivers all rest on and require a positive disposition towards cooperation. They imply, nonetheless, that institutions, and particularly political institutions, did not emerge in the same way and in response to a unique functional problem. They may be a response to foster cooperation and reduce transaction costs, but they may be a response to the need to militarily defend or expand territories and subjects. They may emerge to limit a ruler's predatory activities or they may also reflect aspirations for domestic equality and safety from predation by another domestic group.

The drivers of these four processes of institutional emergence introduce more dynamics and breadth into the history of government than any single functional explanation can ever do. They help explain the process of political institution innovation. We may have (1) a spontaneous generation of institutions from repeated and customary agreements among a set of qualified actors not subject to external interference; (2) transformation over time into consolidated institutions of practices imposed or initiated by rulers; (3) the creation of new institutions by qualified political institutions; and (4) revolutionary political innovations at times of discontinuity in territorial polities and regimes.

Moreover, the four different drivers are important in explaining variations: to explain why societies in some parts of the world evolved more rapidly than others; why the trajectories are many and not identical; why the pace of change is differentiated; and why we observe so many examples of declines, collapses and setbacks. The interactions between the four mechanisms better explain a feature of the history of government: political innovations were generated again and again in different parts of the world at different times and suffered decay again and again, and were rediscovered and readapted and decayed again and again. This is less likely if one single functional pressure and a single generation mechanism are at work. For instance, if limiting the predatory ambition of the ruler was the primary reason for institutional innovation, it would be difficult to understand the frequent deinstitutionalisation and decay of rather effective institutions. Instead, it makes sense to hypothesise that whenever the concern for a military enterprise of a defensive or offensive nature became predominant and the extraction/coercion mechanism was triggered to this effect, the effective institutional arrangements for limiting the predatory ambitions of the rulers suffered deinstitutionalisation and decay. Writing a history of government dealing with the interaction among the four political institution development mechanisms is a fascinating exercise, with a high explanatory potential.

1.8 Conclusion

A few million years ago, our ancestors lived in very small communities organised around kinship and reciprocity. Today we observe societies regulated by many complex institutions. The big bang in this normative structure occurred during the last 20,000 years. Since then, humans organised in groups have developed the ability to bring to success colossal operations, generate a complex morality that emphasises responsibility towards others and is enforced through reputation and punishment, and exterminate other species and their own.

Evolutionary anthropologists, palaeontologists and psychologists agree that the key social institutions predate the anatomically modern *Homo sapiens*. Some of them, such as communities, male kin-bonding, exclusive mating patterns and possibly descent groups, were probably in existence long before the origins of our species. Others developed thousands of years after the first *Homo sapiens*. However, the tendency to cumulatively build ever more complex institutions did not appear until the end of the Pleistocene.[69] Human civilisation probably began when humans conceived of the community as their best instrument for survival in the awareness that a group represents an apparatus far superior to the individual for supplying goods. Population growth and civilisation are associated with and perhaps caused by the complexification of institutions. Our propensity to cooperate and our willingness to punish defectors have, therefore, very old evolutionary roots and are the distinctive evolutionary mark of our species.

Overall, evolutionary biology is critical of cultural and group selection as important forces in nature. Hamilton's idea of 'inclusive fitness' suggests that altruistic and cooperative behaviours can develop if they

---

[69] Foley, *Evolutionary Perspectives on the Origins of Human Social Institutions*, p. 191.

contribute to the fitness not only of the individual but also of related individuals.[70] Organisms should engage in altruistic and cooperative acts only when the benefit to the recipient exceeds the costs to the provider by a factor greater than the reciprocal of the relatedness by common descent between them. The theory predicts that altruism will be rare and decidedly unfitting. Group selection is not an important force as it is not 'an efficient way to select for traits, like altruistic behaviour, that are supposed to be detrimental to the individual but good for the group . . . group selection for altruism would be unlikely to override the tendency of each group to quickly lose its altruists through natural selection favouring cheaters'.[71]

However, many evolutionary biologists accept that human development presents particular features and that 'human social groups represent an almost ideal model for potent selection at the group level'.[72] Studies that focus on natural selection in conditions of the fight for survival in the wildlife of the forest have difficulty in considering other kinds of environments such as those predominating in the conditions of the life of *Homo*. Darwin suggested a group theory in his late work, arguing that the evolution of groups could affect the survival of individuals.[73] In his rarely

---

[70] Hamilton, W. D. (1964a), 'The genetical evolution of social behaviour', I, *Journal of Theoretical Biology*, 7: 1–16.

[71] Coyne, J. A. (2011), 'Can Darwinism improve Binghamton?', *New York Review of Books*, 9 September. See also Wilson, *Sociobiology*. Wilson's positions have, however, changed over time. See Wilson, D. S. and H. E. O. Wilson (2007), 'Rethinking the theoretical foundation of sociobiology', *The Quarterly Review of Biology*, 82: 327–48 and Symons, D. (1989), 'A critique of Darwinian anthropology', *Ethology and Sociobiology*, 10: 131–44.

[72] 'First, the human species is (and possibly always has been) composed of competing and essentially hostile groups that frequently have not only behaved toward one another in the manner of different species, but also have been able quickly to develop enormous differences in the reproductive and competitive ability because of cultural innovation and its cumulative effect. Second, human groups are uniquely able to plan and act as units, to look ahead and purposely carry out actions designed to sustain the group and improve its competitive position . . . in seeking to define the adaptiveness of culture, to analyse directions of cultural change, and to identify the sources of cultural rules, we cannot ignore or downplay effects significant at the group level. On the other hand, the existence of group functions does not erase functions at the individual and family levels, and therefore does not preclude a significant within-group reproductive function.' Alexander, D. R. (1974), 'The evolution of social behavior', *Annual Review of Ecology and Systematics*, 5: 325–83, 336–7.

[73] Darwin, C. (1871), *The Descent of Man, and Selection in Relation to Sex*, London, John Murrey, p. 87.

cited work devoted to the selection of domestic animals and plants, reproducers are not selected according to their best-fitted predominance but because of choices based on economic, aesthetic or other reasons.[74] The human-dominated environment radically modifies natural selection mechanisms and produces results that are very different, if not opposed, to those that natural selection would retain in the wild and over a much longer timeframe. Many Darwinist scholars pay much attention to the possibility of human group selection.[75] Some continue to support group selection to explain the rapid rise of human civilisation and see direct group selection on genes as a process that could give human groups a degree of integration.[76] Other scholars go completely beyond genetic selection and argue that processes related to culture are prone to group selection.[77]

Legitimately, geneticists and evolutionary biologists ask their own question: 'what does the evolution of genes explain?' They do not ask the different question: 'what explains institutions?' The fact remains that inclusive fitness and conditional reciprocation can only explain cooperation among related individuals and in small groups, while large-scale human societies are a theoretical puzzle for only-genes evolution models because they include more cooperation between distantly related people than one would expect. Moreover, the colossal development of humans' normative structures in a relatively short period of 15,000–20,000 years, during which genetic selection has no role, remains mysterious. Genetic theories encounter considerable problems in explaining the origins of punishment and revenge, not to mention morality or complex institutional structures. If 'evolution' means that every individual tries to maximise his own fitness, how did we manage to feel obliged to be honest with others and help them? Similarly, who would incur the costs of punishment if they do not increase individual fitness?

---

[74] Darwin, C. (1868), *The Variation of Animals and Plants Under Domestication*, vol. 1, London, John Murrey.

[75] See the review of the debate about individual and group selection in Kramer, J. and J. Meunier (2016), 'Kin and multilevel selection in social evolution: a never-ending controversy', *F1000Research*, 5: 776.

[76] Wilson, D. S. (2015), *Does Altruism Exist? Culture, Genes, and the Welfare of Others*, New Haven, CT, Yale University Press; Nowak, M. A., C. E. Tarnita and H. E. O. Wilson (2010), 'The evolution of eusociality', *Nature*, 466, 7310: 1057–62.

[77] Richieston and Boyd, *Institutional Evolution in the Holocene*.

Evolution is based on random mutations, their fitness to the environment and the deriving reproductive success. Organisms may become extinct because of an unfavourable development in the environment, while others may get an evolutionary bonus from the same change.[78] The question is what the proper *environment* to evaluate fitness is. If we restrict the environment to the natural conditions of the forest, it is difficult to depart from pure gene-based evolution and from its limited capacity to generate cooperation. On the contrary, if we consider that hominids and early *Homo* evolved in a complex and demanding social environment made up of a dense framework of norms and institutions, this was the environment in which the fitness of random mutations and the reproductive capacities of individuals were decided. Those individuals that more easily adapted to the predominant norms were then more likely to be regarded as best mates and spouses and enjoy the reproductive advantages of such a situation.

Together with genetic selection based on the uniquely cooperative group environment of our hominid and *Homo* ancestors, we need to consider the extraordinary force of cultural selection that operated next to it. Our early and inherently advantageous predispositions to cooperate became objectified, contributing to our revolutionary capacity to always generate new institutional frameworks. This indicates that we have complex and strong imitating capabilities and we are highly sensitive to the positive or negative response of relevant others. Cultural transmission means that the behaviour of the individual largely depends on the behaviours common to the population she lives in and from which she acquires her beliefs. Parents, teachers and peers can shape human behaviour rapidly and easily. We get our genome all at once and it remains unchanged for our entire life, while the acquisition of the adult cultural repertoire takes at least two decades and remains open to further elaboration and change. What one person invents another can imitate, unlike gene transmission. We have a higher possibility of picking and choosing among potential cultural variants and we can modify them. We shape our behavioural repertoire by imitating others, making somewhat biased choices among the cultural variants

---

[78] Biological evolution theory never refers to perfection or efficiency. Evolution is a functional selection mechanism that tolerates imperfection and even inutility. Darwin was worried by organs that were highly imperfect or totally useless, and also by those that were almost too perfect (like the human eye).

we observe and sometimes contributing independently with new adaptive behaviours. However large the diversity of cultural traits is, we are bound to learn those of the culture of our environment and of our time. Cultural evolution has its own particular adaptive properties and particular maladaptation. Rapid social learning allows humans, and only humans, to accumulate innovations more rapidly than individual genetic selection alone could. This may take generations, but it takes place much more rapidly than organic evolution.

How did we develop instruments of cooperation like institutions? We had 7 million years to solve this problem. It is likely that our relatively new status of living in overcrowded communities has exacerbated problems of coordination and cooperation that were not crucial during the long period in which our biological evolution and our brains were shaped. It might well be that in their recent cultural evolution humans have developed more individualistic and egoistic orientations, but based on existing evidence it is difficult to believe that in their long-term biological evolution they have survived thanks to these orientations.

The 'state of nature' and ego-driven evolution remain the premise of rational choice methodological individualism in the social sciences. This envisages an (individual) actor primarily, if not exclusively, concerned with her own advantage and unilateral action, unencumbered by any evolved and embedded normative orientation, endowed with cognitive skills to evaluate the advantages of cooperation from egotistic premises and, therefore, constantly struggling with the problem of cooperation which is excluded from her evolutionary patrimony. This perspective consequently understands norms deductively as resulting only from the rationalistic capacity of humans to devise equilibrium situations and self-enforcing outcomes.[79] It does not engage with the empirical evidence about the evolution of *Homo* and their ancestors and it is, therefore, impossible both to sustain and to falsify it with empirics. However, none of these premises correspond to the available evidence offered by the evolutionary sciences of biology, psychology, palaeontology, anthropology and neurosciences. We should not reify human nature, but remain open to the new contributions of these

---

[79] On the origin of norms in this perspective, see Margalit, E. U. (1977), *The Emergence of Norms*, Oxford, Oxford University Press.

disciplines. We should not resort to the hypothetical 'state of nature' if our evolutionary history does not support this hypothesis. The fact that opportunists exist does not justify the choice to take them as the ontological reference for human nature against all the accumulated direct and indirect evidence of our ancestral cooperative orientation.

An approach combining genetic influence with cultural influence over several recent (from a biological point of view) generations seems necessary, and a model showing gene–culture co-evolution appears a more realistic hypothesis. Theories of human evolution need to take on board the fact that the environment in which it operated was for millions of years a cooperative environment. From the factual point of view, in one way or another, we have adaptively evaded the Hamiltonian rule.

2 | *Approaches to Institutions*

In Chapter 1, I argued that the normative patrimony of humans began very long ago. For more than 2 million years it vertebrated the social environment of our ancestors and *Homo sapiens*, supported a level of cooperation unknown in any other species and probably decided our evolutionary success. How have we conceptualised this normative reality? There is no paucity of definitions of the concept of 'institution' and often they are rather encompassing. In this chapter I shall discuss several ways to conceptualise institutions and elaborate on the implications of each. I will focus on the main characterising elements of the different understandings.

2.1 Deontic Realities

Institutions are most often seen as deontic realities: as 'norms' that include a prescriptive element. Durkheim first engaged in a systematic investigation of institutions as norms in social interaction, focussing on collective representations that are unavoidably harboured at any given time in the mind of the individuals of a population. If such collective representations are highly dominant in a society's representational life – as they probably were for a long time in our evolutionary history – they represent a sort of collective conscience that fosters cooperation. If, on the contrary, collective representations are a recessive element, social cooperation and integration can arise only out of the division of labour and individuals' needs for one another's services. In the first case, the glue of society is constituted of deeply internalised norms that impose themselves on the group; in the second, norms are less uniform and self-imposing and tend to regulate the relations among individuals, often with resort to contracts, rules and sanctions.[1]

---

[1] The entire work of Durkheim concerns institutions. In the preface to *Les règles de la méthode sociologique* (1919, Paris, Librairie Félix Alcan), he defines sociology as the 'science of institutions'.

One can speak of 'individuals' only to the extent that the shared representations lodged within individuals' minds have lost significance relative to those that are instead idiosyncratic, since they arise from and affect experiences particular to them.[2] Therefore, the existence of competing individuals as relatively self-standing, self-activating entities endowed with interests and capacities emerged relatively late in the course of social evolution. In Durkheim's view, compliance with norms cannot rest only on the calculation of advantage and cost in terms of sanctions. Moreover, human beings are not aware of the necessity of norms, of their collective utility. They find it difficult to see the connection between any given norm and social welfare and even more difficult to acknowledge that their own compliance with those norms is necessary to sustain that connection. This rules out an excessive emphasis on the temptation for individuals to evade norms in pursuit of their immediate interests. Society as the sum of norms exists insofar as individuals' compliance is motivated by their sense of having to comply with them.

Norms relate to and mobilise the individual capacity of self-transcendence. In Durkheim's view, this is not innate but socialised by education. Individuals, as role holders, largely disregard their own preferences as to how to conduct themselves in certain situations, or do not even allow themselves to form or consult such preferences. More simply, they arrange their conduct to match dictates that do not originate from themselves but pre-exist them or constrain them, being inscribed in standard scripts that the role holder takes for granted. Role commitments and expectations entail a willingness to refrain from negotiating your conduct with role partners, orientating it to a sense that continuing cooperation is a worthwhile thing in itself, that some sacrifices are worth making to retain the role relationship and that the partner deserves to be trusted even though this makes the role holder vulnerable. Durkheim, therefore, overemphasises the deontic and normative context of norms/rules. His work is the source of all interpretations that underline the moral bindingness, the dutifulness, the legitimacy and the 'ought' associated with norms, and that undervalue the role of a cost/benefit analysis based on sanctions.

In his early works Parsons is much influenced by Durkheim and sees institutions as 'those patterns which define the essentials of the

---

[2] For an insightful analysis, see Poggi, G. (2000), *Durkheim*, Oxford, Oxford University. Press, pp. 52–3.

legitimately expected behaviour of persons insofar as they perform structurally important roles in the social system'.[3] Twenty years later, Parsons underlined more the functional role of institutions within the social system: 'Institutions ... are complexes of normative rules and principles which, either through law or other mechanisms of social control, serve to regulate social action and relationships of course with varying degrees of success.'[4] The Parsonian understanding of institutions as social norms is clearly associated with his normative theory of action.[5] Re-elaborating elements present in the sociology of Marx, Pareto, Durkheim, Tönnies, Weber and Simmel, Parsons defines the framework of action theory starting from the definition of its parameters: the *actors*; the *ends* that they pursue; a *situation* in which they act, subdivided into the *conditions* (the elements that the actor cannot change) and the *means* (the elements that the actor can modify and use to attain goals); and, finally, a *selection criterion* in the relationship between the means and ends.

This scheme operates under two fundamental principles: (1) subjective orientation (that is, the idea that things must be seen from the point of view of the actor, not the observer); and (2) tension between conditions and ends – between the present situation and the goal we want to attain. Parsons underlines the creativity of the actor through the acknowledgement of a means/ends selection criterion much wider than mere maximising rationality. This takes place by integrating the actor/conditions/means/ends scheme within a system of normative regulation, which in part determines the ends of actions and constrains the choices of means. 'Normative orientation' is the idea that something is an end in itself. This excludes beginning the analysis with an attitude of calculation and mere convenience and implies a sense of moral obligation and respect that leads to identifying as means and final ends those that are 'socially approved'. This generates a tension between the integrative function of norms and values and the creative role of the actor. Although the creativity of the actor is a fundamental aspect, the normative system introduces limits to this same creativity.

---

[3] Parsons, T. (1954), *Essays in Sociological Theory*, Glencoe, IL, Free Press, p. 239.
[4] Parsons, T. (1975), *Social Structure and the Symbolic Media of Exchange*, in Blau, P. M. (ed.), *Approaches to the Study of Social Structure*, New York, Free Press, pp. 94–120, 97.
[5] First presented in his *The Structure of Social Action* (1937, New York, McGraw Hill).

The process of internalisation is posed as the basis for order and this reproduces the problem of liberty and necessity. If the normative element is taken away, then the actor can only evaluate conditions and means technically, and his voluntarism is related to the randomness of his ends.

This understanding of institutions defining the 'normative orientations' of actors has been influential in the social sciences both as a source of inspiration[6] and as a critical reference point. All contemporary 'cognitive' approaches take the lead from the critique of the Parsonian equation of the subjective component of action with the normative order of social institutions, criticising the undervaluation of the cognitive process in human action and human interpretative capacity.[7]

A strong normative or deontic component in the understanding of 'institutions' is also present in the work of John Searle.[8] This author defines an 'institution', or more precisely an 'institutional fact', as something that exists thanks to the collective acceptance of a given status. Institutional facts 'typically require structures in the form of constitutive rules X *counts as* Y *in* C and that institutional facts only exist in virtue of collective acceptance of something having a certain status, where the status carries the functions that cannot be performed without collective acceptance of the status'. Once an institution becomes established, it then provides a structure within which one can create institutional facts. Humans have the capacity to impose functions for objects that – contrary to those that perform functions thanks to their mere physical form (such as a stick or a box) – perform the function in virtue of the collective acceptance of their status. Money, a police officer or a professor do not exercise their functions thanks to their physical structure, but because we recognise a status in such objects, in the sense that relevant members of the collectivity believe these powers exist. If everybody were to cease to recognise police officers as such, then they would cease to have the status function

[6] Eisenstadt, S. N. (1968), *Social Institutions: The Concept, in International Encyclopaedia of the Social Sciences*, London and New York, The Macmillan Company – The Free Press, vol. 14, pp. 409–29, 409.

[7] See Granovetter, 'Economic action and social structure' and Giglioli, P. P. (1989), *Teorie dell'azione*, in Panebianco, A. (ed.), *L' analisi della politica. Tradizioni di ricerca, modelli, teorie*, Bologna, Il Mulino, pp. 107–33.

[8] Searle, J. R. (2005), 'What is an institution?', *Journal of Institutional Economics*, 1: 1–22.

and the related deontic powers. Therefore, collective acceptance accounts are constructivist: institutions and institutional facts exist to the extent that they are collectively believed to exist. Collective acceptance ranges from 'grudgingly going along with some social practice to enthusiastic endorsement of it'.[9]

A praxis becomes an institution not only because of its frequent and regular occurrence but also because of its deontic element – the fact of becoming a prescribed behaviour. The prescriptive element is also the key to the sanctioning, which is unthinkable for a praxis without a deontic element. The deontic powers created by institutional facts constitute rights, duties, obligations, authorisations, permissions, empowerments, requirements and certifications. Searle sees a gradual transition from informal but accepted assignments of status functions to full-blown established institutions with written constitutive rules. In both cases the crucial element of deontology is present. The idea of legitimacy in the form of collective acceptance suggests that 'status functions' are nothing but norms.[10] It follows that only facts for which there is no recognised deontology that goes with them are non-institutions.[11]

To this deontic tradition also belongs work by March and Olsen, which was very influential in the rebirth of institutional studies in the last quarter of the twentieth century, the impact of which has been particularly felt in political science.[12] This work's many merits include an analysis of institutional change redressing the underestimation of inter-institutional dynamics, incremental changes and transformative results; a critique of the over-rationalist vision of human action and constructs; and a critique of the historical efficiency of institutions. March and Olsen work with a wide concept of 'institution': 'An

[9] Ibid., p. 10.
[10] In different contributions Searle distinguishes between constitutive and regulative norms/rules. Searle, J. R. (2010), *Making the Social World: The Structure of Human Civilization*, Oxford, Oxford University Press, pp. 12–13. 'Speech acts' and 'declaratives' have a fundamental role in the construction of social institutions; Searle, J. R. (2012), *Speech Acts*, Cambridge, Cambridge University Press.
[11] 'Performative collective acceptance must have been in place for squirrel pelt to become money.' Tuomela, R. (2007), *The Philosophy of Sociality: The Shared Point of View*, Oxford, Oxford University Press, p. 183.
[12] March, J. G. and J. P. Olsen (1989), *Rediscovering Institutions: The Organizational Basis of Politics*, New York, The Free Press.

institution is a relatively enduring collection of rules and organised practices, embedded in structures of meaning and resources that are relatively invariant in the face of turnover of individuals and relatively resilient to the idiosyncratic preferences and expectations of individuals and changing external circumstances.'[13] The institutions they talk about and their acceptance are made up of norms/rules into which people become socialised and the appropriateness of which is 'ordinarily not a case of wilfully entering into an explicit contract ... rules are learned as catechisms of expectations'.[14]

Institutions are defined in terms of the 'logic of appropriateness' that guides the actions of their members. The terminology is one of duties and obligations rather than anticipatory consequential decision-making. 'Some of the major capabilities of modern institutions came from the effectiveness in substituting rule bound behaviour from individually autonomous behaviour.'[15] Moreover, following rules is an effective shortcut mechanism in all those situations in which we face a complex reality and a new environment in which the calculations of risks, costs and advantages, real and potential, would be extremely time consuming and would expose us to unknown consequences. This line of interpretation locates their work within the normativist family, although this is more influenced by organisational theory, organisational culture and the importance of values in understanding organisational behaviour.

The works by Durkheim, Parsons, Searle, and March and Olsen are taken here as representative of the understanding of institutions as normative or deontic entities. They see institutions as 'norms' that do not generate strategic relations; that is, people do not act because of the sanctions or rewards associated with respecting or violating the norms. Norms influence human behaviour without necessarily being the objects of conscious beliefs and desires. If norms were the objects of human beliefs and desires, this would make it easier to explain behaviour, given that it is generally accepted that agents act because of their beliefs and desires.[16] Norms are present in our cognitive system even if

---

[13] March, J. G. and J. P. Olsen (2006), 'Elaborating the "New Institutionalism"', in Rhodes, R. A. W., S. A. Binder and B. A. Rockman (eds.), *The Oxford Handbook of Political Institutions*, Oxford, Oxford University Press, pp. 3–20, 3. Other general definitions can be found in March and Olsen, *Rediscovering Institutions*, pp. 3, 22, 24.

[14] Ibid., p. 23.   [15] Ibid., p. 24.

[16] A point made by Stueber, K. R. (2005), 'How to think about rules and rule following', *Philosophy of the Social Sciences*, 35: 307–23, 309.

the agent is not necessarily conscious of those internal representations as a result of social conditioning and training or of some innate psychological endowment by nature.

2.2 Behavioural Regularities

A core problem with the concept of institution interpreted as norms/rules is the level at which they are accepted or abided by. In this case, the issue is not whether norms/rules guide behaviour by sanction or inner acceptance. The question is whether only effective norms – that is, norms accompanied by compliance – are true norms. If so, then norms/rules without effectiveness are meaningless norms, non-norms. In this perspective, norms are best seen as nothing more than their effects; that is, the behaviours that their being effective determine. To concretise the effectiveness of a norm, the behaviour that the norm generates must be 'regular'. This opens the door to an intertwining of norms and behaviours.

In the context of the behavioural revolution of the 1950s and 1960s, institutions were redefined and seen as 'recurrent patterns of behaviour'[17] and significant scholars have adhered to this understanding.[18] It is claimed that 'a social institution is nothing more than a stable, valued, recurring pattern of behaviour'.[19] Institutions are behavioural regularities shared by all members of a society that point to the conduct to be followed in particular and recurring situations.[20] In the behaviourist tradition, the term 'institution' was substituted with 'structure' and 'system'. Following this line of thought in a systematic way, the conclusion is that institutions are not norms or rules but instead the behaviours that derive from following these norms. Other scholars, rejecting the notion of institutions as norms/rules, conclude that everything that structures

---

[17] See Blondel, J. (2006), 'About institutions, mainly, but not exclusively, political', in Rhodes, Binder and Rockman (eds.), *The Oxford Handbook of Political Institutions*, pp. 716–30.

[18] Note that traditionally this definition was reserved for 'conventions'. See Lewis, D. K. (1969), *Convention*, Cambridge, MA, Harvard University Press.

[19] Goodin, R. E. (1966), *The Theory of Institutional Design*, Cambridge, Cambridge University Press, p. 21; Huntington, S. (1968), *Political Order in Changing Societies*, New Haven, CT, Yale University Press, p. 12. Huntington refers to procedures and excludes practices.

[20] Schotter, A. (1981), *The Economic Theory of Social Institutions*, Cambridge, Cambridge University Press, p. 9.

human behaviour is an institution: 'I define institutions as durable systems of established and embedded social rules that structure social interactions, rather than rules as such.'[21] Not all social structures are institutions, but the boundary between the two becomes hard to draw. Laws and codified rules cannot be ignored, but the latter are institutions only to the extent that they are effectively followed by a set of people. Norms/rules that are not abided by or are poorly abided by are not, therefore, institutions.

Focussing on recurrent patterns of behaviour rather than on norms/rules may mean that institutions *can also be* patterns of behaviour, in the sense that the latter can be taken as signs of hidden norms that work underneath. However, if it is argued that institutions *are* patterns of behaviour, then several problems emerge.[22] On the one hand, we face the problem of whether any regularity of behaviour is an institution and we get engaged in the distinction between regularities that are institutions and regularities that are not. On the other hand, we face the problem of how regular a behaviour must be to count as an institution. Should we downgrade to the non-institutional realm any type of normative phenomena not accompanied by a regularity of behaviour? This line of thought transforms a crucial aspect of institutional analysis, the level of compliance of any given normative fact, into a definitional criterion. Variance in institutions can no longer be evaluated by the level of compliance as low compliance will simply make for a non-institution, not for an institution that is poorly abided by.

In general, one important justification for the study of institutions is that whatever their specific definition, they tend to be more stable, enduring and regular than individual behaviours. The perspective under discussion overturns this link. It is the regularity of behaviours that identifies the deontic element, not the other way around. This has the consequence that it is impossible to utilise institutions so defined to explain the regularity of behaviours.[23] Of course, there are many norms/rules that are not fully respected and many behavioural

---

21 Hudgson, G. M. (2006), 'What are institutions?', *Journal of Economic Issues*, 40: 1–25,2, 13. See also Frey, B. S (1990), 'Institutions matter: the comparative analysis of institutions', *European Economic Review*, 34: 443–9.

22 See Ostrom, E. (1986), 'An agenda for the study of institutions', *Public Choice*, 48: 3–25, 5–6.

23 Tuomela, R. (1995), *The Importance of Us: A Philosophical Study of Basic Social Notions*, Stanford, CA, Stanford University Press, differentiates norms from rules because of their enforcement mechanism (self-enforced or sanctioned) and then sees norms, but not rules, as behavioural regularities.

regularities that can hardly be defined as norms/rules. We should, therefore, be able to specify which types of behavioural regularities are able to define an institution – a difficult and rare operation. More often, the behavioural regularity that violates the norm/rule that is poorly abided by is regarded as the true institution.[24]

This distinction between effective institutions as certified by regular behaviour (for instance, bribing to get X) and ineffective institutions certified as such by the absence of regular behaviours (the prohibition of bribing) opens an additional problematic field. The relationship between the rule not to bribe the officer or not to double park and the 'regular' behaviour of bribing officers and double parking is often seen under the label of the opposition between 'formal' and 'informal' institutions.[25] In the behavioural regularity approach, informal institutions are not a subset of the genus institutions but rather 'true institutions' that oppose, negate and violate the formal ineffective ones. This generates a paradox: informal institutions are, by definition, effective, but we can have formal institutions that are also effective. This puts into logical contradiction the distinction between formal and informal institutions. If we take seriously the idea that recurrent patterns of behaviour only define an effective institution, then there should be no need to distinguish between formal and informal institutions.

In fact, it is often a plea of this approach that more attention should be given to informal institutions as opposed to formal ones. The idea of informal institutions can be applied to virtually any behaviour that departs from, or is not accounted for by, formal institutions; that is, by the prevalent norms or written rules. In a recent contribution, examples of informal institutions include the facts that Brazilian police regularly operate illegal extra-judicial executions; that Latin American presidents enjoy a degree of executive dominance that exceeds the constitutional provisions; that Costa Rican MPs work at the constituency level notwithstanding the fact that the electoral system offers no incentive for this behaviour; that in the selection of American candidates,

---

[24] Aoki, M. (2000), 'Institutional evolution as punctuated equilibria', in Ménard, C. (ed.), *Institutions, Contracts and Organizations*, Cheltenham, Edward Elgar, pp. 11–33, 16.

[25] The distinction is ambiguous because it refers to three different dimensions: formal as legal and informal as non-legal; formal as explicit and informal as tacit; and finally formal as designed and informal as spontaneous: Hudgson, 'What are institutions?', p. 11.

committed voters tend to participate more intensely in the primaries and foster the election of polarising candidates; and that the practice of abortion is frequently prohibited but amply tolerated.[26] This list is an example of the confusion that emerges when considering informal institutions as regularities of behaviour. Widespread violations of codified rules (Brazil), the practice of power extending beyond codified rules (Latin America), departures from expected behaviour or self-interest (Costa Rica) and mere behavioural consequences of codified institutions (USA) all get enrolled in the rank of informal institutions thanks to the claim of 'regularity' that characterises them.

One way to identify informal institutions is to look for instances in which similar formal rules produce different outcomes and then to attribute the difference to an informal institution. An alternative strategy is to identify stable patterns of behaviour that do not correspond to formal rules. However, this approach runs the risk of treating all behavioural regularities as informal institutions. Although some behavioural regularities may alert us to the existence of hidden norms, there is a risk of enrolling mere practices as institutions. Self-interest may be a crucial source of behavioural regularity; general cultural factors have the same capacity.[27]

Intentional and often reiterated efforts to modify rooted cultural traditions and undesired selfish behaviours through codified rules may easily lose institutional reality because of their often-protracted low level of effectiveness. Institutions as regularised behaviours downplay the role of codified rules focussing on the variety of phenomena that may make behaviour diverge from them. This often comes at the cost of missing the difference between clear and unclear sanctions; the presence of rules of interpretation and the absence of them. Norms/rules do not tell the whole story and analysis of them was never without additional explanations of the differential rate of acceptance of any given institution, of how similar institutions work differently and of how different institutions provide similar outcomes in time and space. But solving this

---

[26] Gretchen, H. and S. Levitsky (2004), 'Informal institutions and comparative politics: a research agenda', *Perspectives on Politics*, 2: 725–40.

[27] Pejovich, S. (1999), 'The effect of the interaction of formal and informal institutions on social stability and economic development', *Journal of Markets and Morality*, 2: 164–81, considers these factors as institutions.

problem by enlarging the definition of institutions to almost any regularity of behaviour comes with a high price.[28]

2.3 Games and Equilibria

In the discussion so far, institutions influence humans without being the object of their desires, beliefs and preferences. What characterises equilibrium approaches is a conception of institutions as rules determining the strategic relations among individuals that can be objects of actors' preferences. This emphasis defines 'institutions' as rules of a special kind: 'rules of the game' or simply 'games', and it is typical of rational choice orientations. There is variation among scholars, but even in this case some common elements characterise the approach.

The study of institutions was long neglected by economics because it could not be clearly equilibrium orientated.[29] Neo-institutional economics reshaped the topic to make it compatible with the assumptions of economics,[30] and speaks of 'rules of the game' as external constraints on actors and within which human action is channelled. In politics, the difficulty in studying political action in terms of equilibrium outcomes has obsessed scholars engaged in the search for explanations for the unforeseen high level of equilibrium outcomes.[31] An extensive literature focussed on why the predictions of cyclical voting and majorities are not occurring. Institutions are often seen as the key to explaining the occurrence of the equilibrium as a stable outcome. To keep institutions congruent with preference theory, they are defined as 'congealed tastes' or 'condensed conventions', as preferences about the

---

[28] On this point, see Bendix, R. (1973), *State and Society*, Berkeley, University of California Press, p. 11.

[29] This is not true for economists such as Thorstein Veblen, Karl Polanyi, John R. Commons, Adolf A. Berle, John Kenneth Galbraith and others, who, however, are marginal in mainstream economics.

[30] Masahiko Aoki has engaged in a research programme labelled 'Comparative Institutional Analysis' promising to go beyond both neo-classical and neo-institutional economics. See Aoki, M. (1996), 'Towards a comparative institutional analysis: motivations and some tentative theorizing', *The Japanese Economic Review*, 47: 1–19 and Aoki, M. (2001), *Comparative Institutional Analysis*, Cambridge, MA, The MIT Press.

[31] Starting with the contributions of Arrow, K. J. (1951), *Social Choice and Individual Values*, New York, Wiley, and Black, D. (1958), *The Theory of Committees and Elections*, Cambridge, Cambridge University Press.

rules that are congealed.[32] These congealed preferences consist of attitudes, beliefs, expectations and preferences about 'the way things are done around here'. Such institutions, therefore, are 'chosen' as much as policy proposals are.

Explanation of the existence of unexpected equilibria has taken various forms: the presence of ex-ante agreements; a norm of universalism to share things as a project for all members; the value of partisan labels in discouraging defection; the advantages of belonging to a majority; and sequential procedures that restrict the alternatives against which a specific proposal can be compared. Other institutional features can produce 'equilibrium' and stable outcomes: specific rules of preference aggregation concerning the power to set the agenda[33] and interaction among several institutions in the separation-of-powers approach.[34]

Shepsle names an institutionally enriched equilibrium concept a 'structure-induced equilibrium'. This is defined as an equilibrium that can depart from 'unnecessarily impoverished' explanations based on maximising behaviours.[35] In this case, the emphasis is more on the game as a technical analytical instrument than on the rules. Institutions are not things that make equilibria possible but are equilibria themselves. Institutions are ways to aggregate the preferences of selfish individuals as 'self-selected modes of constraint' for agents with well-defined preferences on policy proposals. To achieve an equilibrium outcome, a proposal does not need to defeat all possible alternative proposals, which easily leads to the instability outcome, but only those proposals that the 'rules' permit it to be compared with. In other words, institutions in general restrict the number of alternatives that can be compared with each other. Permissible amendments, a division of

[32] Riker, W. H. (1980), 'Implications from the disequilibrium of majority rule for the study of institutions', *American Political Science Review*, 74: 432–44.

[33] Romer, T. and H. Rosenthal (1978), 'Political resource allocation, controlled agendas, and the status quo', *Public Choice*, 33: 27–43.

[34] For a review, see Shepsle, K. A. and B. R. Weingast (2012), 'Why so much stability? Majority voting, legislative institutions, and Gordon Tullock', *Public Choice*, 152: 83–95; Shepsle, K. A. (2006), 'Rational choice institutionalism', in Rhodes, Binder and Rockman (eds.), *The Oxford Handbook of Political Institutions*, pp. 23–38; and Shepsle, K. A. (1986), 'Institutional equilibrium and equilibrium institutions', in Weisberg, H. (ed.), *The Science of Politics*, New York, Agathon, pp. 51–82.

[35] Shepsle, K. A. (1989), 'Studying institutions: some lessons from the rational choice approach', *Journal of Theoretical Politics*, 1: 131–47, 135–6.

labour among committees and their competences, and other kinds of similar rules have this effect.

In this perspective, the 'rules of the game' that define an institution include rules that (1) identify the players, (2) determine prospective outcomes, (3) permit alternative methods of deliberation and (4) specify the way in which preferences among *allowable* alternatives of *eligible* participants occur. 'An institution is a script that names the *actors*, their respective *behavioural repertoires* (or *strategies*), the *sequence* in which the actors choose from them, the *information* they possess when they make their selection and the *outcome* resulting from the combination of action choices.'[36] Institutions are game forms which, if we add the *preferences* of actors, transform the game form into a real game. In this formulation, the world is imagined as being characterised by a set of people (the choosing agents) engaged in choosing an institution or several institutions to shape the 'game' of their interactions; that is, setting the rules they must abide by. These people have no perfect information but they know a lot about themselves and about the others. This leads to an ex-ante selection of rules (i.e. game form) which, if obeyed, will not come to be regretted by any of the parties ex post.

The tenets of this approach are twofold. First, not all participants in the games are the same; they are differentiated because the rules confer the privilege of certain moves on a certain specified subset of actors. Some people have *prerogatives, competences* or even *powers* that others do not have. This is a critique of the anonymity assumptions of social choice models. Second, rules often delimit what (kind of) alternatives are available for choice. Certain alternatives are unavailable. This is a modification of the assumption of neutrality among alternatives. With these notions as a background, a structure-induced equilibrium may be defined as an alternative (a status quo ante) that is *invulnerable* in the sense that no other alternative allowed by the rule of the procedure is preferred by all the individuals, structural units and coalitions that possess a veto or voting power. The idea of a structure-induced equilibrium is seen as a move in the direction of incorporating institutional features into rational choice approaches. Structure and procedures combine with preferences to produce outcomes.

[36] Shepsle and Weingast, 'Why so much stability?', pp. 12, 24; Tsebelis, G. (1990), *Nested Games: Rational Choice in Comparative Politics*, Berkeley, University of California Press, pp. 92–5.

As usual, in this review I am only interested in the conception of institution that underlies the approach. I suspect that no one doubts that institutions *permit and foster equilibrium* outcomes. It is a different thing to say that *institutions originate as equilibria*, mainly as Nash equilibria. The idea that games and game theory can be used to define the *genesis* of certain types of institutions is convincing. The definition of the situation in which none of the actors has an interest in moving from the choice they have made seems particularly promising to produce stable outcomes that are then taken as the original birth of an 'institution'. This is likely to not be an exhaustive theory and one should perhaps specify which types of institutions are profitably seen to emerge in this way. Hierarchically shaped and authoritatively imposed institutions are not likely to originate in this way. However, 'equilibrium' is a very general term – vague enough to resist considerable strains. Its generality permits us to argue that the origin of any institution must rest on some kind of equilibrium. This is valid both for institutions such as customs, conventions and social norms, the self-enforcing mechanisms of which refer to a collective outcome that can be defined as an equilibrium. But it can also apply to all those codified and designed institutions that have been decided on by a subset of qualified actors. Even the emergence of those institutions that are imposed by the few on the many can always be described as resulting from a game form through which the few must reach an equilibrium.

However, it is a very different thing to argue that *institutions are 'equilibria'*.[37] This idea generates logical inconsistencies. First, institutions as 'forms of the game', 'rules of the game' or 'outcomes of the game' include an embedded functional theory and often many other things such as information, choices and available strategies. Moreover, in this line of interpretation (political) institutions are, therefore, an outcome that in theory can be extended to any additional actor entering the game.[38] Nevertheless, this cannot be said to be valid for those actors not taking part in it. Consequently, either (1) the institutional outcome

---

[37] On the dualism of rule/equilibrium, see Greif, A. and C. Kingston (2011), 'Institutions: rules or equilibria', in Schofield, N. and G. Caballero (eds.), *Political Economy of Institutions, Democracy and Voting*, Berlin and Heidelberg, Springer-Verlag, pp.13–43.

[38] Following the logic of the n-actors prisoner's dilemma supergame in chapter 4 of Taylor, M. (1976), *Anarchy or Cooperation*, London, Wiley; revised as *The Possibility of Cooperation* (1987, New York, Cambridge University Press).

reached involves all the members of the group, or (2) the equilibrium outcome must be constantly re-formulated whenever new members enter the game, or (3) it only involves a set of relevant or qualified actors who have the possibility of *generalising* the outcome norms/rules to non-participating actors. The first hypothesis raises the transaction costs to a preposterous level. The second hypothesis requires that any new actor different to those who originally reached the equilibrium will take part in the redefinition of the equilibrium, bringing his preferences and strategies into it, in which case no equilibrium would ever evolve into anything different from a provisional solution. In the third hypothesis, the generalisation of the cooperation norms/rules resulting from the game remains a mysterious process, which, however, cannot be guaranteed by the game outcome. The process of generalisation is inherently different to the process of interaction that engenders the norm/rule. It implies a 'socialisation' or 'command' capacity that is not inherent in the cooperative game.

If we posit the hypothesis that the generalisation process derives from the equilibrium, acquiring a force and value of its own so that new actors somehow spontaneously, unreflexively or automatically adhere to it without constantly gaming and calculating, then the equilibrium is no longer an individual, rational adaptation of the game form but something else. It teaches the players a lesson so that, instead of repeatedly calculating their payoff, they would save time by following the lesson learned. It acquires a normative content, it becomes a standard, a norm, the way to do things, the usual practice, an exogenous rule/norm that is accepted and that you do not need to achieve anew every time. Therefore, an institution, exactly because of its capacity to extend its normative effects to a continually changing group membership, cannot be defined theoretically as an equilibrium. Institutions conceptualised as equilibria are normatively neutral and do not incorporate the deontic element of a prescribed behaviour. If equilibria do so, then they are no longer equilibria. In conclusion, there is a logical incompatibility between the concepts of equilibrium and institution.

If institutions are defined as 'structurally induced equilibria', it is not clear whether the equilibrium-generating structure is (1) another institution or (2) a rule or sub-routine of the same institution. The equilibrating 'structure' could be external, in which case we can simply say that an institution with the conferred power to order another institution produces equilibrium outcomes.[39] Alternatively, it could be internal, in which case there would not be much use in the concept because institutions would be able to produce equilibria with their own rule systems. If a structure-induced equilibrium is equilibrium 'induced' by structures and structures are rules and procedures, institutions come to be defined as equilibria induced by rules and procedures; that is, rules induced by rules. This gives the impression of a tautological formulation of what an institution is.

2.4 Cognitive Templates

The views discussed so far provide a 'thin' understanding of institutions in which they appear primarily as norms and rules. There are more 'thick' conceptions of institutions which include within the institutional phenomenology memories, practices, routines, conventions, roles, organisational forms, technologies, beliefs, myths, paradigms, cultural and cognitive templates, and mental frames. These are infused with values; they have lost their mere instrumental value; they generate strong personal interests and diffuse loyalties; they adapt in an isomorphic way to environmental myths; and they eventually consist in and represent highly persistent normative and symbolic systems.[40]

Institutions can be seen as 'institutionalised' practices with the accent on the institutionalisation process rather than on the specific content of the practice. A social relationship among a set of actors is institutionalised when the actors are behaving not following individualistic rationality. That is, the actors are willing to pay a cost rather than destroy the

---

[39] For instance, if in a parliamentary system the cabinet repeatedly fails to master parliamentary support, then the president can dissolve the assembly. On these interaction rules, see Chapter 6.

[40] On sociological institutionalism, see Di Maggio, P. J. and W. W. Powell (1991), 'The iron cage revisited: institutional isomorphism and collective rationality in organizational fields' and Meyer, J. W. and B. Rowen (1991), 'Institutionalized organizations: formal structures as myth and ceremony', both in Powell, W. W. and P. J. Di Maggio (eds.), *The New Institutionalism in Organizational Analysis*, Chicago, IL, University of Chicago Press, pp. 41–62 and 63–82. See also Jepperson, R. L. (2000), 'The development and application of sociological institutionalism', in Berger, J. and M. Jr. Zelditch (eds.), *New Directions in Sociological Theory: The Growth of Contemporary Theories*, Lanham, MD, Rowman & Littlefield, pp. 229–66 and Greenwood, R., C. Oliver, K. Sahlin and R. Suddaby (2008), 'Introduction', in *The Sage Handbook of Organizational Institutionalism*, London, Sage, pp. 1–46.

relationship or face an accusation of non-compliance with appropriateness standards.[41]

If by institutionalisation we mean the process through which these practices and routines persist and become infused with values while others decline, we can imagine several mechanisms. Institutions persist because they 'increase returns' (the qwerty keyboard argument). Institutions persist because, over time, commitments to them increase and help to define the identity of those who belong to them. Institutions persist because they 'objectify' in the sense of being presented as objective ways of doing things in a given context.[42]

Institutionalisation implies (1) an increasing clarity, agreement and formalisation of a behavioural code, (2) description, explanation and justification of behavioural rules and (3) the definition of which resources are legitimate in different settings and who has access to them and control over them. Institutionalisation unfolds in three steps: 'externalisation', 'objectification' and 'internalisation'. Externalisation is the production, through social interaction, of symbolic structures, the meanings of which come to be shared by the participants. Objectification is the process through which this production becomes an objective external factor, a reality experienced by and in common with others. Internalisation is the process through which this objectified world feeds back, basically retrojecting into the actor's consciousness through the process of its socialisation.[43] On the contrary, de-institutionalisation implies that existing rules, practices, descriptions, explanations, justifications, resources and powers are becoming more contested and possibly discontinued. There is increasing uncertainty, disorientation and conflict. Under these conditions it is necessary to use more incentives or more coercion to make people follow the prescribed procedures and routines and to punish deviance.

This emphasis sees institutions primarily as cognitive or cultural factors, identifying them with the shared conceptions or mindsets that constitute social reality and the frames through which meaning is

---

[41] Mayer, W. and B. Rowan (1977), 'Institutionalized organizations: formal structure as myth and ceremony', *American Journal of Sociology*, 83: 340–63.

[42] On the process of institutionalisation seen from the point of view of strategic actors, see Urpelainen, U. (2011), 'The origins of social institutions', *Journal of Theoretical Politics*, 23: 215–40.

[43] Beger, P. L. and T. Luckmann (1967), *The Social Construction of Reality*, New York, Doubleday Anchor, was very influential for this emphasis.

attributed and constructed. Institutions so defined are based on values and embedded in culture. In line with this understanding, contemporary sociological institutionalists define institutions in a very broad sense, including not just norms/rules or procedures but also the symbol system, cognitive scripts and moral templates that provide the 'frame of meaning' guiding human action.[44] They often surround organisations with a variety of institutions such as institutionalised myths, rationalised institutional rules, institutionalised contexts and institutionalised organisations.[45] Culture itself tends to be defined as an institution, being seen as a network of routines, symbols or scripts providing templates for behaviour. These culturally specific practices, akin to myths and ceremonies, do not necessarily enhance the formal means–ends efficiency. Institutions are culturally constructed conceptions. Society is institutionalised knowledge and culture.

Behaviour is not rational and strategic but bounded by individual worldviews. Institutions influence behaviour by providing the cognitive scripts, categories and models that are indispensable for action. They provide the terms on which meaning is assigned in social life and in this way define the preferences and the very identity of actors themselves. The interaction between individuals and institutions is mutually constitutive.

More generally, the revolution in cognitive sciences has fostered a rebirth of a variety that we could label 'cognitive institutionalism'. Learning at the social level is seen as 'shared or collective learning' composed of two factors: a static one – shared mental models resulting from communication; and an evolutionary one – the transmission and accumulation of knowledge across generations. A mental model is to be understood as the final prediction that the mind makes or expectation that it has regarding the environment before getting feedback from it. Learning is the complex modification of mental models according to feedback received from the environment, an evolutionary process of trial and error, as failure to solve a problem leads to trialling a new solution. Indeed, the persistence throughout history of dogmas, myths, superstitions and ideologies based on flawed beliefs requires as much attention to be paid to learning that produces such beliefs as to learning

---

[44] Sometimes institutions are viewed primarily as cognitive and discursive phenomena. Phillips, N., T. B. Lawrence and C. Hardy (2004), 'Discourse and institutions', *Academy of Management Review*, 29: 635–52.

[45] Mayer and Rowan, 'Institutionalized organizations'.

that correctly interprets the problems confronting humans. Elucidation of the learning process is the crucial step to adequately explain the emergence, evolution and effects of institutions, and it is what makes the qualitative difference between a cognitive approach and other approaches.[46]

2.5 Institutions as Organisations

The understanding of institutions in a thick and organic sense often derives from organisational studies and from the blurred distinction between organisations and institutions. In many research perspectives, organisations are equated with institutions; in others, organisations are regarded as one type of institution among others.

Any organisation is defined by its specific *membership* and *goals* and by the modalities of their achievement through *differentiation* (division of labour, specialisation and the presence of a centre of authority and control) and *integration* (the process that reconducts to a unity of intent the efforts of individuals in their respective roles).[47] All organisations, such as stock companies, armies, schools, hospitals, prisons and churches, are deliberately constructed to reach and attain specific goals. All have bodies constituted to define or modify these ends. All have norms/rules to define the people who have a right to participate in the definition/modification of the goals and in the more practical policies for their attainment. The ideal-type configuration of the classic Weberian bureaucratic organisation includes ten features, most of which are in fact rules/norms.[48] Simon sees an organisation as

---

[46] On the role of learning, see Mantzavinos, C., D. C. North and S. Shariq (2004), 'Learning, institutions, and economic performance', *Perspectives on Politics*, 2: 75–84, 76–7.

[47] Gross, E. and A. Etzioni (1985), *Organizations in Society*, Englewood Cliffs, NJ, Prentice-Hall.

[48] These are as follows: (1) functionaries only obey objective office duties; (2) within a well-defined office hierarchy; (3) with precise office competences; (4) they are hired (not elected) through selection mechanisms; (5) based on qualifications as ascertained by exams and tiles; (6) they are rewarded with a contract with a salary, pension rights and so on; (7) they see their office as the unique or predominant profession; (8) they have career prospects; (9) they work in a context of separation of the administrative means and without personal appropriation of the office; and (10) they are submitted to office discipline and controls. Weber, M. (1978 [1922]), *Economy and Society*, edited by G. Roth and C. Wittich, Berkeley, University of California Press, vol. 2, pp. 956–8.

a multi-level entity in which at each level there are corresponding values or factual 'premises' that allow individuals that cover a role to take decisions that are coherent with the overall design of the organisation. At any moment, a comprehensive task of the organisation exists that can be decomposed into a plurality of simpler sub-tasks that are linked together. The organisation is a way to simplify decisional processes through the definition of the decisional premises which relate to any role.[49] Other typologies of organisation make primary reference to the beneficiary of the organisation – distinguishing between (1) mutually beneficial organisations (parties, trade unions, voluntary associations), (2) profit organisations (firms) and (3) public welfare organisations (firefighters, police and so on).[50] Others combine the principle of adhesion with the mechanism of control, distinguishing between (1) coercive organisations which resort to force and violence and foresee an 'alienated participation' (e.g. prisons), (2) utilitaristic organisations based on exchange of resources (e.g. firms) and (3) normative and symbolic organisations based on fideistic adhesion and symbolic means of control (e.g. churches).[51]

As far as norms and rules are concerned, I believe a fundamental distinction relates to the extent to which the organisation is built on the assumption that it represents the preferences and goals of its members or is constituted by members who have in principle no voice in the preference and goals of the organisation. In the first case, conflicts emerge concerning the goals and the best ways to achieve or modify them. Norms/rules are necessary to align the goals of participants, achieve command through accepted modalities and limit the means through which different interests can be pursued. In the second case, the participation of the members is defined by contract and remuneration and the goals of the organisation are set by a structure of authority not answerable to the members. Norms/rules are more technical devices for the improvement of

---

[49] Simon, H. A. (1957), *Administrative Behavior*, London, Macmillan, pp. 110–22.

[50] Blau, P. and R. W. Scott (1962), *Formal Organizations*, San Francisco, CA, Chandler, pp. 40–5.

[51] Etzioni, A. (1961), *Modern Organizations*, Hempstead, Prentice Hall and (1975), *A Comparative Analysis of Complex Organizations*, New York, Free Press.

performance and the resolution of technical issues concerning how best to achieve the defined goals, while conflicts of interest and corresponding ideological divisions are less central, and technical problem-solving norms/rules prevail.[52]

2.5.1 Are Organisations and Institutions the Same Thing?

Organisations of any type have norms/rules as an essential and constitutive dimension,[53] which, however, does not exhaust their property space. Organisations include people and their interactions, are physical entities with time and space locations and they have seats, buildings, properties and financial budgets. They are legal personalities. In firms, schools, hospitals, legislatures and courts, rather similar sets of basic norms/rules combine and interact with real people, resources, traditions, culture and values to create new, emerging properties that neither belong to the simple norms/rules nor to the atomised individuals but instead to the organisation as a whole.

For these reasons, in some works no distinction is made between the two concepts: organisations are institutions and institutions are organisations.[54] In particular, organisational sociology studies undervalue the difference between the two. Rules and norms develop together with organisational structures, and changes in organisational forms reflect changes in norms and rules. Organisations are shaped by the cultural norms and rules in which actors are embedded and this environment limits the options for what organisations can do and how they can change.[55]

---

[52] However, organisational studies underline that the elements that lead to efficiency may produce inefficiency in specific instances, and that bureaucratic procedures may inhibit the realisation of organisational goals. See Merton, R. K. (1940), 'Bureaucratic structure and personality', *Social Forces*, 18: 560–8.

[53] For a distinction among types of rules in organisations, see March, J. G., M. Schulz and X. Zhou (2000), *The Dynamics of Rules: Changes in Written Organizational Codes*, Stanford, CA, Stanford University Press, pp. 5–15.

[54] In particular, Selznick, P. (1957), *Leadership in Organization*, London, Harper and Row; Williamson, O. E. (1990), *Organization Theory: From Chester Barnard to the Present and Beyond*, New York, Oxford University Press; Hall, P. A. and R. C. R. Taylor (1996), 'Political science and the three new institutionalisms', *Political Studies*, 44: 936–57: 'In general, historical institutionalists associate institutions with organizations and the rules or conventions promulgated by formal organizations' (p. 938).

[55] Di Maggio and Powell, 'The Iron Cage Revisited'.

A different perspective proposes to keep together the institution/ organisation phenomenology under the label of institution by distinguishing between a 'structural', a 'procedural' and a 'behavioural' dimension of institutions. In this view, organisations like political parties are institutions in structural terms, voting rules are institutions in a procedural sense and conventions are institutions in a behavioural sense.[56] However, the three categories are not mutually exclusive. To exist, structural institutions (i.e. organisations) necessarily include procedural institutions and behavioural ones (norms and rules).

Organisations can also be defined as a type of institution – *a special type of institution*. If organisations inevitably require norms/rules to be set up and function, then 'it is evident that organisations are a special kind of institutions, *with additional features*' (my emphasis). Organisations are special institutions that involve '1) criteria to establish their boundaries and to distinguish their members from non-members, 2) principles of sovereignty concerning who is in charge and 3) a chain of command delineating responsibilities within the organisation',[57] but include additional features beyond the type (1), (2) and (3) norms/rules. In this case, institutions are the large genus of which organisations are a species. However, the problem comes exactly from these additional features, which are definitely non-norms/rules. Moreover, in this case 'institutions' define a set of objects that includes themselves to the extent that they include organisations that also include institutions. This is not tenable on mere logical grounds. That organisations have, involve or require institutions as rules/norms does not mean that organisations are a type of institution.

In any case, the assimilation of institutions and organisations gives birth to a perspective in which the 'institution' is precisely the specific interaction output of norms/rules, practices, routines, people and cultural traits. This way of looking at 'institutions/organisations' has advantages. It explains why similar rule/norm settings generate different outcomes in different cultural contexts, and why similar outcomes can result from different rule/norm settings. It also helps our understanding of how certain institutional isomorphisms exist among different organisations operating in the same cultural context. In all these

---

[56] Van Hees, M. (1997), 'Explaining institutions: a defense of reductionism', *European Journal of Political Research*, 32: 51–69, 56–60.
[57] Hudgson, 'What are institutions?', p. 8.

cases, it is the 'people/culture/values/expectations' element that makes the difference to how rules/norms operate. Specific forms of thinking and of collective understanding, values, assumptions, cognitive frames and so on are relevant to the definition of the identity and activities of the organisation. They offer the individual members adequate answers to questions such as 'who are we?', 'what do we do?' and 'what is the meaning of what we do?'.[58] Moreover, in organisations there are compliance searches that go beyond what role expectations would suggest and that usually rest on power resource asymmetries. They meet with resistance and a counter-mobilisation of resources, transforming the organisation into a political arena. This implies that within organisations what is foreseen by the rules/norms, by the competence organigram and by the formalised system of roles is only a part of their real functioning.

However, these research advantages come at the price of considerable confusion *when one tries to generalise about institutions*. If institutions equal organisations, then institutions have structure and culture. This generates inconsistencies when dealing with institutions that show neither ends, nor strategic action, nor structural differentiation, nor integration of preference mechanisms; that is, when dealing with institutions not embedded in an organisational form. Rules/norms do exist without any organisational base. Constitutions, electoral systems and penal codes have no organisational basis. Neither would one search for the organisational basis of property, marriage, rights, customs and social norms. If organisations always have norms/rules, not all norms/rules are or have organisations. The conclusion is that in order to help the study of organisations, we adopt a thick definition of institutions that is unsuited to understanding the whole institutional reality. Organisational studies phagocytise institutional studies, making them functional to their heuristic endeavour.

2.5.2 *Are Organisations and Institutions Different Things?*

If institutions and organisations are kept analytically separate, one way to conceptualise the difference is to stress that organisations are agents

---

[58] Ferrante, M. and S. Zan (1994), *Il fenomeno organizzativo*, Rome, La Nuova Italia Scientifica, p. 130.

(or actors, or players) and that institutions are rules/norms.[59] A similar line of thought suggests that the difference is to be reduced to the difference between ends and means, to the extent that agents act according to ends while considering the means (the institutions).[60] Obviously, institutions in a thin and atomistic conception as rules/ norms cannot be actors, while organisations are actors having common purposes, promoting independent interests, reflecting historical leg- acies and so on.

Unfortunately, even proposing a neat distinction between the two is unconvincing. The fact is that the boundaries between an organisation and the environment – its structure, membership, roles, networks, decision rules and so on – are defined by institutions in a thin sense, by 'rules/norms'. Organisations (parties, firms, universities, hospitals and so on) can be considered collective actors only to the extent that we can demonstrate that they are coherent and capable of unified strategic action. This rests on the internal ordering of the organisation, which is made up of selection and decision rules for the aggregation of prefer- ences and a level of agreement concerning these rules. We are back to the point that organisations and institutions cannot be separated neatly because organisations always have institutions – the thin institutions of rules/norms.

Therefore, in analytically discussing the concepts of 'institution' and 'organisation' we get trapped in a 'Sophie's choice' dilemma, in a choice between two entities that are both necessary but necessitate the destruc- tion of the other to continue to exist.[61] If we include organisations in the same semantic space as the concept of institutions, we are bound to bring within the latter the many additional features that organisations carry as defining properties. If, on the contrary, we exclude institutions from the semantic field of organisations, we de-vertebrate organisa- tions of their embedded institutional structure. One can think that the two solutions refer to different research agendas and issues which use

---

[59] A line followed by North, D. C. (1990), *Institutions, Institutional Change and Economic Performance*, Cambridge, Cambridge University Press, pp. 4–7 and North, D. C. (1994), 'Economic performance through time', *The American Economic Review*, 84: 359–68, 361. See also Knight, J. (1992), *Institutions and Social Conflict*, Cambridge, Cambridge University Press, p. 3.

[60] Khalil, E. (1995), 'Organizations versus institutions', *Journal of Institutional and Theoretical Economics/Zeitscrift fur die gesamte Staatswissenschaft*, 151: 445–66, 447 and 449.

[61] Styron, W. (1976), *Sophie's Choice*, New York, Random House.

the same term differently. Alternatively, one can pragmatically ask which of the two engenders lower analytical costs.

If we consider institutions and organisations not as separate entities but as analytical dimensions of analysis, we can imagine that every socio-political entity has an organisational and an institutional dimension, or an 'organisational structure' and a 'normative structure'.[62] The two dimensions have only a relative independence. Elements typical of the organisational dimension (membership and goals, culture and understandings, division of labour, specialisations, a centre of authority and control, integration mechanisms) can also be seen in the light of the norms/rules that sustain them. Nevertheless, the two dimensions combine in different ways and some entities have a stronger or weaker institutional basis and a stronger or weaker organisational basis. An electoral system is a codified institution which is almost entirely without an organisational dimension, while a firm is a strong organisational entity with a relatively modest internal institutional ordering. A refectory is weak on both dimensions, while a big modern hospital is a corporate entity with strong institutional norms/rules and a strong organisational dimension. Phenomena for which we cannot identify either an institutional or an organisational component are either mere individual behaviours (pay your bill, wash your teeth and so on) or totally unstructured collective behaviours, such as mobs, revolts, traffic jams and *statu nascenti* social movements (Table 2.1).

As mentioned earlier, this mental exercise is not fully convincing, but it is useful in that it evidences that the institutional dimension has priority over the organisational one. In the 'no institutional dimension' column, no case can be fitted. Even the weakest organisational dimension requires some institutional component to be present. Therefore, *for the theoretical constitution of the field of 'institutional studies'* a hard choice must be made, and this is to the advantage of an institutional priority and an organisational downgrading. Consider the concatenation of the following propositions:

(1) minister A issued provision X;
(2) the holder of a ministry has the competence to issue provisions;

---

[62] Martin, T. W. (1968), 'Social institutions: a reformulation of the concept', *Pacific Sociological Review*, 11: 100–10.

Table 2.1 *The institutional and organisational dimensions of entities*

| | | Institutional dimension Rules/norms | | |
		none	weak	strong
	none	behavioural outburst (stock exchange bubbles, mobs, traffic jams, etc.)	funerary conventions	electoral systems
Organisational dimension: office/ people/ properties	weak	impossible	refectories	court systems
	strong	impossible	firms	hospitals

(3) the organisation of government is made up of ministerial roles which, among other things, have the competence to issue provisions.[63]

In this sequence, proposition (1) is a mere factual statement that alone is without any institutional meaning. Proposition (3) defines the organisation of government in one of its main functions. Only proposition (2) is an institution that both explains/legitimises individual acts and defines a component of the organisation. Giving heuristic priority to institutions means interpreting acts first starting from their normative underpinning, and interpreting organisations first starting from the normative sets that define their goals, roles, competences, membership and so on. Undoubtedly, other motives or forces enter the interpretation of behaviours, and other factors affect the functioning of organisations. The question is what should be given interpretative priority.

In my view, it is analytically better to have clear ideas about institutions and to pay a price for the richness of organisational studies than

---

[63] The example is inspired by Battegazzorre, F. (2012), *Saggi sopra la teoria delle istituzioni politiche*, Genoa, Coedit, pp. 26–7.

to give priority to organisations at the cost of blurring the idea of institutions. Perhaps those who focus on the study of organisations find it preferable to deal with an encompassing concept of institutions. Those who are more focussed on the study of institutions are advised not to blur them within the pan-institutionalism of organisational approaches. This conclusion is more evident for the study of political institutions, as is discussed in the next chapters.

2.6 A Note on Historical Neo-institutionalism

Historical institutionalism is a predominant political science version of the new-institutionalist approach and it is one that gives special attention to 'political institutions'. I do not reserve a special place for it, which requires a note of explanation.

A large set of studies have recently gone under this label and they constitute a refinement of previously unlabelled traditions in both methodological and substantive terms. Historical neo-institutionalism has criticised 'old institutionalism' for consisting mainly of detailed configurative studies of different administrative and political structures, and for often being too legalistic, theoretically weak and poorly comparative. This literature has contributed to large debates about the role of time and change over time and to critiquing efficiency arguments about institutional development. Historical institutionalist studies have made important contributions to the consideration of history in process terms, of path dependence and critical junctures, of self-reinforcing or positive feedback processes, of sequencing arguments and threshold effects, and of modalities of institutional change.[64] This approach has a distinct advantage in the study of dynamic processes of institutional change as it is not committed to a frantic search for equilibria and it is freer to generate historically grounded empirical generalisations.[65] Moreover,

---

[64] See Thelen, K. (2003), 'How institutions evolve: insights from comparative historical analysis', in Mahoney, J. and D. Rueschemeyer (eds.), *Comparative Historical Analysis in the Social Sciences*, Cambridge, Cambridge University Press, pp. 208–40; Mahoney, J. and K. Thelen (2010), 'A theory of gradual institutional change', in Mahoney, J. and K. Thelen (eds.), *Explaining Institutional Change: Ambiguity, Agency and Power*, New York, Cambridge University Press, pp. 1–37; Héritier, A. (2007), *Explaining Institutional Change in Europe*, Oxford, Oxford University Press.

[65] Immergut, E. (1998), 'The theoretical core of the New Institutionalism', *Politics and Society*, 26, 1: 5–34, 26.

given their less demanding assumptions, historical institutionalists can also take institutions for granted in a conventional sense and focus on their impact on something else, such as the causal effect on policy outcomes.[66] Historical institutionalism puts emphasis on a new programme concerning how institutions shape political strategies and influence political outcomes, and it argues that this role is much greater than that suggested by rational choice models. It underlines that through – problematic rather than exogenously given – preference formation not only strategies but also actors' goals are shaped by institutions.

These important achievements are not discussed in this section. As with any other approach, here I only focus on the understanding of the phenomenon of 'institutions' that is typical of the approach. From this point of view, the contribution of this approach to the theoretical characterisation of institutions, and namely of political institutions, is limited and less elaborate than that of sociological and rational choice institutionalism.

When it comes to defining the object of the approach – institutions – it is argued that

in general, historical institutionalism works with a definition of institutions that includes both formal organisations and informal rules and procedures that structure conduct. . . .

Clearly included in the definition are such features of the institutional context such as the rules of the electoral competition, the structure of the party system, the relationships among the various branches of government and the structure and organisation of economic actors like trade unions. . . .

Our definition emphasises intermediate-level institutions, such as party systems and the structure of interest groups like unions, that mediate between the behaviour of individual political actors and national political outcomes. But couldn't more macro-level structures – class structure, for example – also qualify as institutions? Clearly such structure can impose significant constraints on behaviour.[67]

---

[66] Scharpf, F. W. (2000), 'Institutions in comparative policy research', *Comparative Political Studies*, 33: 762–90.

[67] The quotations are from Thelen, K. and S. Steinmo (1992), 'Historical institutionalism in comparative politics', in Steinmo, S., K. Thelen and F. Longstreth (eds.), *Structuring Politics: Historical Institutionalism in Comparative Analysis*, Cambridge, New York, Cambridge University Press, 1–31, 2, 10, 11.

In a sober account of the contrasts between a calculous and a cultural approach to institutions the question is raised

How do historical institutionalists define institutions? By and large, they define them as the formal and informal procedures, routines, norms and conventions embedded in the organisational structure of the polity or political economy. They can range from rules of a constitutional order or the standard operating procedures of a bureaucracy to the conventions governing trade unions' behaviour or bank-firm relations. In general, historical institutionalists associate institutions with organisations and the rules or conventions promulgated by formal organisations.[68]

If we judge it from the point of view of the analytical theory of 'institutions', and particularly of 'political institutions', this paradigm does not refer to or is inspired by a vision of institutions which is its own. The approach adheres to the general idea that *everything that structures behaviour is an institutional phenomenon*. Institutions as rules and norms and institutions as organisations are often assimilated. Little is said about the specific nature of political institutions with respect to other kinds of institutions such as conventions, routines and social norms.

The extended debate about historical institutionalism has very much focussed on new ways to approach the study of politics in which institutions are central, but has not contributed much to the clarification of the specific object of analysis. The debate concerns primarily the approach, not the type of institutions. Presented as a new research paradigm, historical institutionalism focusses more on research goals and tasks than on a special understanding of political institutions. The definition of the latter remains quite encompassing. This is problematic given the special attention the approach gives to political institutions, and it is only understandable if we consider historical institutionalism as a research programme and a paradigm in which the institutionalist content is not realised in the study of the special institutions that are political, but in the perspective from which every relevant socio-political phenomenon is studied.[69] The neo-institutionalist approach does not identify with a specific understanding of political institutions.

---

[68] Hall and Taylor, 'Political science and the three new institutionalisms', p. 938.

[69] Peters, B. G. (1998), 'Political institutions, old and new', in Goodin, R. E. and H. D. Klingemann (eds.), *A New Handbook of Political Science*, Oxford, Oxford University Press, pp. 205–20, defines neo-institutionalism as an approach, a new methodology and new variables rather than a specific understanding of what 'institutions' are.

2.7 Conclusion

The concept of 'institution' discussed in this chapter is much stretched and covers a wide set of meanings and an even wider set of objects. With such encompassing visions of institutions, it becomes difficult to define them *a contrario* – to define what is a non-institution.[70] If the definition is very wide, then obviously institutions matter, but it is also impossible or very difficult to say anything precise about them. To combine customs and conventions, social norms and role expectations, cultural templates, shared notions of appropriateness, cultural cognitive frameworks, political parties and the legal system, regimes and cleavages in the same category of institutions is to theorise about objects that do not belong to the same genus. The risk is that of theorising about 'non-existent aggregates that are bound to defy, on account of their non-comparable characteristics, any and all attempts at ... generalisations'.[71] If institutions are so widely different, there can hardly be a theory of 'institutions' in a general sense. Most often contributions extend the specific understanding of 'institutions' in a given context and disciplinary approach to the whole world of institutions.[72] It is unfortunate when a specific emphasis or approach presents itself as a general theory of institutions without specifying the application context of its understanding.

We can conclude that what constitutes an institution is not generalisable and depends largely on the researcher, the subject of research and the research question. Different conceptions of institution, from 'game

---

[70] A concern already expressed by Rothstein, B. (1996), 'Political institutions: an overview', in Goodin and Klingemann (eds.), *A New Handbook of Political Science*, pp. 104–25 and Blondel, 'About institutions, mainly, but not exclusively, political', pp. 717–18. The only example I know of an author who explicitly tells us what is not an institution is provided by Knight, *Institutions and Social Conflict*, p. 3: 'Thus, rules of thumb such as the maxim "pay my bills on the day I get my pay-check", "get an hour of exercise five days a week", and "get a physical once a year" are not institutions ... they are purely private constraints, idiosyncratic to the individual actor.'

[71] Sartori G. (1991), 'Comparing and miscomparing', *Journal of Theoretical Politics*, 3: 243–57.

[72] And the different approaches are worlds apart. There is no single citation common to two authoritative reviews of sociological and rational choice institutionalism. See Lawrence, T. B. (2008), 'Power, institutions and organizations', in Greenwood, R., C. Oliver, K. Sahlin and R. Suddaby (eds.), *The Sage Handbook of Organizational Institutionalism*, London, Sage, pp. 170–97, and Shepsle, 'Rational choice institutionalism'.

form' to organisations to mental templates, serve vastly different research programmes and different types of situations. 'Because of definitional looseness surrounding institutions, inevitable difficulties ... are associated with conducting institutional analysis.'[73] Undoubtedly, there are inherent and constitutive difficulties in institutional analysis. The alternative is to take a clear stand on these problems and try to disentangle the definitional maze by making clear at least a few fundamental distinctions among types of institution. This requires facing the risks implicit in the attempt to define the core properties of each of them, and this is what I turn to in the next chapter.

[73] Parto, S. (2003), 'Economic activity and institutions: taking stock', *Infonomics Research Memorandum Series*, Maastricht, p. 28.

3 | A Framework for Institutional Analysis and a Typology of Institutions

In reviewing diverse understandings of institutions in Chapter 2, I concluded with scepticism about the possibility of generalising about all possible institutions. This difficulty derives from the imbalance between the wide definitional scope, the many empirical referents and the level of generality of findings. Improving on this situation requires an analysis of the various dimensions of institutional phenomenology and a re-composition of them into different and more homogeneous 'types' of institutions. In particular, the particularities of political institutions, the object of this work, cannot be fully appreciated without a discussion of different types of institutions. Without such a framework, we are likely to observe a flourishing variety of incompatible theories.

In Section 3.1 of this chapter, I draw the core 'dimensions' or 'properties' of institutional analysis from the different approaches reviewed in Chapter 2 and discuss them separately. In Section 3.2, I reconstruct different types of institutions based on specific combinations of these dimensions or properties. In Sections 3.3 and 3.4, I discuss the fundamental distinction between 'norms' and 'rules', how they relate to one another and the specific dynamics of changes in them.

The categories I have chosen to identify the dimensions for the analysis of institutional phenomenology are likely to be controversial and contestable.[1] However, it is by contesting these categories and their outer limits that we can clarify the relevant continuities and discontinuities that might make them or other categories analytically useful.

---

[1] To a certain degree, the dimensional analysis proposed here is inspired by the component analysis of institutions in Crawford, S. E. S. and E. Ostrom (1995), 'A grammar of institutions', *American Political Science Review*, 89: 582–600. Their grammar of institutions includes five components: Attributes, Deontic, AIms, Conditions and 'Or else' (ADICO), where 'or else' can be read as sanctions. Norms can be defined as ADIC, rules as ADICO and shared strategies as AIC. My analysis goes in a different direction, however. Among the many differences, I do not consider shared strategies to be institutions precisely because of the missing deontic element.

3.1 The Dimensions of Institutional Analysis

The previous chapter allowed the dimensions of analysis on which each approach puts an emphasis to emerge. These core dimensions were *stability*, *normativity*, *sanctionability* and *enforcement*. To these, I add an additional core dimension that is rarely considered, the level of *layering/interconnectedness* of institutions, which also varies across institutional types. Finally, other often-mentioned dimensions include the *intentionality* of their generation, their *endogeneity* and their *function* and *efficiency*. Institutions can be intentionally devised or develop unintentionally or spontaneously. They can be characterised as resulting from endogenous or exogenous forces and change processes. They are often defined by referring to the 'functions' they perform and to their efficiency in performing them. This leaves us with eight dimensions of institutional analysis to discuss:

(1) Stability
(2) Normativity
(3) Sanctions
(4) Enforcement
(5) Layering/interconnectedness
(6) Intentionally designed versus spontaneous
(7) Endogenous versus exogenous
(8) Functions/efficiency.

3.1.1 Stability

Generally speaking, institutions are more stable than behaviours. This is a statement no scholar or school disagrees with. They have a high degree of inertia and it is difficult for actors to depart from the established paths. Institutions tend to be more permanent, less variable, more resilient to change and more stable than any individual's preferences and values can ever be. The question is which types of institutions are more stable and which less stable.

3.1.2 Normativity: Preceptive and Directive Force

The existence of institutions means that certain kinds of human conduct are no longer optional but in some sense required and obligatory.

Institutions generally incorporate a normative element, a deontic component, a prescribed direction of behaviour and an expected conformity. The range of 'appropriate' actions is by far narrower than that of possible actions. Normativity is the context of standards of oughtness or appropriateness.

The normative strength of any given institution varies depending on two factors: its *preceptive force* and its *directive force*. The preceptive force is defined as the capacity of an institution to leave a prescriptive meaning and trace in the consciousness of individuals. The directive force is the capacity of an institution to determine the conduct of individuals. When the preceptive force of an institution is maximal, it becomes an ineludible directive force. When it is minimal, its directive capacity declines. However, we should not see directive force as deriving entirely from preceptive force, in which case the distinction would be redundant. Certain norms/rules are so thoroughly and ruthlessly enforced that they effectively determine the conduct of people even if their preceptive strength in their consciousness is minimal. Other norms/rules maintain a certain preceptive meaning, while in fact being without directive force. For instance, the ancient norms concerning the penal extra-territoriality of buildings of worship even today have a certain preceptive meaning. They are nevertheless deprived of almost any directive force for judges and police forces. On the contrary, custom control rules are effectively abided by without having much felt preceptive force.

The 'informal institutions' that are often invoked to explain the deviation from formal ones should be checked for their normativity. If corruption and bribing are widely practised up to the point that the rules/norms that prohibit them are made ineffective, this does not mean that corruption and bribing become institutions. If people violate these norms, it may be a frequent behaviour or an effective practice but not necessarily a prescribed one.

3.1.3 Sanctions

Non-compliance and explicit violations of norms/rules are associated with hostile reactions, punishment or sanctioning. These can go from an embarrassing silence or a disgusted facial expression to the death penalty. Norms/rules that do not generate any of these effects cannot be defined as effective institutions. Even the dimension of sanctionability requires more precise treatment. Sanctions have two fundamental components. The first is the ex-ante clarity of infringement. The second is the ex-post certainty of the penalty.

3.1.3.1 Ex-Ante Clarity

Clarity refers to the degree of ex-ante precision of the definition of the infringement. Ex ante, it may be more or less clear which norms/rules are to be applied. If institutions are deeply internalised, the question is of little consequence. For all kinds of norms/rules that are not profoundly embedded in the consciousness, this clarity is crucial. For institutions understood as cognitive scripts, moral templates and frames of meanings, the ex-ante clarity of the infringement may be very low.

3.1.3.2 Ex-Post Certainty

This dimension refers to the certainty of the ex-post implications of abiding by or disobeying existing institutional prescriptions. Sanctions that are perceived as certain are predictable. Doubts about the willingness of the other to punish, mercy, forgiveness and so on may define a circle of uncertainty around rewards and punishments.

The ex-ante clarity and the ex-post certainty of sanctions are core elements in the distinction between norms and rules, as will be more extensively argued later in this chapter. If infringement of norms/rules is clearly defined and the likely consequences well known, the information will go a long way towards making the set of feasible actions coincide with the institutionally defined subset. However, the infringement may be clear while its ex-post implications are uncertain. Even worse, we may fear the implications of unclear infringements. Different types of institutions vary in both these dimensions, which opens the way to the calculus of positive and negative incentives for a specific course of action and, hence, its likelihood of being chosen by actors. Note that conceptions that see institutions as cultural scripts, cognitive templates, frames of meanings and so on that are internalised as constitutive elements of the individual actor considerably dilute the element of sanctioning and let it fade towards states of psychological uneasiness.

3.1.4 Enforcement

How norms/rules are enforced is a further differentiation mechanism. Institutions may depend on self-enforcement; that is, they may be enforced by the 'first party', which is the actor itself. They may be enforced by a 'second party', by peer-group reactions involving reputation, blame, shame and so on. Institutions may be enforced by a 'third party'; that is, by an authority that enjoys such a position within a given membership group, organisation, association, firm and so on. These include private enforcers such as referees, arbiters and disciplinary bodies. Finally, institutions can be enforced by a 'fourth party', which is usually the specialised enforcement system of the state.

Stability, normativity, sanctionability and enforcement affect the level of compliance with single norms/rules. The level of compliance was mentioned earlier when discussing the distinction between 'formal' and 'informal' rules. More will be said about it later when discussing the great divide between rules and norms. In short, my position is that the degree of compliance/deviance can distinguish different types of institutions but should not be used to distinguish institutions from non-institutions.

3.1.5 Layering/Interconnectedness

Institutions are layered vertically and interconnected horizontally to different degrees. The word 'institution' is used to denote concrete, complex and large-scale entities or organisations and at the same time denotes the specific rules and norms that regulate the activity of these same entities. Vertically, 'institution' indicates anything that goes from a single norm of conduct, custom or convention, the articles of statutes, or rules of procedure up to complex codes and interrelated sets of institutional rules and norms, and finally to complex organisations with dense institutional orderings. We use the word 'institution' for the French Assembly, the German Constitutional Court and the American presidency and with the same term we identify the standing orders of the French Assembly, the rules of accessibility of the Constitutional Court's jurisdiction and the veto powers of the American president. If we claim that a political regime or the market are institutions, we refer to an extremely complex set of atomistic institutions combined into a more complex institution. The diligence of a good father/mother of a family is different from the whole of family law and both are part of civil law. Institutions are imbricated into one another.

A hierarchical layering of institutions distinguishes *atomistic accounts* from *molecular* and *holistic accounts*.[2] Atomistic accounts consider institutions as singular entities, singular norms and rules. Molecular accounts go beyond the atomistic forms. They have constitutive elements (atomistic norms/rules) but also their own structure made up of the other norms/rules that link the molecule together. Holistic accounts of institutions include whole institutional 'regimes', organisational entities and general principles. In this case we may tend to move from an understanding of the whole to an understanding of the parts.

How can institutions as atomistic norms/rules be combined in higher-level institutions such as the market, the regime and the monarchy? More complex institutions are constituted by summing up simple institutions. Alternatively, higher-level institutions may constitute entities far more complex than the sum of their parts, which shows emerging properties that belong to none of them. In this case, the norms/rules cannot be analysed in isolation. In most situations, in fact, interactions among norms/rules are explicitly foreseen as other norms/rules. Rules combine configurationally rather than operating individually and we need to include norms/rules that explicitly regulate this interaction. The terms 'rule regime',[3] 'rule configurations'[4] and 'institutional arrangements'[5] have been used to tackle the problem of layering and interconnectedness. In Table 3.1 I make my own proposal, taking examples from typical political institutions. I keep the term 'institution' as the general label and distinguish between *norms/rules* as single or atomistic institutions, *institutes* as sets of related atomistic institutions and *institutional regimes*.[6]

---

[2] Lane, J.-E. and S. Ersson refer to 'atomistic' and 'organic' conceptions of institutions in their (2000), *The New Institutional Politics: Performance and Outcomes*, New York, Routledge, pp. 5–7.

[3] March, Schulz and Zhou, *The Dynamics of Rules*, pp. 91–2.

[4] Ostrom, 'An agenda for the study of institutions', pp. 14–15.

[5] Hollingsworth, R. J. (2000), 'Doing institutional analysis: implications for the study of innovations', *Review of International Political Economy*, 7: 595–644, 601 and following.

[6] Institutionalist legal theory distinguishes different levels of layering. See Suarez-Rodriguez, J. J. (2016), 'Le fondement des principes juridiques: une question problématique', *Civilizar*, 16: 51–62; Atenza, M. and J. Ruitz-Manero (1993), 'Tre approcci ai principi di diritto', in *Analisi e diritto*, Torino, Giappichelli, pp. 13–16; Di Carlo, L. (2017), *Teoria istituzionale e ragionamento giuridico*, Torino, Giappichelli, pp. 59–63.

Table 3.1 *(Political) institutions by their layering/interconnectedness*

Rules/norms	Institutes	Institutional regimes
Single or atomistic institutions	A set of related atomistic institutions combined by addition	A set of related institutes that let new norms/ rules or institutes of interconnection emerge
The selection rule for the head of state	Responsibility institutes	Parliamentary regimes
Formateur's norms/rules	Decision institutes	Constitutional
Confidence/censure votes	Delegation institutes	monarchies
Dissolution of the legislature	etc.	etc.
Collegiality norms		
etc.		

A single *norm/rule* is highly specific and often contextual. By *institute* I refer to a set of atomistic institutions that relate to the same field, topic or functional problem (the family, the contract, the bicameral structure, etc.) and combine by addition to constitute the 'institute'. Institutes are more general than single norms/rules and may include different application modalities. Institutes such as the family, the contract and the selection of the chief executive are not necessarily characterised by the same single institutions in different times and places. The institute of the contract maintains itself and travels through time and space while being embodied by different single norms/rules that change considerably. *Institutional regimes* are more general and encompass a more complex set of rules/norms and institutes, and this complexity generates new rules/norms and even new institutes which are not simply additive but emerge from the inter-institutional layering and interconnectedness. At an even higher level of abstraction, one could locate 'institutional principles'. Freedom of thought, the rule of law and privatistic good faith cannot be described either as atomistic norms/rules or as institutes or institutional regimes. They are 'principles' in the sense that they are normatively pregnant and axiologically strong. They imply more semantic indeterminacy as epistemic categories applicable to a high number of spheres. Moreover, institutional principles are not expressed in a conditional form, while norms/rules generally are.[7] I do not discuss 'institutional principles' in this work.

Moving from single norms/rules to institutional regimes, we climb a ladder of conceptual abstraction and we increase the level of defectibility of our concepts. Norms/rules are more precise and therefore less defectible in the sense that they do not permit too many exceptions. The generality of institutes exposes them to being defeasible by another institute, with the consequence of a need for a technique to balance different institutes (on which there is more in Chapter 5). Institutional regimes allow even more exceptions and deviations, hybrid cases and mixed cases. The way in which rules/norms and institutes interact in an institutional regime is, therefore, subject to far more variations and exceptionalisms.

The distinction between single norms/rules, institutes and institutional regimes is particularly appropriate and useful for the analysis of political institutions. Nevertheless, the proposed layering may be useful and clarify the differences also in the fields of social and economic institutions. For instance, we should avoid the specific norms/rules on inheritance by minors, the general institute of responsibility for minors and the even broader family regime being undifferentiated in the same basket.

3.1.6 *Intentionally Designed versus Spontaneous*

Beyond the five elements of stability, normativity, sanctionability, enforcement and layering/interconnectedness, the disagreement

---

[7] For rules, the conditional form is essential. Rules derives from the insertion of the circumstances of the case in the form of a conditional clause within the syntagma of the principle. For instance, the principle of freedom of art gets translated into the normative rule 'if one activity is artistic, then it is free' or 'it is exempted from taxation', which is the conditional formulation. The principle is not conditional, but the rule is. On this latter point, see Alexy, R. (2002), *A Theory of Constitutional Rights*, Oxford, Oxford University Press.

among different approaches widens. Some approaches incorporate theoretical statements about why institutions exist, what function they perform, how they emerge or change, or how efficient they are. A close connection exists between the four properties of institutions of being 'intentionally designed or unintended', 'endogenous or exogenous', and performing specific 'functional tasks' in a more or less 'efficient' way.

Concerning the issue of whether institutions originate from intentional design or evolve spontaneously, it is clear that without a differentiation between types of institutions, it is impossible to decide. Certain types of institutions are intentionally designed in a given moment, while others evolve over time without intentional design:

> It must be admitted that the structure of our social environment is manmade in a certain sense; that its institutions and traditions are neither the work of God nor of nature, but the results of human actions and decisions. But this does not mean that they are all consciously designed, and explicable in terms of needs, hopes and motives. On the contrary, even those which arise as the result of conscious and intentional human action are, as a rule, the indirect, the unintended and often the unwanted by-product of such actions.[8]

The 'artificer bias', the tendency to postulate a designer whenever we encounter what looks like evidence of orderliness and patterned structure, is always present but it is stronger when the overall pattern produced is not only well structured but also appears to be functional; that is, it responds to some need or goal.

Institutions that emerge without the execution of a plan need to be interpreted as unintended consequences of human action. However, not every unintended consequence qualifies as an explanation of the emergence of institutions. The accidental product of actions by one or many individuals does not qualify as an explanation of patterned outcomes like institutions. We have to distinguish and contrast explanations based on *human intentional design*, explanations as *mere human accidents* and explanations as *invisible-hand explanations*. Invisible-hand explanations need to clarify the mechanism that aggregates dispersed individual actions into the patterned outcome. It is only when the social pattern or institution to be explained

---

[8] Popper, K. (1963, 5th revised edition), *Conjectures and Refutations: The Growth of Scientific Knowledge*, London, Routledge, p. 342.

has a structure beyond a certain degree of complexity that an invisible-hand explanation has a point.[9]

Designed institutions often pass through too many hands before they are fully implemented. New members of committees, administrative bodies or departments conform to the traditions, rules and existing practices (or what they think they are), and sometimes contribute ideas and rules of their own. However, they often leave before these ideas and rules can be put into practice or before it becomes obvious that they did not work well. Therefore, the development of institutional rules is often a result of the interplay between 'fatherless traditions and orphaned decisions'.[10]

In this process, intentionally designed institutions become prone to unintended consequences. An intentional design of an institution could be an adequate causal explanation of its emergence, but the accumulation of unintended consequences may lead us to conclude that the original intended design is not a satisfactory explanation of its existence, durability and functioning. In conclusion, certain types of institutions unquestionably emerge from spontaneous dynamics (e.g. conventions, social norms), while others clearly derive from explicit design (e.g. electoral systems, professional codes). Nevertheless, all institutions are prone to fatherless traditions, orphaned decisions, unintended effects and mere accident.[11]

---

[9]   Margalit, U. E. (1978), 'Invisible-hand explanations', *Synthèse*, 39: 263–91, 267.

[10]   Bovens, M. (2007), 'Analysing and assessing accountability: a conceptual framework', *European Law Journal*, 13: 447–68, 457.

[11]   The birth of the American Constitution, probably one of the most deeply pondered documents in history, is so described: 'Even that most theoretically informed, deliberate group of men who assembled in Philadelphia in 1787 to reform the articles of the Confederation and who are credited with having produced a brilliant constitutional design actually improvised at every step. They abandoned reform for reconstruction. They composed their bicameral legislature to resolve the impasse between small states and large. The supremacy of federal authority over the states was the unintended consequence of a dispute over a different issue . . .. The institution of judicial review was omitted from the document, was assumed to be inherent in it by some . . . and was probably not contemplated by others. The presidency, truly an original contribution to government, was the result of a coup against the majority of the constitutional convention by partisans of a strong executive operating in two committees of the convention; most delegates were wary of executive power, believing that parliament was the palladium of liberty . . .. The framers of 1787 could justify the design that emerged, but they could hardly claim to have planned the result.' Horowitz, D. (2002), *Constitutional Design: Proposals Versus Processes*, in Reynolds, A. (ed.), *The Architecture of Democracy: Constitutional Design,*

3.1.7 Endogenous versus Exogenous: The Circularity of the Role of Institutions

In studying any social phenomenon, we artificially open an observation window with respect to the continually flowing stream of social history. We assume that the social process can be divided into subunits that have a clear beginning, middle and end. But for most entities 'there is only an endless middle' as they consist of a 'continuous stream of historical events'.[12] Taking a picture at a given time of the starting distribution of preferences, options or whatever else is as artificial as it is heuristically necessary. Social scientists work in vicious circles. Institutions affect the scope of action of actors, influencing their behaviours and beliefs. At the same time, actors create, maintain or destroy institutions, devising strategies to oppose them or trying to avoid their constraints. Thick institutions can also shape and constitute the actor's identity through the normative structure of her personality. So, depending on where we start, institutions may be cause and effect, covering the entire social reality or only limited niches of it. Theories of the origins of institutions may be different from theories of their effects. Process changes are sometimes endogenous and sometimes exogenous.

With reference to political institutions, Przeworski argues that all institutions are endogenous: 'their form and their functioning depend on the conditions under which they emerge and endure' and, therefore, 'if endogeneity is strong, then institutions cannot have a causal efficacy of their own . . ... To tell whether institutions matter we must be able to isolate their effects from that of the conditions under which they function'.[13] Because of this, similar institutions may lead to completely different outcomes and it is difficult to separate the impact of the conditions from that of the institutions. In the example Przeworski discusses, the institution is the type of regime ('democracy' or 'dictatorship') and the effects are gross domestic product (GDP) levels and rates of change; that is, holistic institutions and macro-economic

---

Conflict Management, and Democracy, Oxford, Oxford University Press, pp. 15–36, 17–18.

[12] Blossfeld, H.-P. (1996), 'Macro-sociology, rational choice theory and time: a theoretical perspective on the empirical analysis of social processes', *European Sociological Review*, 12: 181–206, 189–90.

[13] Przeworski, A. (2004), 'Institutions matter?', *Government and Opposition*, 39: 527–40, 527, 528 and 532.

outcomes. The conclusion witnesses the scepticism about institutional engineering across widely different environments and the critique of the idea that importing institutions from one context to another will yield the same result.

In these general terms, the argument is hard to beat.[14] However, not only the study of institutions but also the study of everything in the social sciences evidences this embedded endogeneity. Nothing is exogenous in social reality. We can explain institutions with culture or explain culture with institutions. Nothing which is humanly devised, intentionally or unintentionally, can be fully extrapolated and made exogenous from the environment that generates it. Only physical laws and natural disasters probably are. Are individual preferences, values and interests to be conceived as exogenous to the context within which they are shaped? Are behaviours to be seen as such? We can *methodologically* see them in this way but we cannot *ontologically* claim they are so. Therefore, the problem of endogeneity is not particular to the study of institutions.

We may conclude that the endogeneity/exogeneity of any phenomenon is the result of a methodological choice. The decision does not concern the ontology of norms/rules (or of everything else, for that matter) but their heuristic role. We can choose whether to regard an institution – or any other social phenomenon – from the point of view of its generation, which inevitably is endogenous to the environment generating it, or from the point of view of its impact and effect, in which case it is probably methodologically preferable to see it as exogenous to the environment. A large literature has studied the effect of electoral systems on party systems and voters' choices, but undoubtedly electoral laws are chosen and devised by political parties and their leaders. Institutions can be seen as both independent and dependent variables.

A different possibility exists: that institutions are neither exogenous nor endogenous but are instead endogenous for some actors and exogenous for others. New institutions may be endogenous for the actors who devise them and exogenous for those who, without

---

[14] An alternative option to isolate the effects from the conditions is to do more historically and geographically confined work, where conditions will never be the same but neither will they diverge dramatically. To engage in statistical analysis across extremely dissimilar cases of holistic institutions and macro-outcomes is, perhaps, too demanding a test.

having participated in the devising, are asked to orient their behaviours in the context of the new institution. Even in this case, a better clarification of which institutions we are talking about may help. Institutions generated by repeated games and equilibrium outcomes among qualified actors participating in their design sound like a strong case for an understanding of institutions as endogenous products of actors' interactions. For customs, habits, cognitive frameworks and social norms, it is convincing that these self-enforcing institutions are more likely to be endogenous in the sense of being highly affected by environmental conditions. We may find appropriate the idea of them 'evolving' more than being created and changed. On the contrary, if by institutions we mean role expectations, private rules or legal rules, these can be changed and revised more easily and frequently, and they can be more convincingly interpreted as exogenous for many individuals who have not participated in their design.

There are numerous examples of institutions endogenously generated by a group: children setting the rules necessary to play football in a square; fishers devising norms for sharing the exploitation of the fishery; peasants devising how to regulate the common water supply. If the institution-generating group includes all the members to which the institution will apply, then the institution is endogenous to the environment. If it does not, then the institution was created 'endogenously' but will then be presented or imposed on new members, who will recognise it as exogenous. And the more time elapses and institutions endure, the larger the set of actors will be who consider them exogenous. It is a mistake to merge all types of institutions in a single box and to generalise about their endogeneity or exogeneity.

3.1.8 Functions/Efficiency

The literature on institutions often has a strong functional tone. The function of institutions is regarded as an aspect of both their definition and their explanation. Institutions provide cognitive shortcuts offering predefined solutions to classes of social problems, economise on transaction costs, reduce opportunism, foster the prospects for gains deriving from cooperation and other forms of agency slippage, maximise wealth and well-being for those who generate them, protect property rights, check and control the 'state' and so on. There are plenty of good reasons why they should be there to satisfy needs and perform functions. If institutions are meant to face functional problems, their evolution will be driven by how efficiently they do so. Proposers of functional definitions/explanations of institutions (and of their maintenance or change) claim that their approach answers the question of why institutions should exist at all, while previously we have taken their existence for granted and focussed on how they work and what sort of incentives they determine.[15]

Seeing institutions in functional terms as large-scale social devices of adaptation, control, coordination and cooperation involves studying them with the complexity of functionalist theories, with the definition of which functions are *systemically crucial* in fulfilling basic societal needs or requisites. We need to adhere to a functionalist theory of societal development to identify these functions that 'any society as a whole must meet in order to survive'.[16] In other words, the connection between a functional analysis of an institution and a genetic account of its presence requires an evolutionary relation. The process of selection needs to be understood as a large-scale evolutionary mechanism that screens all the institutions in a given period and lets pass to the next phase only those that are best adapted to perform the identified function.[17] To the extent that an evolutionary mechanism of selection is at work, the question of intentional or unintentional emergence is of less importance. It is functional evolutionary mechanisms that deliver 'good' and 'durable' institutions. In this perspective, when an institution declines or breaks down, we need a theory of its functional obsolescence coupled with a theory of how the independent action of

---

[15] Keohane, R. (2001), 'Governance in a partially globalized world', *American Political Science Review*, 95: 1–13.

[16] Martin, 'Social institutions', p. 103.

[17] For a general discussion of institutions maximising social efficiency and Pareto optimality, see Knight, *Institutions and Social Conflict*, pp. 27–37: 'Theories of social institutions that emphasise these collective benefits cannot provide micro foundations for the explanation in terms of individual rational action. If they insist on grounding their explanations in collective benefits, they must describe the mechanism that transforms the effects of social institutions into collectively beneficial forms ... must describe the mechanisms that restrict self-interested behaviour exclusively to mutually beneficial forms' (p. 40).

a multitude of people not aiming deliberately to abolish the institution makes it functionally redundant and disposable.[18]

A first problems is that a definition that incorporates a functional theory generates an empirical world constituted by the referents that do indeed perform the specified functions. For instance, if institutions are meant to reduce transaction costs or foster cooperation, everything that produces this outcome is, by definition, an institution. Presumably, everything that does not perform these functions is to be regarded as a non-institution. Conventions and customs (e.g. funerary and dining etiquette, dress codes) hardly solve problems, and efficiency considerations poorly apply to them because individuals who follow customs and conventions incur costs and it is unclear which advantage follows. More generally, functional definitions leave out phenomena that have the character of institutions but do not necessarily perform the functions indicated in the definition, for instance institutions that do not reduce transaction costs or foster cooperation but generate conflicts. The answer to the objection that institutions can be malign rather than benevolent, 'bad' rather than 'good', is that historical processes eliminate institutions that are not appropriate solutions.[19]

However, institutions that prove unstable, inefficient, conflict-generating or unable or not aiming to solve collective action problems have long endured. Slavery can be functional for something, but hardly in the eyes of slaves. Lotus feet, the custom of applying tight binding to the feet of young girls to prevent further growth, could hardly find a functional justification.[20] Clitoridectomy, the common form of female genital mutilation in Asia, the Middle East and west, north

---

[18] Note that in functionalist arguments the existence of institutions is never a deductive consequence of equilibrium models. The equilibrium analysis is merely a background theory that provides an account of institutions in the terms of a selection argument. On this point see Kourikoski, J. and A. Lehtinen (2010), 'Economic imperialism and solution concepts in political science', *Philosophy of the Social Sciences*, 4: 347–70.

[19] March and Olsen, *Rediscovering Institutions*, p. 15.

[20] The practice of foot binding originated among upper-class court dancers during the Five Dynasties and Ten Kingdoms period in Imperial China (tenth to eleventh centuries), spread in the Song Dynasty and became common among all but the lowest classes as a means of displaying status and a symbol of beauty. It resulted in lifelong disabilities. Attempts to ban foot binding started with Manchu Emperor Kangxi in 1664, but only in the early twentieth century did it begin to die out, partly because of changing social conditions and partly as

and east Africa, can hardly be related to systemic functional needs. Few scholars believe that the decay and oblivion of Roman law from the sixth to the twelfth century was an efficient development driven by it no longer serving functional needs. The institution of duelling and its elaborate code of honour lasted for centuries in Europe. Rationales can be advanced for it and, of course, it can be modelled as a rational behaviour,[21] but it is unquestionable that it was regarded as dysfunctional by the public authorities and one can hardly believe that it was functional from the systemic point of view. Many political institutions are unlikely to be functional in reducing transaction costs as they often deliberately increase them through Lockean prudence balancing.[22]

These examples can be multiplied over time and space. Either institutions of this kind are denied the status of institutions because they are not functional or dysfunctional institutions are temporary and destined to disappear. We are left to wait – in some cases for about 1,000 years – until evolutionary mechanisms lead to their obsolescence. Functional institutions that decay need explanations too. Approaching institutions in terms of their beneficial functionalist effects underscores the fact that institutions also result from distributional conflicts and power asymmetries in society. Although institutions can have beneficial effects on social life, they always distribute these additional benefits differently. Therefore, such gains cannot be the basis for a social explanation of institutions, which should instead reflect the combination of aims of interested actors who like the institutions to produce the outcomes that are best for them.[23]

---

    a result of anti-foot-binding campaigns. It was formally banned in 1911–12 after much controversy.

[21] Duels 'helped to stabilize significantly volatile notions of both rank and gender'. Low, A. J. (2003), *Manhood and the Duel: Masculinity in Early Modern Drama and Culture*, New York, Palgrave Macmillan, p. 3. For the modelling, see Kingston, C. G. and R. E. Wright (2010), 'The deadliest of games: the institution of duelling', *Southern Economic Journal*, 76: 1094–106.

[22] On dysfunctional state institutions, see Börzel, T. A. and T. Risse (2015), *Dysfunctional Institutions, Social Trust, and Governance in Areas of Limited Statehood*, Berlin, SFB-Governance Working Paper Series, No. 67, Collaborative Research Center (SFB) 700 and Wallis, J. and B. Weingast (2008), 'Dysfunctional or optimal institutions? State debt limitations, the structure of state and local governments, and the finance of American infrastructure', in Garrett, E., E. Graddy and H. Jackson (eds.), *Fiscal Challenges: An Interdisciplinary Approach to Budget Policy*, Cambridge, Cambridge University Press, pp. 331–65.

[23] See Knight, *Institutions and Social Conflict*, p. 40.

To conclude, it is implausible that functional hypotheses can represent the emergence and/or maintenance and decay mechanisms of all types of institutions. Definitions that incorporate a functional component risk dragging the concept of institution into the broader ocean of societal functions and correspondingly fraying its definition. They imply an evolutionary selection mechanism based on efficiency requirements that are not micro-founded but must resort to societal needs. They profoundly affect the empirical reality to which they apply, disregarding dysfunctional institutions, and the decay of functional institutions. They apply tautologically to the institutions that the definition itself declares are functionally selected. They methodologically exclude the possibility of seeing some institutions as resulting from asymmetries of power and conflicts of interest. If efficiency is regarded as a dimension of institutional survival, we are left with a host of historical examples of doubtful efficiency or we are committed to finding the functional efficiency of every existing institution. The idea that institutions perform predefined social functions must be severely qualified.

3.2 Types of Institutions

At this stage, we can discuss different types of institutions by looking at them through the dimensions of analysis indicated in Section 3.1 of this chapter. My solution is summarised in Table 3.2, in which the core and additional dimensions of institutional analysis are reported for each type. Functions and efficiency are left empty because of the difficulty in using these properties to differentiate institutions in a useful way.

3.2.1 *Culturally Stabilised Systems of Meanings*

If culture as a symbol system, cognitive script or template that provides the frame of meaning guiding human action is considered an institution, it undoubtedly tends to be very stable and changes only partially and gradually. Institutions of this sort must be highly internalised. Their normativity is strong, although highly diffused. Their sanctionability is low; they are 'orientations' not subject to instrumental calculations and largely independent of legal or social sanctioning. Individuals involved in a rationalistic calculation of the costs of not abiding by them would

Table 3.2 Types of institutions and their key properties

Types of institutions	Dimensions	Stability	Normativity (level of internalisation)	Certainty (degree of ex-ante precision of infringement)	Sanctions (un/certainty of ex-post rewards and punishment)	Enforcement (who enforces)	Layering/interconnectedness	Designed or self-developing	Change process	Function?	Efficiency?
Cultural stabilised systems of meanings	Culture as a symbol system, cognitive scripts and moral templates that provide the frame of meaning guiding human action	High	Internalised	Low	Uncertain	First party. Self-enforcing	Holistic, highly interconnected, not layered	Undesigned	Endogenous		
Conventions, customs	Tradition, habit or 'arbitrary' agreement	High	Internalised	Low	Uncertain	First and second party. Self-enforcing and social peer pressure	Not layered, not interconnected	Undesigned	Endogenous		
Social norms	Shared notions of appropriateness and legitimately expected behaviour	High/medium	Internalised and imposed	Medium	Some certainty	First and second party. self-enforcing and social peer pressure	Not layered, not interconnected	Undesigned	Endogenous		
Practices, routines	Repetitive unthinking acts	Low	Imposed and internalised	Medium	Uncertain	First-, second- and third-party enforcers	Weakly interconnected	Both undesigned and designed	Endogenous and exogenous		
Role expectations	Beliefs concerning the qualities, behaviours and characteristics suitable in a specific position	Medium	Imposed and internalised	Medium/high	Some certainty	First-, second- and third-party enforcers	Interconnected	Both undesigned and designed	Endogenous and exogenous		
Private rules	Codes of private associations	Low	Imposed	High	Certain	Third-party enforcer	Layered and interconnected	Designed	Mostly exogenous		
Legal rules	State law and regulations	Low	Imposed	High	Certain	Fourth-party enforcer	Highly layered and interconnected	Designed	Mostly exogenous		

find it difficult to identify ex ante with clarity their infringement and to calculate the certainty of the expected rewards/punishments. There is no specialised enforcement agency and these institutions are embedded and self-enforcing. Institutions of this kind are non-designed and their change is necessarily endogenous.[24] They cannot be single or atomistic institutions as they constitute highly interconnected wholes.

Following this characterisation, it is difficult to conceptualise them as institutions at the same level as others. Of course, language, culture and aspects of symbolic, cognitive and meaning systems generate action constraints and conformities. However, I doubt there is much heuristic advantage in considering them institutions that can be assimilated to other types. Culture is such a widespread and pervading element in our social life that it is perhaps preferable to reserve a domain of its own for studying it. I will argue that this is recommended when dealing with political institutions.

3.2.2 Conventions and Customs

Conventions and customs are traditions, habits or arbitrary agreements among the members of a group. They describe a convergent behaviour within a social group such as the habit of standing up at certain moments during a mass, taking off one's hat when entering a house as a guest, not shaking hands with gloves on, rules of etiquette, rules of clubs, funeral conventions, marriage conventions, reciprocating gift conventions and the like. They are clearly somewhat stable, non-designed and subject to endogenous change processes. Their normativity is predominantly internalised and self-enforced, but a sanctioning system is effective as violating conventions may generate some reputational consequences from second-party peers. Conventions can profitably be conceived as spontaneously generated through learning processes, repeated game-shaped interactions or mechanisms of socialisation. They are atomistic institutions often unrelated to one another. In my understanding, there is limited layering and interconnectedness among different customs/conventions. However, conventions have a cost and it is unclear why we incur that cost with only moderate advantage.

---

[24] There are a few historical examples of wholesale exogenous attempts to change the cultural templates of entire populations. They usually prove resilient to imposed change and tend to re-emerge.

3.2.3 Social Norms

Social norms permeate every relationship among humans in any known time. They do so in three ways. Following the *logic of appropriateness*, they define appropriate behaviours and offer cognitive shortcuts in any new context. Following a *logic of identity*, they often define the sense of individual 'honour'. Following a *logic of consequences*, they shape the available alternatives associated with costs and advantages. In this sense, they are the confining conditions of any conception of strategic action. In this way, they make most types of social relationships 'predictable', even when they shape attempts to escape and cheat them.

Social norms are shared notions of appropriateness and legitimately expected behaviour, and they are *not role-dependent* (on role expectations, see later in this chapter). They are socially transmitted and internalised by actors but they may also be discovered and learned in all those cases in which actors face a somewhat radical change in the social environment. Social norms are more fundamental in grounding the identity of actors and in determining their options for strategic action than conventions and habits are. The degree of ex-ante perception of infringement of them is more acute. The certainty and precision of possible punishment vary enormously and are never clearly defined ex ante. Sanctioning usually involves reputation mechanisms, social disapproval, loss of trust and recognition, reprobation, withdrawal of cooperation and esteem, and social ostracism.

Social norms affect the sense of honour of the actor, understood as his image in the eyes of relevant others: 'Social norms operate through the emotions of shame in the norm violator and of contempt in the observer of the violation.'[25] Their enforcement mechanisms, therefore, include both self-enforcement (first party) and peer-group pressures (second party). Like conventions and customs, they are undesigned and poorly affected by hierarchy. Deliberate attempts by hierarchies to modify or radically change certain social norms are, nonetheless, not infrequent. A large part of the historical process of codification takes the form of rules devised explicitly to modify prevailing and undesired social norms. Any generalisation in this case is daring, but these efforts

---

[25] Elster, J. (2007), *Explaining Social Behavior: More Nuts and Bolts for the Social Sciences*, Cambridge, Cambridge University Press, p. 355.

are often ineffective unless they are consistently repeated over time and often over generations. Therefore, their change processes are predominantly endogenous.

In given circumstances, social norms impose themselves on the actor in view of the potential costs of violating them, while in other circumstances they 'belong' to the actor as a normative endowment that is not subject to cognitive evaluations and calculations. It is hard to decide the matter *in abstracto*. For how long it is proper to look directly into the eyes of our interlocutors does not seem to be an object of reflection, evaluation or calculation. Appropriate behaviour in queuing may be less self-imposing. As argued before, any functional analysis of social norms and any consideration of their efficiency seems inappropriate. Without a substratum of social norms, the costs of cooperation would probably be preposterously high. Nevertheless, there are plenty of examples of costly and undesired social norms – of social norms that are more obstacles than facilitating conditions.

3.2.4 Practices and Routines

Practices and routines are often enrolled in the category of institutions. They represent a rather ambiguous category which is hard to define lexicographically. In general, their distinctive character is that of being *repetitive* and *unthinking* acts.[26] The terms 'routine' and 'practice' also have a derogatory meaning: boring, unexciting, uncreative activities. Their normativity is questionable. Of course, conformism pressure exists to do things as they have always been done, but it is hard to say that an administrative practice or a daily routine at work or home has strong normativity. Sanctioning too presents elements of ambiguity in both the clarity of infringement and the certainty of sanction. Practices and routines are learned and poorly internalised. We adapt to those prevailing quite easily once we learn them. Enforcement is highly contextual. Sometimes, breaking established practices and routines is praised rather than sanctioned. After all, any innovation is a breaking of past practices/routines. Depending on the circumstances, we may feel scared at the idea of departing from routine, while in others we may

---

[26] The literature on practices/routines is limited. See Reckwitz, A. (2002), 'Toward a theory of social practices: a development in culturalist theorizing', *European Journal of Social Theory*, 5: 243–63.

think this is an asset enhancing our status in the group. I see in practices and routines a stronger element of rational appreciation and calculation. It is often the case that they are deeply criticised by those who follow them. They may be designed by hierarchy but may also be spontaneous and self-developing, and they can change following two modes. The boundary between practices and routines that deserve to be enrolled among institutions and those that do not is hard to draw. Plenty of them are little more than mere conformism and sometimes opportunism. In short, the category is too broad in my view to be profitably used. It can perhaps be useful in organisational studies of individuals in confined cooperation and organised according to specialisation, the division of labour and integration.

3.2.5 Role Expectations

Role expectations are beliefs concerning the qualities, behaviours and characteristics suitable in a specific position. They express duties, powers, faculties and obligations that pertain to a given position or office independently of the person occupying it. They define, reduce and limit the 'appropriate' strategic action options, but only in the time, place and circumstances in which the actor plays the role. Outside that role, they are non-operational. Role expectations are somewhat stable. Their normativity concerns more their directive force than their preceptive force. With roles, we move a step forward towards a precise definition of the expectations and of the sanctioning and enforcement mechanisms. Although in principle they can become internalised, the fact that they are adopted only when performing the role makes them also imposed. They involve a clear perception of infringement and considerable certainty of the implications of not abiding by them. In the role, we are observed and evaluated by others. Enforcement, therefore, primarily takes the form of second-party enforcement (peer pressure), but also that of third-party enforcement, a hierarchy or authority that can assemble evidence of good or poor role performance. They can be both undesigned and designed by the hierarchy. Change processes are predominantly exogenous as no actor can self-define the expectations of a role. In many cases, hierarchy can modify the institutions to a certain extent by setting new standards.

Their level of externality with respect to the actor is more complex to evaluate. In some cases, they can simply be known and learned from the environment and, in fact, role expectations may sometimes be codified, as in ethical and professional deontology codes. In this latter case, hierarchy can sanction them more easily. Role expectations are, therefore, in a somewhat intermediate position between social norms and written rules. They often have an intimate link with written rules that define the role. Expectations concerning parents' roles in their relationship with a child, or the professor's role regarding a pupil, despite extending beyond the rules of family law or university regulations, cannot be easily disentangled from them. This mixed nature is what separates role expectations from social norms.

3.2.6 Private Rules

I use the term 'private rules' to refer to the vast field of normative requirements explicitly expressed in the form of written statements which are not state laws or regulations. The term 'private' is not satisfactory, but I could not find a better one. To identify written rules with 'the law' is clearly mistaken. The number of written rules is vaster than that of state laws and regulations. A considerable number of these written rules are in fact only 'practical rules' that guide behaviour towards a correct utilisation of resources for a technical end, such as the rules on how to properly assemble a machine or properly use it and prescriptions about the utilisation of medicaments. These rules do not pertain to relations among individuals – that is, to social relations – and therefore lack both social normativity and social sanctioning.

On the contrary, every association, political party, club, firm, university, hospital, foundation, and sports, recreational and cultural circle has internal written rules: statutes, ethical and professional codes, dress rules, health and safety rules, and so on. Tennis clubs' rules about dressing and party rules about conferences are not state laws or regulations, although in some cases they are bound to be in a relation of compatibility with the latter. It is, therefore, important that we do not assimilate 'private' rules to legal rules sanctioned by the court system and state apparatuses. They extend far beyond them and constrain most instances of our lives.

Private rules are easier to interpret as external to actors. Their stability is low as they are subject to easy modification by a hierarchy or the membership of a group. What the rules are is generally clear or easily discoverable. The consequences of violating them are predictable. They are enforced by a third party, usually the hierarchy or a specialised body with this function invested with inquiring and arbitration powers concerning the behaviour of members, possible internal conflicts and relations with other organisations and entities, and so on. The punishment may take harsh forms, but it usually has an upper limit in expulsion from the organisation or association. Private rules are intentionally designed and in most cases it is possible to identify the original designers and successive modifications. They have a documented history. The change process is therefore exogenous to the rules themselves. Layering and interconnectedness is usually much higher than in any of the previous categories. Private rules tend to be complex, their interpretation generates precedents and they often strongly interconnect with legal rules regarding the level of deviation and departure from them.

Private rules present some characteristics that belong to every type of rule, some of which are specific:

(1) *Scope*. Private rules are membership rules without territorial validity.
(2) *Temporality*. The time of a normative rule is essential to enforce the principle that makes the recent rule prevail over the preceding one.
(3) *Hierarchy*. Within each normative source, superior rules always prevail over inferior ones and rules of recognition help establish this order.
(4) *Coherence*. Rules that are contradictory or that prescribe impossible conducts are without directive force.
(5) *Knowledgeability*. Rules must be known by all potential subject members.

A distinctive element of private rules is, therefore, the development of agencies that are responsible for issuing new rules and repealing old ones, agencies that operate the execution of valid rules and agencies that adjudicate alleged breaches or failures to implement the rules. The ultimate enforcer is a third-party enforcer; the hierarchy, supported by referees, disciplinary committees and boards of arbitration.

3.2.7 State Law and Regulations

Legal rules are written rules supported by a powerful enforcement and sanctioning apparatus. They include (1) rules forbidding or enjoining certain types of behaviour under penalty; (2) rules requiring people to compensate injured people in certain ways; (3) rules specifying what must be done to make wills or other arrangements that confer rights and create obligations; (4) rules determining what the rules are and when they have been broken; and (5) rules that define who can modify existing legal rules, when and how.

The principles of *temporality*, *hierarchy*, *coherence* and *knowledge-ability* stated for private rules are valid for legal rules too. But some additional elements set the difference between private rules and legal rules.[27]

(1) *Scope.* Legal rules have territorial validity. Therefore, in principle they cannot be violated by private rules, although partial exceptions are defined in arbitration clauses.

(2) *Recognition.* Legal rule production must necessarily refer to a unitary, subjective and identifiable centre for normative production. Norms of other kinds do not have any subjectively identifiable production centre and private rules have a plurality of them.

(3) *Administrative implementation.* Legal rules are enforced through administration. For instance, applying the rule that prescribes confidentiality concerning practices, products or innovations in sensitive or high-tech firms requires precise registering of what must be kept confidential. The right to property for certain intellectual products requires a precise definition of the property from which arises the need for patents and copyright register offices. Customs, conventions, social norms, routines, practices, role expectations and private rules, not to mention cultural meanings, are directly operative and require no 'administration'. If they fail to be directly operative, their ineffectiveness is demonstrated.

---

[27] Normative legal theory mentions other aspects: 'determinacy', 'generality', 'completeness' of normative coverage, 'clarity', 'non-retroactivity', 'exigibility' and 'congruence between text and normative praxis': di Carlo, *Teoria istituzionale e ragionamento giuridico*, pp. 96–7. None of these are essential for my argument here.

Legal rules have varying stability but in general they are objects of continual modification, with special bodies explicitly devoted to this task. Their normativity is imposed so that the directive force that derives from enforcement is in general higher than their preceptive force. Their sanctionability is high on both dimensions. Enforcement is left to a fourth-party enforcer, a sophisticated judicial system managed and administered by officials explicitly assigned to this function and a coercive state apparatus. They are designed and change processes are generally exogenous, although interpretative evolutions may also modify them. A distinctive element of legal rules is, therefore, the development of agencies that are responsible for issuing new rules and repealing old ones, agencies that execute valid rules, and agencies that adjudicate alleged breaches or failures to implement the rules.

3.3 Types of Normativity: Norms and Rules

In the scheme in Table 3.2, the underlying dimension that separates types of institutions is the distinction between 'norms' and 'rules'. On the one hand, we have the everyday practice of people, which implies interactions based on norms; on the other hand, we have a body of 'institutional facts'; that is, of regulative representations managed and administered by officials. In both cases there is no way to interpret *the institution* with reference to the finalised individual action because the fundamental role of an institution is to integrate and harmonise motivations and ends, which may be very different. In this sense, what unifies norms and rules is not the subjective orientation of those who are subject to their influence but precisely their standardising the outcomes of different motives. Many other factors, however, differentiate them.

Norms refer to and include orientations about how people should behave towards each other, and they acquire their status because they are simply shared. They are abided by and respected without or with only mild supervision and enforcement through mutual awareness of their implicit deontology. When people invoke a 'norm' as an explanation for a behaviour, they imply that a person has done something either because of an internalised ethical command or because she believes or thinks that many other people do the same and therefore expects the same to be done. In this latter case, people's expectations and behaviours seem to cause other people to behave in a certain way. If a group of people is willing to punish deviance from an established practice, then avoiding that behaviour may easily become a group norm. Agents are inclined to please others by engaging in expected behaviours and not engaging in unexpected or unusual behaviours.[28]

Social conformity like imitation of behaviour may be a strong force behind the development of norms. However, even calculating individuals, if they calculate well, should end up using normative shortcuts. When people obtain a benefit by performing a certain kind of a behaviour based on means/ends rationality, they tend to continue that behaviour. On the contrary, behaviour generating harm is more likely to be discontinued. While punishment and reward can take any form (from a smile to killing), it is reasonable to assume that people try to avoid punishment and seek rewards. If people in a group believe that other people are inclined to reward them if they do something, doing that something may become a norm.

Rules acquire their status from the fact that they *are made* in a specific way, in accordance with rules that specify how to make rules. The institutional facts that derive from codification are such that they are interpreted as something else thanks to reference to the normative framework made up of rules.[29] In other words, being mentioned in a testament or issuing a ministerial act does not mean much if there is not a rule framework that states that those who are mentioned in testaments are heirs and ministers have the competence to issue acts to be abided by.

Legal theorists and legal historians have debated at length the issue of the boundary between socio/moral norms and written rules. The debate polarises those scholars who insist that the 'legal' and the 'social' are clearly different domains (which implies that criteria are

---

[28] Jones, T. (2006), '"We always have a beer after the meeting": how norms, customs, conventions, and the like explain behavior', *Philosophy of the Social Sciences*, 36: 251–75, 257–9.

[29] MacCormick, N. (2007), *Institutions of Law: An Essay in Legal Theory*, Oxford, Oxford University Press, pp. 11–12. Note that in legal theory terminology 'institutionalisation' usually means 'codification'. See Hage, J. (2009), 'What is a legal transaction?', in Del Mar, M. and Z. Bankowski (eds.), *Law as Institutional Normative Order*, Farnham, Ashgate, pp. 104–21, particularly pp. 105–6. This labelling deprives the realm of social norms of the 'institutionalisation' process as understood by social scientists.

needed to properly define the legal) and those that regard the two fields
as both belonging to the broader domain of general normativity. The
question is whether there is anything inherent in legal rules that establishes their distinctiveness with respect to other instances of social
normativity. This is the same debate in which social scientists find
themselves, with the difference that they tend to see the legal order as
a minor and simple part of normativity, while legal theorists are more
concerned with the role of law in connection with other kinds of
normative sources.

The monistic understanding of the law and of the legal system that
social scientists accuse of excessive formalism and abstractness is an
invention of continental European nineteenth-century legal theory.
Kelsen's approach best exemplifies this.[30] In this tradition, a legal
rule is nothing but the *attribution of meaning* – an 'imputation' – to
something that has no meaning of its own. Therefore, what happens in
the social realm, or rather whether rule-abiders comply with legal
norms or not,

has no legal significance ... there are no pre-legal actions, models of conduct
or lifestyles that should be encapsulated and enforced by legal norms. Any
conduct may become legal, not because of an alleged pre-legal normative
value but because this conduct has not been assigned a sanction ....
A primary legal norm is nothing but the amount of coercion that, within
a legal proposition, is attached to a given action and that therefore makes this
action illicit.

Therefore, the truly distinctive feature of law is the sanction that a body
of legal officials formally administers under the guidance of a basic
norm, which is the peak of the legal system and determines who is
entitled to issue valid legal norms.[31] In this perspective, the 'purity' and
formalism of legal doctrine rests in its departure from any ideological
root (as present in *iusnaturalism*) or empirical root (as is evident in *legal*

---

[30] Kelsen, H. (1934), *Reine Rechtslehre: Einleitung in die rechtswissenschaftliche Problematik*, Leipzig, Deuticke. The English version I refer to is the translation of the second revised version of 1960: (1967), *The Pure Theory of Law*, Berkeley, University of California Press.

[31] 'If we ignore this specific element of the law, if we do not conceive of the law as a special social technique, if we define the law simply as order or organization, and not as coercive order ... then we lose the possibility of differentiating law from other social phenomena.' Kelsen, H. (1945), *General Theory of Law and the State*, Cambridge, MA, Harvard University Press, p. 26.

realism theories) and, therefore, on a coherent theory that separates law from morality and politics.[32]

The positivistic understanding of the distinctive features of the law with respect to other sources of normativity has been contested by different schools of legal theory. For the latter, the building blocks of law consist of the norms and models developed within concrete forms of life and sanctions are meant to confer binding force on these shared standards. Eugen Ehrlich, the key early figure in the new field of the sociology of law, used the term 'living law' to indicate the variety of local norms such as those found in Bukovina in the late phase of the Austro-Hapsburg Empire. The 'living law' concept includes decisions issued by the government together with other rules and usages in associations, and shared practices of associations not recognised and even disapproved by the state.[33] Therefore, 'living law' includes common practices like the sanctioning mechanisms of diamond merchants and even the practice of queuing at the cinema. Adopting this perspective, there can be a 'law beyond the law'; that is, a law different to that which is codified and contained in statutes and judgments. There can be a 'law without the state', focussing on what else law does beyond its traditional role, up to the point of detecting the existence of plural and even alternative legal systems that do not have or do not need to have the backing of the state (e.g. *lex mercatoria*, the governance of the internet). There can eventually also be an 'order without law'; that is, deeper sources of normative orders of any kind associated with the emergence of patterned orders.[34] Finally, there can even be an 'order within law'; that is, the orders shaped by the notion of legality and of legal obligation that pervade our society.[35]

---

[32] Other scholars in the positivist tradition criticise the pure theory à la Kelsen by qualifying it. Hart's distinction between primary rules (rules of conduct) and secondary rules (rules of interpretation) leads him to conclude that primary rules are not a purely artificial construction but they embody pre-existing social models of conduct, while secondary rules do not. Hart, H. L. A. (1961, 1994), *The Concept of Law*, Oxford, Oxford University Press.

[33] Ehrlich, E. (1936), *Foundational Principles of the Sociology of Law*, New York, Russel and Russel.

[34] See Ellickson, R. (1991), *Order without Law: How Neighbours Settle Disputes*, Cambridge, MA, Harvard University Press.

[35] Nelken, D. (2014), 'Legal sociology and the sociology of norms', in Donlan, S. P. and L. Heckendorn Urscheler (eds.), *Concepts of Law: Comparative, Jurisprudential, and Social Science Perspectives*, Burlington, VT, Ashgate, pp.

The term 'legal pluralism' denotes the coexistence of multiple normative orders – legal and non-legal normativities. This challenges the idea that there must be a single rule of recognition, and that if a norm is a rule for action, we must first know what the norm is and only afterwards ask what its source is.[36] It is impossible to identify an external, uncommitted, neutral or value-free standpoint from which the concept of law can be elaborated.[37] Intermediate positions admit the existence of principles but exclude nevertheless the capacity to make the rule of recognition defectible.[38] More radical positions claim that law indicates any form or pattern of social control, in which case there is eventually no criterion that can distinguish law from other normative orders.[39] The most radical departure from positivism argues that state law is an integral part of society, one ordering among many others to the extent that any hierarchy among them depends merely on differences of power.[40] Among legal pluralists, therefore, law is understood as a continuum that goes from the clearest forms of state legal rules to the vaguest forms of informal social control.

Therefore, legal theorists have engaged more than social scientists in discussing types of norms/rules depending on their formal/informal character, the existence of secondary rules for the group of people entitled to administer primary rules and the type of sanctions issued, and so on.[41] These developmental classifications conceptualise in plural terms the general normative dimension of life, make it explicit that law and legal institutions existed before the state or have existed outside such an entity, dynamise the connection between social norms and codified rules, clarify the rather late and specific role of the modern state as producer of codified rules, emphasise the pluralism of

138–51; Mitchell, L. E. (1999), 'Understanding norms', *University of Toronto Law Review*, 49: 177–258.

[36] Raz, J. (2009), *The Authority of Law: Essays on Law and Morality*, Oxford, Oxford University Press.

[37] Dworkin, R. (2004), 'Hart's postscript and the character of political philosophy', *Oxford Journal of Legal Studies*, 37: 119–37.

[38] MacCormick, *Institutions of Law: An Essay in Legal Theory*.

[39] Mattei, U. (1997), 'Three patterns of law: taxonomy and change in the world's legal systems', *American Journal of Comparative Law*, 45: 5–44.

[40] Woodman, G. (2009), 'Ideological combs and social observations: recent debates about legal pluralism', *Journal of Law and Society*, 42: 21–59.

[41] See, for instance, the typology proposed by Donlan, S. P. and L. Heckendorn Urscheler (eds.) (2014), 'Introduction', in *Concepts of Law*, pp. 5–6.

normative sources through history, and ask what character law takes in de-centralised polities when and where there are multiples sites of power.

There seems to be a deadlock in these debates: those who want to specify the distinctiveness of legal rules fail to explain why a given legal order in a given historical and geographical situation should be regarded as legitimately supreme. Those who defend legal pluralism risk including any type of social normativity in the category of the legal and conclude that every order is a legal order and that there is no criterion for putting legal orders in a hierarchy.[42]

The debate mixes two issues. One is whether the law is a distinctive system with respect to other sources of normativity; the second is whether it is possible to self-legitimate it (the positivist stance). One can reply yes to the first and no to the second. One can acknowledge the contingent predominance of a legal system while at the same time recognising its supremacy and distinctive features now and here. The distinctiveness of law can be identified: authority to regulate any type of behaviour; supremacy over other types of regulations of the same behaviours; and openness as a capacity to confer binding force on rules that belong to other systems.[43] At the same time, it is possible to admit that there are other types of normative orders, that these might have been dominant in other times and places, and that in principle no argument can be clearly made why the current system of law should have the pre-eminence that we observe it has now and here.

Social scientists do not find it problematic to combine these two ideas. The modern state was historically able to become the exclusive holder of the official lawfulness not possessed by any other social normativity. This was not the situation in the past and it may become less so in the future. The law in the positivist understanding represents a dominant evolved form and at the same time the legal rules that historically prevail are the result of political struggles. The 'purely legal' is neither an eternal nor a coherent intellectual artefact.[44]

---

[42] Croce, M. (2014), 'Is law a special domain? On the boundary between the legal and the social', in Donlan, S. P. and L. Heckendorn Urscheler (eds.), *Concepts of Law*, pp. 153–67, 161.

[43] Raz, J. (1999), *Practical Reason and Norms*, Oxford, Oxford University Press, p. 150.

[44] Schmitt, C. (2004), *On the Three Types of Juristic Thought*, Westport, CT, Praeger.

In fact, a positivist understanding of legal rules makes sense only once a political order has been decided to be legally valid, a constitution is in force and competing orders are made illegal or extra-legal, or at best licensed and subordinated. The 'pureness' derives from the acceptance of the order as objective. If the justification of law depends on political power (and the political institutions that embody it) and power can be organised in different ways (more or less centralised, for instance), so then can law. In other words, this means that law takes a different character depending on the organisation of power.[45] On the other hand, the insistence of legal pluralists and legal sociologists on merging legal rules within the broader field of multiple normative sources risks blurring any specificity and, in the end, missing not only the difference but also the inherent tension between the rule and the norm.

The production of guaranteed and stabilised rights and compliances in the form of legal rules as opposed to other kinds of normativity exploded in size and depth during the nineteenth century and further accelerated in the twentieth. Individuals increased their dependency on this production function. Even the satisfaction of their primary life needs must become the object of legal guarantees. Moreover, the new fields of regulative activity are quite different from the traditional ones in that they are less orientated to the protection of social order from disruption and are more programmatic and finalistic. The recipients of the rules are invited to perform a behaviour orientated towards certain goals but are left free to decide the executive modalities of their behaviour.[46] This has increased the inherent tension between the rule and the norm.

3.4 Norms and Rules: Orthograde or Contro-grade Change

To delineate the essential difference between norms and rules, we should perhaps start with the question of why at any given time certain institutions are written and codified, while others are not. Certain types of behaviour are spontaneous and self-reinforcing, and

---

[45] Del Mar, M. (2014), 'Beyond the state in and of legal theory', in Donlan, S. P. and L. Heckendorn Urscheler (eds.), *Concepts of Law*, pp. 19–42, 31.

[46] On this point, see Grimm, D. (1993), 'Diritto e politica', in *Enciclopedia delle Scienze Sociali*, Torino, Istituto dell'Enciclopedia Italiana Treccani, vol. 3, pp. 113–19.

their adaptation is endogenous and does not require active hierarchical intervention to occur. Changes of the matter in line with a spontaneous tendency to change in the absence of external influences can be labelled *orthograde changes*. Other forms of change of the matter require an intervention that forces them to occur because they are resistant to intervention. Rules are the institutions that introduce constraints on action or induce changes in action that would not otherwise take place. Such changes would not occur unless there was an intervention. Changes of the status of a system that must be forced externally to counteract the natural tendency to change can be called *contro-grade* changes.[47]

The role of contro-grade constraints consists in what, because of its existence, cannot happen. Codified institutions are inducements to contrograde behaviour by making certain behavioural patterns impossible or very costly. The constraints reduce the degree of orthograde behaviour. Customs and conventions, social norms and some role expectations are orthograde institutions that in specific cases require efforts to modify them by contro-grade institutions. Codified institutions are constraints introduced in fields where orthograde spontaneous behaviour must be strongly contained to prevent undesired outcomes or to foster desired ones. The production of contro-grade incentives is, therefore, necessarily reserved for authorities.

The analytical connection between codified institutions as contrograde rules and spontaneous non-codified institutions as orthograde norms generates three areas of normativity. In the first area, a spontaneous and self-enforcing normativity prevails not accompanied, sustained or reinforced by codified rules or strong enforcement mechanisms. Orthograde institutions of this kind can afford to be normatively vague, procedurally obscure and characterised by opacity of infringement and uncertainty of sanctions.

Next to these, institutions exist for which the norms correspond closely to the isomorphic codified component. This area of overlapping between rules and norms is best exemplified by the primordial rules/norms not to kill, steal, damage the innocent and so on. The codified rules are

---

[47] On orthograde and contro-grade changes in the natural sciences, see
Deacon, T. W. (2012), *Incomplete Nature: How Mind Emerged from Matter*,
New York, W. W. Norton & Company Inc., pp. 221–3.

a reinforcement and a clarification of deeply felt norms, making more precise the way to ascertain the infringement and deliver the sanctioning.

Finally, there is that form of codified normativity that represents the deliberate introduction of contro-grade constraints. These do not coincide at all or are poorly supported by isomorphic norms. It is reasonable to expect that they are not deeply felt. Exactly because they are contro-grade institutions, they need to specify the hierarchical source and the mechanisms of production and validity. They are more precise and detailed, and precisely specify inducements and sanctions for non-conformity, and the roles that must decide on the empirical occurrence of non-conformity (see Table 3.3).

The extent to which codified rules and non-codified norms overlap is a crucial dimension of territorial and temporal variation. In a traditional society, the predominance of non-codified norms and a high coincidence with the few codified rules guarantee a considerable degree of conformism and compliance. On the contrary, in modernised and secularised societies the development of an ever-growing codification of rules and procedures not sustained by isomorphic corresponding norms is likely. This is accompanied by a declining level of compliance and perhaps a vicious circle of over-formalisation that generates even further non-compliance.

Table 3.3 *Areas of normativity*

Orthograde norms	Coincidences of orthograde and contro-grade normativity	Contro-grade rules
Norms.	Codified rules coincident with isomorphic norms.	Codified rules that do not correspond to isomorphic norms.
Felt and embedded in tradition and social relationships, but not sustained by specific and precise codified rules.	The rules reinforce the norms by specifying infringement instances, sanctions and inducements, and the roles that administer them.	Non-embedded in social relationships and not deeply felt. Specific, detailed and highly sanctioned because deviance is likely.

The presence of 'norms not backed by rules', 'norms backed by rules' and 'rules not backed by norms' results in a process of change that can take three directions. Norms not backed by rules define the sphere where normativity is left to its own adaptive dynamics. Norms supported by rules define a sphere of normativity where an orthograde tendency is reinforced by codification and leads to lower tension and deviance. Rules not backed by norms define the increasingly programmatic nature of codified production and its tendency to aspire to orientate behaviours in a planned direction. There is a tendency to increase the detailed codified normativity that always invades larger parts of the spontaneous normativity. Rules without a strong orthograde underpinning are directed against felt norms with the intent to modify them. *In this case, the directive capacity of rule enforcement is orientated against the preceptive capacity of norms.* Deviance is likely to be high. In the battle of rules against norms it is possible that the latter are mobilised against the former, determining their ineffectiveness and inefficacy. If ineffective rules were to be disregarded as institutions, following the line of some of the previously discussed schools, we would be without the possibility of observing the tension between the two. At the same time, the distinction among the three areas of normativity improves on the rather vague distinction between formal and informal institutions and their respective levels of conformity.

Written rules leave a historical record that allows reconstruction. Written rules usually include prescriptions concerning the procedures and the timing for them to be changed. Norms do not require this; they are by far more difficult to discover and define, and they leave more tenuous traces of their changes. They can often only be identified thanks to their tensions with contro-grade codified normativity. If we separate norms from codified rules, then we can study the relationships between the two and when and why in different contexts we have the same norms but different codified rules, different norms and different rules, and the same rules but different norms. Therefore, codified rules offer a heuristic advantage even for the study of norms. For this reason, I believe that it is unfortunate that political science has recently so much departed from any reference to codified normativity. We must go beyond it, but we should not disregard it. The cost is a loss of anchorage for the study of other kinds of normativity.

3.5 A *Vade Mecum*

Any programme of dynamic analysis of institutions loses its focus if it is without an analysis of their ideal-type forms. If we distinguish more clearly the type of institutions we are dealing with, some of the problems mentioned are simpler to handle, although they do not disappear. Enrolling all institutions in an undifferentiated basket through encompassing definitions means generalising about a heterogeneous set of phenomena. Institutions differ in their stability, normativeness, sanctioning, enforcement, layering, intentionality and exogeneity, not to mention their putative functions and efficiency. More fundamentally, they differ in their orthograde or contro-grade nature. Depending on which institutional phenomenology the researcher has in mind and takes as an example, different and often incompatible theories of institutions and institutional change emerge.

This chapter has evidenced that it is difficult to generalise about types of institutions that are so different: institutions generated by autonomous actors' interactions; institutions pre-existing and external to actors; institutions that define the actors; self-enforced institutions and institutions enforced by third or fourth parties; inherited institutions characterised by marginal change; and institutions consciously designed by other institutions. We should require every study to specify the institutions it is talking about and to avoid framing its conclusions as a general theory of 'all' institutions.

In this chapter, I have downplayed certain dimensions of analysis. Functional interpretations and efficiency considerations can be empirically discussed for different types of institutions, but they cannot be a definitional property of institutions themselves. In so doing, we unduly restrict the normative realm to only those institutions that are supposed to perform functions and we include among institutions everything that may perform a function. In both cases, we get a blurred set of empirical references.

If efficiency is a definitional property of institutions, we exclude inefficient ones and we must implicitly accept some form of institutional evolutionary theory that justifies the efficiency outcome. If we turn back to the history of institutions, it is difficult to justify this optimism.

Some institutions are intentionally designed and others are more self-developed. However, neither are spared the unintended consequences of the original design. Therefore, we should not consider the original mechanism of institution development as part of their definition.

We must differentiate institutions from behaviours, culture, polities and so on. Otherwise, several interesting problems pertaining to the relationships between these phenomena are defined away. A radical behaviouralist approach that sees institutions as 'recurrent patterns of behaviours' is unsuited as it makes institutions of no use to interpret what social sciences are about: patterns of behaviour.

While many approaches underline the fact that institutions forge or constitute the actor, I am unwilling to generalise that interest or identity formation is a definitional property of institutions. In this case, everything that may shape the individual actor's identity becomes an institution and, again, we lose analytical insight rather than gaining it. At the highest possible level of abstraction there is no doubt that culture as a symbol system, cognitive script and moral template (not to mention language) provides the frame of meaning guiding human action through which individuals cope with reality. But if we consider these cultural phenomena 'institutions', they overlap with any other kind of institutions that depend on the cultural templates that make them meaningful and understandable.[48]

Equilibrium models may be a theory of the origins of certain types of institutions. However, equilibria do not incorporate a normative element, and if they do, they are no longer equilibria. The crucial dimensions of analysis discussed in this chapter and in Table 3.2 do not apply to equilibria.

I reject considering organisations as institutions. We should depart from conventional language and avoid calling complex organisations such as parliament, courts, political parties, bureaucracies, universities and hospitals institutions. These entities do *have* institutions for their internal ordering, but to include them among institutions generates logical and empirical inconsistencies. Not surprisingly, practically none of the dimensions of analysis in Table 3.2 are applicable to organisations but only to their internal rules/ norms.

The difficulty in specifying the institutions one is talking about is deadly for political studies. The tendency of each discipline and

---

[48] On this point, see Rothstein, *Political Institutions*, p. 145.

approach to consider its own institutions as typical of the entire set attributes to political institutions problems that do not pertain to them and, at the same time, does not identify the specific problems that do. We must avoid the success of the terms 'institution' and 'institutionalism' resting on the vagueness and ambiguity of the concept and its capacity to stretch in any direction. Today these terms are more fashionable than the terms 'structure' and 'function' were in the 1950s and 1960s. They may suffer the same fate when the labels expand to an excessive denotation and begin to dilute, leaving the field open to specialists in rediscoveries. Political scientists cannot afford this risk with the concept of institution. Determining which institutions are political and what their specificities are is a task political scientists cannot delegate to either economics or sociology.

While recognising the possibility of different terminology and different definitions, let me conclude with a simple set of rules of good conduct for the political scientist dealing with political institutions, a simple *vade mecum* that may enhance the intersubjective exchange of knowledge:[49]

(1) Any definition of 'institution' should prove its utility in the identification of a class of phenomena that we deem an important object of analysis.

(2) Given that the semantic field of the term 'institution' is too wide, any definition should specify the type of institutions to which it intends to refer.

(3) The definition should not be too complicated and should avoid resorting to terms the meaning of which is even more controversial than the term 'institution' itself.

(4) The definition of the concept of institution should remain the same whether institutions are utilised as dependent, independent or intervening variables, and whether we explain their emergence, their purpose, their enforcement or their change and decline.

---

[49] As a source of inspiration for some of these rules, see Sjoblom, G. (1993), 'Some critical remarks on March and Olsen's "Rediscovering Institutions"', *Journal of Theoretical Politics*, 5: 397–40 and Sjoblom, G. (1994), 'Notes on the Concept of "Institution"', Paper presented at the XVI World Congress of the International Political Science Association, 21–25 August, Berlin.

(5) Definitions of institutions should not include what they are supposed to explain. If institutions *are* recurrent patterns of behaviour, they cannot, without tautology, explain human behaviour. If culture is part of the definition of institutions, we cannot claim that culture shapes institutions.

(6) Any definition that incorporates a theory of the term to be defined is to be rejected. These definitions cannot be validated given that they auto-define the empirical referent that could validate them, and attribute to all institutions the specific theory that appears in the definition.

   (6a) The definition of 'institutions' should not incorporate a theory of their functions.

   (6b) The definition should not include properties of institutions that vary across types of institutions: consciousness of design, implementation, unexpected outcomes, invisible hands and so on.

(7) Theories of the 'origins' of institutions should be differentiated from theories of their effects.

(8) The concept of 'institution' should be differentiated from that of 'organisation'.

(9) With reference to political institutions, the capacity of the institutions to define the identity of the actors should not be a definitional property.

In the classification in Table 3.2, no specific reference is made to political institutions. Part II of this work and its four chapters are devoted to them.

On Political Institutions

What are political institutions; that is, the norms and rules that are 'political'? I propose the following short-cut definition: norms and rules that allow a bounded group – be it a voluntary membership group or an involuntary territorial group – to select one request for compliance among a set of different instigations that are contradictory at the level of the group are 'political'.

Let me take an extreme example to clarify the point.[1] If a group of friends heatedly discuss whether to go to the theatre, to the pub or to see a movie in the evening, the request for behavioural compliance that extends from some members of the group to the entire group is indeed contradictory at the individual level, as no one can simultaneously go to more than one place. But it is not necessarily contradictory for the group, as the possibility of different subgroups choosing different options does not jeopardise the friendship relationship. On the contrary, let us imagine the case of a city facing an approaching enemy army and dividing over the best strategy to respond to the challenge. One subgroup suggests surrendering and paying the price of subjugation; another prefers the option of fighting the enemy in an open-field battle and a third proposes reinforcing the walls and facing a siege. In this case, the city cannot survive as a group as it is weakened and eventually destroyed by the fact that some individuals respond positively to one instigation while others respond to a different one.

In short, if different requests for compliance are only contradictory at the level of the individual (in the sense that each individual can only respond to a single request but not to two or many) but not at the level of the group, then there is no special 'political' problem. Different subsets of the members of the group can effectively follow one instigation while others follow other instigations without it having negative consequences for the group. On the contrary, when different

---

[1] See Bartolini, S. (2018), *The Political*, Colchester, ECPR Press, pp. 72–4.

instigations to action are contradictory at the level of the group, a single request for behavioural compliance must be chosen, it is proclaimed to be the 'command' and it becomes compulsory and binding on all members of the group.[2] Here it does not matter whether the final command is one option prevailing over the others, a merger of different options, a compromise or an imposition. What matters is that one unitary command is eventually chosen. The capacity of a group bonded by some social relationship to overcome solicitations that are contradictory at the level of the group always depends on the development of norms and rules that allow this selection process. These are what I call 'political institutions'.

In Chapter 4, I discuss the theoretical definition of 'political institutions' sketched above, which sets them aside from the other institutions discussed in Chapter 3. Political institutions are norms and rules that transform a set of contradictory instigations to action into a single command; that discipline the struggle to achieve positions that can transform contradictory instigations into a command; that constrain the ruler's search for generalised and stabilised behavioural compliance in any confined group; and that concern the procedure through which public powers produce private powers (as guaranteed rights), not the concrete outcomes of these procedures. I then distinguish different kinds of norms/rules: norms/rules of conduct versus norms/rules of recognition and norms/rules of conferral. It is argued that political institutions are norms/rules of conferral and are not rules of conduct or of recognition, and that confusion is generated when the types are mixed.

In Chapter 5, this definition of political institutions drives us to a discussion of the main 'institutes' that constitute them. Individual and atomistic political norms and rules are so many over space and time that a detailed discussion is impossible. While norms/rules identify micro-political institutions, with the term 'political institute' I identify those clusters of norms/rules that preside over the solution to a functional political problem; namely, norms and rules of selection, responsibility, inclusion, representation, decision, competence, accountability, devolution and redress. In my view, these nine institutes cover and exhaust the field of political normativity. Each of them is discussed analytically and historically in the chapter.

---

[2] The 'law of conservative exclusion' of de Jouvenel, B. (1963), *The Pure Theory of Politics*, Cambridge, Cambridge University Press, pp. 111–12.

Micro-norms/rules and institutes do not suffice to exhaust the field. The vertical layering of political institutions is such that we must pay attention to how we conceptualise even higher-order institutional realities such as territories, constitutions and regimes. In Chapter 6 I explore the possibility of composing these higher-order macro-institutions, starting with micro-norms/rules and institutes and their mutual compatibility and balancing. The chapter underlines that a necessary precondition for power-sharing is the monopolisation of destructive resources and of 'legitimate' violence over a territorial space: the 'territorial institution'. In territories in which destructive means have been successfully monopolised and there are no challenges to the ruling function, 'fundamental norms' or 'constitutions' may develop that delineate the *institutional regime*. The territory, the constitution and the institutional regime are macro-institutions that are located at the highest level in the vertical layering of institutions and are complex combinations of single norms/rules and institutes. At the same time, as macro-phenomena they are characterised by emerging properties that cannot exclusively be reduced to lower-level properties. Different regimes rest on the prominence of some institutes over others. In some cases, the predominant institutes damage and offend the others excessively. In other cases, the institutes balance each other in various ways. In the chapter I suggest that institutional analysis generalisations should concern political institutes, their balancing and combination and the likely effects. Actors' preferences and constellations of actors (e.g. political structures such as party systems and interest intermediation systems) should be kept separate as much as possible from institutional analysis. Adding them results in generalisations concerning the interaction between political institutions and political structures; that is, in the analysis of 'political regimes'.

Chapter 7 concludes this work by focussing on the specificity of political institutions as opposed to any other type of institution. I discuss particular aspects of political institutions such as their primordiality and scope, their generative character, weak normativity and sanctionability, their particular enforcement mechanisms, their contestedness and their intentional inefficiency. I conclude that it is improper to assimilate, and even worse to derive, the properties of political institutions from other kinds of economic, administrative or social institutions. For political institutions, the political element outweighs the institutional one, giving them their unique character.

4 | *What Political Institutions Are*

In the taxonomy of institutions in Table 3.2 in Chapter 3, political institutions have no special place. It can be argued that they are institutions like any other and consist of cultural templates, habits and conventions, social norms, routines and practices, role expectations, written rules, and so on. However, I believe that their being closely related to the political phenomenology gives them a special flavour, and in this chapter I will argue what that is.

4.1 A Theoretical Definition

The compound term 'political institutions' may be understood as referring to things that belong to the genus of institutions and at the same time to the particular species of the political. Contrarywise, political institutions may refer to things that belong to the genus of the political and to the species of institutions. Either way, between institutions and the political there is an intersection area, which implies that there are institutions that do not belong to the realm of the political and political realities that do not belong to the realm of institutions. The properties of this intersection area are not easy to define, particularly if we do not start with a clarification of the nature of political phenomenology.

If the question is *which* are the 'political' institutions, we encounter no scarcity of listings, usually involving human rights, constitutions, state formats, executives, legislatures, judiciaries, election systems, democracy, legal systems, the free market economy and corporatism.[3] More detailed listings may include items such as parliament/cabinet relations, types of regimes, legislation rules, agenda setting, investiture, confidence and dissolution rules,

[3] From Lane and Ersson, *The New Institutional Politics*, p. 52.

presidential vetoes, and so on. Further perusing the literature, we encounter strange bedfellows: interest organisations, parties and party systems;[4] entire 'regimes';[5] 'cleavages';[6] class structure; the standard operating procedures of a bureaucracy;[7] civil society political institutions;[8] and even public policies and political economies.[9] The list of the 'which' grows, generating a bewildering variety of objects and with it some perplexity too. To answer the 'which' question is perhaps not the right strategy. The 'which' does not easily turn into the 'what'.[10] On logical grounds, if we do not agree on 'what' political institutions are, it is hard to say 'which' political institutions exist. However, on the question of 'what' political institutions are, the theoretical elaboration is meagre.

In Scott's comprehensive review of all the schools and disciplines dealing with old and new institutionalisms, it appears that none of them focus on 'political institutions' and references to them are scanty and often derivative.[11] March and Olsen's influential book[12] primarily deals with institutions within organisations and makes few references to political institutions in common-sense language. A recent handbook entirely dedicated to political institutions, *The Oxford Handbook of Political Institutions*,[13] includes only one article (at the very end) devoted to discussion of the concept,[14] while all the other chapters deal with varieties of institutionalism

---

[4] Thelen and Steinmo, *Historical Institutionalism in Comparative Politics*, p. 11.
[5] Przeworski, 'Institutions matter?'.
[6] Greif, A. and D. Laitin (2004), 'A theory of endogenous institutional change', *American Political Science Review*, 98: 633–52.
[7] March and Olsen, *Rediscovering Institutions*, p. 21.
[8] Harris, J. (2006), 'Development of civil society', in Rhodes, Binder and Rockman (eds.), *The Oxford Handbook of Political Institutions*, pp. 131–43.
[9] Capoccia, G. (2015), 'Critical juncture and institutional change', in Mahoney, J. and K. Thelen (eds.), *Advances in Comparative Historical Analysis*, Cambridge, Cambridge University Press, pp. 147–79, 147.
[10] As happens with the concept of 'political action'. A listing of common-sense political actions does not turn into a theoretical meaningful definition of them. Bartolini, *The Political*, pp. 11–13.
[11] Scott, R. W. (2008, 3rd edition), *Institutions and Organizations: Ideas and Interests*, Thousand Oaks, CA, Sage Publications.
[12] March and Olsen, *Rediscovering Institutions*.
[13] Rhodes, Binder and Rockman (eds.), *The Oxford Handbook of Political Institutions*.
[14] Blondel, *About Institutions, Mainly, but Not Exclusively, Political*, pp. 716–30.

and concrete political institutions, among which national health insurance, civil society and national pension systems are discussed.

Political scientists, who have always been busy with the analysis of specific political institutions, have participated less in the new theoretical effervescence of the field and contributed less to the theoretical specification of the features of political institutions as opposed to social and economic institutions. 'Old' political institutional studies were criticised for their excessive formalism, lack of theoretical foundations and descriptive character, and new paradigms have resorted to the label of 'neo-institutionalism'. The change is a revisiting with new lenses, often influenced by the neighbouring disciplines of economics and sociology. As was argued in Chapter 2, neo-institutionalist efforts in political science have focussed more on the definition of an approach than on a theoretical discussion of the specificity of political institutions. As a result, the theory of political institutions remains much influenced by new developments in institutional economics and organisational sociology. In these, political institutions have been phagocytised into broader problems of the emergence, persistence, change and functions of all types of institutions.

What is the specificity of institutions that are defined as 'political' as opposed to those which are not? There are a variety of general definitions. Political institutions are critical for restraining leadership and holding political elites accountable, and for identifying proper selection procedures for choosing people in various positions of political leadership. They differ from markets in that their actors cannot simply engage in exchange but make decisions under some framework such as majority rule. For some scholars the most important task of political institutions is to 'get property rights right', to establish rule systems that promote efficient economic organisation. Political institutions are distinctive in that they are fundamentally about the exercise of public authority, which entails access to unique coercive powers. They live in a far murkier environment than the economic realm, lacking the measuring rod of price and entailing the pursuit of often incommensurable goals with opaque processes. They are defined as 'formal arrangements for aggregating individuals and regulating their behaviour through the use of explicit rules and decision processes enforced by an actor formally recognised as possessing such power'[15] and are seen as systems of rules that apply to the future behaviour of actors.[16]

The list could be made longer, but one would not get much out of excavating shreds of decontextualised definitional sentences, except to be unfair to the authors proposing them. Alternatively, a full elaboration of these different positions would turn this work into a textual exegesis, which is not my aim. Therefore, I will pursue my own perspective by elaborating on some of these positions to advance a theoretical definition of political institutions compatible with the theory of politics and political action delineated in my work *The Political*. Referring to that piece will help in following the analysis that ensues, but I will here summarise a few core points for those who are not familiar with it.

4.2 Producing Behavioural Compliance through Commands

In *The Political* I discussed elementary political action in terms of its motivational underpinnings and its mechanisms of deployment. As the political is essentially the production and distribution of behavioural compliance within any membership or territorial group, the search for compliance therefore characterises political action in its elementary form. Actor A, in trying to gain the compliance of actor B, can sanction, persuade, condition and manipulate. In analytical anarchic or natural fields of interaction – characterised by the absence of any monopolisation of the function of behavioural compliance production – the individual's search for others' compliance is bounded only by the resources of the actor and his capacity and propensity to use them.

Limits or constraints on this capacity/propensity to use resources to achieve compliance exist. Moral principles and social norms can limit the propensity of actor A to use certain resources and mechanisms. Resorting to manipulative techniques may cost you social honour; certain sanctions may be highly socially dishonourable. Conditioning the environment may entail costs of reputation. So, the naked search

---

[15] Levi, M. (1990), 'A logic of institutional change', in Cook, K. S. and M. Levi (eds.), *The Limits of Rationality*, Chicago, IL, University of Chicago Press, pp. 402–19, 405.

[16] Offe, C. (2006), 'Political institutions and social power: conceptual explorations', in Shapiro, I. et al. (eds.), *Rethinking Political Institutions: The Art of the State*, New York, New York University Press, pp. 9–31, 10.

for behavioural compliance analysed in *The Political* needs to be complemented with those situational constraints that take the general name of institutions as norms/rules. They set limits to an actor's capacity and disposition to use her own resource endowment to achieve compliance by making certain kinds of action courses normatively prescribed.

In my view, however, although they limit and constrain political action in its search for compliance, these constraints relate to social, moral, honour or interest norms/rules that affect individual conduct and they are not 'political' institutions.[17] They are not political institutions because in the presence of conflicting instigations to action among actors, this type of institutional constraint cannot solve the problem of coordination or can solve it only through voluntary action. In anarchic and natural fields, therefore, the only institutions we can observe are either non-political or non-institutions; that is, either mere agreements among actors or impositions of outcomes derived from the imbalance of their resources.

In authority and governmental fields of interaction, where a monopolistic provider and distributer of compliance exists, a large and growing number of requests for behavioural compliance originate not from a personalised other but from an impersonal norm/rule that is faceless in most cases, or for which a face is simply the carrier of the impersonal command. In these cases, it is not A that asks B to do H but it is a norm/rule. The sanctioning, persuasion, conditioning and manipulation that preside over the production of compliance generalised for the entire group and stabilised in time cannot be generated by the action of A over B but must be collectively imposed on all the membership or territorial field. And it cannot be different because the compliance that A can impose on B through her own resources and actions cannot be extended to C, D, E and so on unless it stabilises and generalises itself as a mechanism of compliance generation and of distribution of due quotas of compliance for the entire group.

Rulership, too, cannot be unbounded but finds limitations in all those dimensions in which an exchange is needed between rulers and

---

[17] Available political action and normative constraints cannot be easily distinguished. This is a valid point, but, without an analytical distinction between the two, the knowledge enterprise cannot advance. Recognising that empirical action is embedded in normative frameworks does not require them to be treated together as indistinguishable. For heuristic purposes, we can pursue the analytical exercise of trying to disentangle them.

the ruled for purposes of defence, justice, counsel and support. The mutual obligations resulting from these go towards the superior offering counsel and support, or towards the inferior offering defence and justice. Counsel, support, defence and justice express themselves through several constraints that regulate the complexity of these functions and they define in general terms the proper domain of political institutions as institutionalised counsel and support, defence and justice.[18]

The emergence of a generalised and stabilised production of compliance is a contested and contentious process. This is due to the indeterminacy and instability of fundamental political predicaments: (1) who are the members authorised to take decisions and who are subject to these decisions? (2) Which are the rules to be used to set rules? (3) Why should people conform to the prevailing command? Political institutions emerge when a group cannot endure following contradictory instigations and requires the issuing of commands for its survival as a group. Political institutions are rules/norms that allow the transformation of competing instigations into single commands (or merge competing instigations into a single command). The presence of a monopolistic provider of command and compliance generates the problem of his selection and the rules that discipline it. This leads to a first general definition: norms/rules are political that

(1) transform a set of contradictory instigations to action into a single command valid for a membership (authority field) or a territorial group (governmental field);
(2) discipline the struggle to achieve positions that can transform contradictory instigations into commands;
(3) constrain the ruler's search for generalised and stabilised behavioural compliance in any confined group.

Let me stress a point before we proceed further. Among some of the colleagues who have reviewed this work, the use of the term 'command' in the text has generated some discomfort and uneasiness. In part, this

---

[18] To avoid misunderstanding, let us stress that the presence of political institutions does not reduce to nothing the role of individual actors' resources. They may get their way through political institutions as they would have done through direct action, but the distinction between the two modalities of compliance generation becomes crucial in the more differentiated forms of government.

may be due to misunderstanding. It is not claimed here that politics *is* command. As is clear throughout the text, politics includes negotiations, cooperation and agreements, compromises, voting, protest, and so on. What is claimed here is that *political institutions are those instruments that, in the presence of different and likely conflicting options, allow the definition of a single outcome solution in all those situations in which the group is not allowed to follow different solutions.* The ways in which this outcome is achieved may be very different but the final result is a single outcome that acquires the nature of a command for the territorial or membership group.[19]

4.3 Norms/Rules of Conduct, Recognition and Conferral

To characterise more precisely the nature of these political norms/rules, let us imagine a group that organises itself in such a way that the only means of social control are accepted and self-enforcing norms/rules of mutual obligation. These self-generated norms/rules of conduct must contain some restriction on the use of violence, theft and other misdeeds that tempt human beings. Those who would eventually reject the mutually agreed institutions must be a relatively small minority that fears the social pressures of non-reciprocation or of punishment that are available in such an elementary social setting. It is also likely that only a small community in a stable environment can successfully live in such a regime of norms supported by common sentiments and beliefs.

In fact, norms/rules of conduct of this type have limits.[20] Doubts may arise as to what the norms and rules are or as to their precise scope. In this case, there is no procedure for settling this doubt by reference to something else, an authoritative text of some kind, or an official whose declarations on this point are authoritative. But even admitting

---

[19] If, on the contrary, the uneasiness is primarily lexicographic, one can use different and more palatable terms: direction, directive, injunction, dictate, instruction, ordinance, precept, imposition, regulation, law and so on. However, these seem to me different forms of 'command', which remains the best general term for all of them.

[20] Norms/rules of conduct include *definitional norms/rules* and *permissive norms/rules*. The first define the criteria for inclusion of a conduct within the broader norm. For instance, if you share information with the enemy, you are a traitor; if you are adult, you are responsible; and so on. Permissive rules/norms concede positions of advantage, rights, privileges, powers and immunities. This distinction is of limited importance for my argument here.

widespread knowledge of which are the norms/rules of conduct to be applied, there may be disputes concerning whether any specific action or inaction has or has not violated any given norm. Overcoming these uncertainties requires the development of other norms/rules that constitute an authoritative source to adjudicate who has violated which norms/rules, and what punishment is appropriate. A chief, shaman, priest, judge/court or an ordeal is empowered to make an authoritative determination of the fact that a rule, and which rule, has been broken and, therefore, the precise determination of which are the rules. These different norms/rules are not norms/rules of conduct. Let us call them *norms/rules of recognition*, exactly because they help to 'recognise' the offence/violation and to decide on culpability and the penalty.

In a world of norms of conduct and recognition, the situation greatly improves as we have the instruments to decide which are the norms/rules, when they are violated and what can ensue because of the violation. However, a problem remains. Changing these norms can only be a slow process of growth and adaptation to new circumstances in which conducts, once regarded as optional, would then become first habitual and then obligatory, or deviations once severely dealt with within the group slowly become tolerated. In a simple world of norms of conduct and recognition, eliminating old rules and introducing new ones is a long, demanding process that inevitably is left to spontaneous adaptations and to gradual interpretative changes; in fact, it is left to orthograde change. To overcome the static bias inherent in norms of conduct and of recognition, other norms/rules are needed empowering specific bodies or persons to repeal old norms/rules, to introduce new ones and modify existing ones. These rules of change have a diversified character but all imply a complex and precise procedure to be followed for the conferral of such authority. I call these *norms/rules of conferral*.

Therefore, we can distinguish between *norms/rules of conduct*, *norms/rules of recognition* and *norms/rules of conferral*.[21] Norms/rules of conduct impose duties. They either forbid or require certain actions. They lay down standards of behaviour and are constituted by the deontic modalities of obligation, prohibition and permission. They

---

[21] Hart terms the distinction between primary and secondary rules as rules of conduct versus rules of interpretation. See Hart, *The Concept of Law*, pp. 91–4, and Hart (1961), *The Law as a Union of Primary and Secondary Rule*, Oxford, Oxford University Press. I divide the category of secondary norms/rules into norms/rules of recognition and norms/rules of conferral.

exist in any type of community. The early groups discussed in Chapter 1 lived based on norms of conduct, the origins of which were customary, and with elementary norms of recognition supporting them. The latter could be made by proof derived from trial by ordeal (by combat, fire, water and so on) or by judgement made by shamanism and other magico-religious practices, and so on. In modern systems with multiple sources of normativity – socio-moral normativity, roles in complex organisations, written constitutions, legislative enactments and judicial precedents – rules of recognition are quite complex and require a hierarchy where some rules overrule others. Rules of recognition define the procedural sources and steps and the sanctioning mechanisms for violations of rules of conduct. They are ancillary to the norms/rules of conduct. They specify the ways in which violation of the rules of conduct may be ascertained. They are mainly procedural and remedial.

Norms/rules of conferral confer public powers. They confer prerogatives and powers not in the form of guaranteed individual powers (the rights to …) but in the form of collective powers. *Norms/rules of conferral are what we should properly understand as political institutions.* For instance, the norms/rules that prohibit unrecorded financing of political organisations or sexual harassment take the form of norms/rules of conduct. The power to verify the correspondence of a concrete conduct to the normative parameter of illegal financing or sexual harassment takes the form of rules/norms of recognition. The power to issue these norms/rules and to modify, abolish and repeal them results from norms/rules of conferral.

This discussion clarifies why it is mistaken to identify political institutions with rules of conduct. Arguing that political institutions consist of behaviours dictated by the 'logic of appropriateness', considering the logic of appropriateness as the logic of political action,[22] or attributing to political institutions the property of being a 'socially shared standard' or 'infused with (social) value'[23] means assimilating political institutions to rules of conduct. The extension of a normativist approach

---

[22] 'Much of the behaviour we observe in political institutions reflects the routine way in which people do what they are supposed to do.' 'Political institutions are collections of interrelated rules and routines that define appropriate actions in terms of relations between roles and situations.' March and Olsen (1989), *Rediscovering Institutions*, pp. 21 and 160.

[23] Selznick, *Leadership in Administration*, p. 17.

centred on social norms and filtered through administrative and organisation studies to the realm of political institutions leads to the conclusion that most behaviour in politics follows a logic of appropriateness – that norms/rules are followed and roles are fulfilled. In the end, political institutions are assimilated to norms/rules of conduct; that is, they are like all other social institutions.

The thesis that most political behaviours follow the logic of appropriateness appears problematic to the scholar of politics. And the idea that the fundamental activity of political institutions is to educate individuals as informed citizens seems perhaps excessively benign and insufficiently sensitive to the evil face that political institutions sometimes show. Expected and appropriate behaviour are poorly defined in politics; reneging on commitments is not a forbidden or sanctioned practice; tricks and stratagems constellate political life.

For political institutions, the questions of who infuses and shares values and how large the infusion and the sharing are remains open and crucial. Political norms/rules always remain contentious and controversial and alternative solutions are present and discussed. In politics, the appropriateness cannot exclusively be referred to a logic of morality or sociality but also, and perhaps primarily, to a logic of 'effectiveness' of political action with respect to the goals it sets for itself.

What is most important is that norms/rules of conduct do not define norms/rules of recognition and conferral. In the best instances they regulate behaviour, but they do not confer any specific power or competence to arbitrate and eventually reduce contradictory instigations to action. Defining political institutions through some sort of socially shaped 'rule of conduct' betrays the often-discussed tendency to incorporate political institutions in the broader and undifferentiated pool of social integrative institutions. This approach 'socialises' political institutions to an excessive extent. In politics, there might be rules of conduct that are socially defined, but political institutions are not these rules of conduct.

Norms/rules of conferral confer the power of introducing, repealing or modifying existing rules/norms of conduct, of recognition and even of conferral (in the case of political institution reforms). Undoubtedly the rules and norms of conferral that lead to the production of other norms/rules set 'appropriate' procedures. In certain circumstances – not all – the norms/rules of conferral that permit the transformation of potentially incompatible requests into a single command may be widely accepted and therefore shared and valued. As was argued earlier, it is nonetheless a mistake to make this social acceptance and sharing a defining property of political institutions.

Rules/norms of conferral may be differentiated into three subtypes. *Rules/norms with attributive power* create a source of normative production and define an institutional subjectivity; for instance, the king rules by divine right; he includes the body of the nation; the prime minister defines the political agenda of government; political parties contribute to the representation of citizens' wills; and so on. *Rules/ norms of competence* concretely define the matters of intervention of the titular political authority – what an authority can or must do or is prohibited from doing – for instance, a feudal lord grants immunities such as the rights to collect taxes and tolls, hold judicial proceedings and coin money; the mayor of a city authorises building permits. *Norms/rules of exercise* precisely describe how powers can be exercised and which limitations may exist; for instance, the mayor of a city can authorise building permits only after having consulted the communal technical office and the office of fine arts protection or after evaluating impact assessment reports. In this exercise of theoretical definition, there is no need to further pursue this differentiation.

Conferral norms/rules allow the definition of the allocation of public powers. Private powers allow individuals to sell, marry, exercise a profession or an economic activity, profess a religion, make wills and get a pension. Public powers concern the power to legislate, to appoint, to adjudicate, to veto and so on about the concrete distribution of private powers and rights. *This means that political institutions should not be confused with the powers/rights they confer but should be identified as the norms/rules that concede them.* Therefore, the definition of a right, subjection or constraint, immunity or incapacity, privilege or non-right and the determination of specific policies, corporatist agreements, welfare states, pension systems and so on result from political institutions but they are not political institutions.[24] This

---

[24] Hohfeld's theory of correlatives identifies eight types of norms. The one of interest here is power-type norms. The correlative of power is 'subjection' and its negation is 'incapacity'; Hohfeld, W. N. (1913), 'Some fundamental legal conceptions as applied in judicial reasoning', in Patterson, D. (ed.) (2003), *Philosophy of Law and Legal Theory: An Anthology*, Oxford, Blackwell, pp. 295–321.

last paragraph leads to a further refinement of the definitional statements: norms/rules are political that

(4) concern the procedure through which public power produces private powers (like guaranteed rights), not the concrete outcomes of these procedures.

At this stage, my complete theoretical definition of institutions that are political includes four linked elements. Political institutions are those norms/rules that

(1) transform a set of contradictory instigations to action into a single command valid for a membership (authority field) or a territorial group (governmental field);
(2) discipline the struggle to achieve positions that can transform contradictory instigations into commands;
(3) constrain the ruler's search for generalised and stabilised behavioural compliance in any confined group;
(4) concern the procedure through which public power produces private powers (like guaranteed rights), not the concrete outcomes of these procedures.

I will pursue this line of thought about the differentiation of political institutions in Chapter 5. I shall now elaborate on some of the specificities of political institutions as rules of conferral which I have only briefly mentioned in this definitional phase. From the elementary and abstract definitions provided above, several implications follow. The remaining sections of this chapter will more precisely and thoroughly discuss them.

4.4 Concentrating/Sharing Political Power in Analytical Terms

In contemporary political science literature, the term 'power-sharing' has been appropriated by the consociational (or consensual) approach and by the politics of divided societies. This is 'conceptually constricting'.[25] It is a far more encompassing concept. Whether, to what extent and how political power is concentrated/shared defines the core problem of political institutions. This is crucial because differentiating political institutions always takes place within a context of

[25] Horowitz, *Constitutional Design*, p. 23, fn. 7.

monopolisation of coercive and destructive resources. We need to stop and reflect on this particularity.

Concentrating resources and the corresponding potential powers generate different expectations in different domains. Classic political sociology differentiates economic, symbolic and coercive resources and the corresponding powers:

(1) *economic power* is based on concentration in a few hands of economic resources, material instruments and means of subsistence;

(2) *symbolic power* rests on the concentration of symbolic resources able to produce values such as social honour, ethical-religious norms and identity (including political identities);

(3) *coercive power* rests on the concentration of resources that generate and inflict destructive damage, and concerns physical security and integrity, the possibility to use one's own body, and freedom to possess and use one's material instruments.

Monopolising economic and symbolic powers is difficult, and it is most often seen as normatively undesirable. We usually seek positive balancing forces in the plurality, the dispersion and the competition of centres of economic and symbolic power. We believe that a free society can exist only if economic and symbolic powers are not (excessively) concentrated. This is not the case with coercive means. In the case of coercive resources, the monopoly of one actor A may determine the full subjection of the others, but ending the monopoly of coercive resources by A is not associated with an improved situation for B.

Given that the resources at stake are destructive resources, a situation of competition between several actors to exercise coercion and physical violence may worsen the situation of B. B would be subject to coercive power in any case and may even be subject to a sequence of violent events generated by the competitors for the monopolisation. B may develop an interest in supporting and fostering the acquisition of the monopoly of coercion for one single actor disposing of destructive resources. In other words, *contrary to the expectation concerning economic and symbolic powers, in the case of coercive resources competition has no beneficial effects for the third party.* In a situation of asymmetry between actors in economic or symbolic resources we may aim to rebalance the asymmetry, but asymmetry in destructive resources is a necessary condition for the development of more equality in the other spheres (see Table 4.1).

Table 4.1 *Equalising resources in different domains*[26]

	Economic resources	Symbolic resources	Destructive resources
(Extreme) inequality of resources	Economic domination *Slavery*	Symbolic domination *Imposition of religious, linguistic, moral, etc. conformity*	Coercive domination *Possibility of differentiating political institutions*
(Extreme) equality of resources	Exchange benefits *Synallagmatic relations and contracts*	Exchange of recognition *Recognition of pluralism of identities*	Coercive anarchy *Permanent violent conflict. Differentiation of political institutions is unlikely*

[26] This table is inspired by Stoppino, M. (2001, 3rd edition), *Potere e teoria politica*, Milan, Giuffré, pp. 191–2. The interpretation is rather different.

One ruler for one territory may entail different forms of political power organisation, in some of which political institutions may share and/or limit the political power of the ruler. The equalisation of coercive or destructive resources does not have this potential and only leads to coercive anarchy. We are terrified by the pluralisation and equalisation of destructive resources, which are associated with permanent civil war and strife, violent conflicts and a likely reduction of the equalisation of other resources.

This leads to the conclusion that, unlike any other kind of resource, the only mechanism for balancing necessarily concentrated destructive resources is not their equalisation and competition but political and institutional pluralism; that is, forms of political power-sharing or limiting the territorial monopolisation of destructive resources. Compensation for asymmetries in other resources can only occur in the context of the monopolisation of destructive resources. Therefore, if we were to attribute a 'function' to political institutions it would be their role in taming and constraining the monopoly of destructive resources that cannot be shared.

The particularity of the Western experience is that it has added a further type of resource that could compensate other asymmetries. These are resources linked to the equalisation of institutionalised political power, political institutions, which early on were embedded in the institution monopolising destructive resources over a given territory. The interesting question is, therefore, how and when has it happened that specific sets of political norms/rules were created that introduced uncertainty and insecurity in the holding and future exercise of public authority?

Unlike property rights, political power is attached either to specific offices or positions of public authority and, technically, does not belong to anybody. Therefore, in politics the primary aim of every holder of public authority is to stabilise it over time and generalise it over people. Given that rulership stabilises itself in the context of a monopoly of destructive resources, as was argued earlier, the most natural outcome and the most frequent in history is that rulers resort to such a monopoly of violence to resist any differentiation of political institutions.

One way to eliminate uncertainty about the future control of political power is to avoid creating political institutions at all, and rely on de facto (dictatorial) achieved power without adopting rules/norms for the change of public authority, not even elementary lineage hereditary rules, which already define a potential enemy (the Macbethian nightmare).

A second strategy is to create institutions that are *insulated* from future revisions by alternative future public authorities, such as specific hereditary rules, nepotism, patrimonialism and divine or religious blessing. In doing so, the current holder of public authority also limits her own control of such institutions, not only the control of potential future holders.

A third strategy to stabilise public authority is to create institutions so *biased* in favour of a part or person through patronage, co-optation, bribing and corruption that the passage of public authority to others is very difficult. The strategy of hierarchical control over existing institutions and agencies based on discretionary decisions by the current holders may be extremely risky if they were to lose that control, as this would offer their adversaries the same degree of discretion in destroying and reshaping the institutional biases.

Therefore, it is not surprising that those in monopolistic control of the means of destruction have so often resorted and do resort to a strategy of devising *inexistent, insulated* or *biased* political institutions. We should instead be surprised by the contrary: the existence of political institutions that discipline public authority in such a way as to guarantee uncertainty about its future exercise.

In circumstances in which inexistent, insulated or biased political institutions are too risky or fail, public authority holders and their opponents develop compromises that protect the opponents from the threatening power of the incumbents. For the vital need to protect from outside and out-group conflictual relations, a maximum of power concentration and a minimum of power-sharing would appear an efficient solution. Taming and limiting the power and prerogatives of rulers, however, has opposite requirements. It is crucial for opponents, subjects/citizens and interest groups to establish some sort of defence against the possibility that the public authority will negatively affect their rights and interests. Given that the public authority could in principle modify the status quo in any possible direction, it is crucial for commitments to be established as to the limitation of this capacity. To this effect, elite circulation and uncertainty about the tenure of public authority are essential.

In historical analysis the main problem is how it has happened that specific sets of political institutions introducing uncertainty have developed *without jeopardising the necessary precondition of the con-tinued monopolisation of the means of destruction.* We should regard this as the normative standard against which to evaluate political institutions. In this case, we would perhaps be less surprised about the apparent inefficiency of some of the solutions adopted to face this problem.

Continuing the analytical investigation, it seems to me that political institutions differentiate along four dimensions of power concentration/sharing. These include two *principles of inclusion* and two *principles of limitation.*[27]

The two principles of institutional inclusion are:

(1) *The circulation of the elite.* This involves the achievement of rules that guarantee a circulation of the governing elite and instability in the tenure of political power. This implies making top political positions 'removable' – that is, with fixed terms – and 'responsible' to some sort of other body. It also means imposing that key political positions are not reserved for special ascriptive groups but are, at least in part, open to different (and competing) groups of actors.

(2) *Enlargement.* This involves the enlargement of politically relevant actors; the spread of political rights of participation in the polity. This implies bodies that represent more and different people and groups, granting or mandating their consultation and participation (be they estates, corporations, the military, ethno-religious groups, the bureaucracy, parties, citizens and so on).

The two principles of limitation are:

(1) *Scope restraints.* This involves achieving norms/rules that substantively restrain the capacity and scope of rulers to act unilaterally. This usually requires certain spheres of decisions to be excluded from the range of possible choices and precluded from command (like human rights, religious practices, vulnerable groups, civic and political liberties, etc.).

(2) *Implementation restraints.* The monistic formation of command is constrained by partitioning power among different bodies (e.g.

---

[27] In 'Safeguarding democracy: power sharing and democratic survival', *American Political Science Review*, 111: 686–704, Graham, B. A. T., M. K. Miller and K. W. Strøm (2017) identify three dimensions of power-sharing that result from a factor analysis of nineteen indicators.

bicameralism); by decentralising implementation instruments; by requiring cooperation among different layers of territorial author- ity; by submitting command to ex-post or ex-ante review by inde- pendent and non-partisan judicial institutions; or by requiring the cooperation of independent agencies (regulatory, monetary, etc.).

Circulation of the elite, enlargement of political actors and scope, and implementation restraints are all what political institutions are about. On the contrary, power concentration takes one or more of the opposite directions: (1) stabilising political tenure and limiting political elite circulation; (2) restricting the relevant political actors; (3) extending the scope of command decisions; (4) strengthening the monistic formation of command by abolishing or weakening the coun- ter-powers of any nature (territorial, constitutional, expertise, etc.). The more political power is concentrated, the more political institu- tions de-differentiate in the sense of becoming biased, insulated or eventually inexistent.

From the point of view of those in authority positions, power- sharing institutions are problems for command. For those excluded from such positions, they are safeguards. The concentration/dispersion of political power generates a tension between problems seen as obs- tacles to effective rule and the same problems seen as guarantees against unchecked rule. Different kinds of power-sharing may enhance the chances of non-rulers accepting rulership while undermining its effectiveness.

In terms of institutional stability, one may think that power- sharing institutions, once they have emerged, are more resilient to change than power-concentrating institutions. The more concen- trated the institutional power of public authorities, the higher the possibility of radical departures from the status quo and the more likely that new power holders, if successful, may modify this status quo thanks to the concentration of power. If an institutional arrangement can be easily altered by the power holders, the arrange- ment can also be easily modified by their successors. On the con- trary, in an institutional structure characterised by mechanisms of power-sharing, new deals can be introduced with greater difficulty but they tend to be more stable over time. Changes are more diffi- cult, but once introduced they tend to be more resilient to further change. This points to the inherent conservatism and long-run stability of power-sharing institutions as against the inherent radical changeability and instability over time of power-concentrating institutions.

4.5 Concentrating/Sharing Political Power in Historical Terms

The combination of the (necessary) monopolistic control of coercive resources with the (possible) differentiation of political institutions is difficult and not very frequent. The recent doctrine of the 'separation of powers' is a rationalisation of accumulated experiences. Political power-sharing institutions have a much longer history and this is largely a Western history. It was substantiated in a set of accumulated steps that left innovations, habits, memories, practices and expectations concerning balancing in the management of different types of resources. They eventually contributed to a separation between the exercise of political power and the mere exercise of coercive power through an elaborate set of rules/norms: in Weberian terms, the separation between the 'legitimate' use of violence – legitimate because confined and bounded by rules and norms – and the mere use of it. This separation is always tentative and at stake; setbacks exist. Nevertheless, the memories, practices and expectations derived from past experiences accumulate to generate reactions against these setbacks.

In my view, there are six main historical critical junctures that contributed to the equilibrium among opposing forces and different roles and eventually fostered and sustained the institutionalisation of experiences of power-sharing in the West. They are (1) the secular/religious dualism at the collapse of the Roman empire; (2) the codification experiences of the Germanic kingdoms; (3) the emergence of independent cities; (4) the invention of institutions of consensus in the Middle Ages; (5) the crisis of universalism in the 'long sixteenth century' (1500–1700); and (6) the differentiation of European legal systems. Let us review their contribution to pluralism and power-sharing institutionalisation.

4.5.1 *Secular/Religious Dualism*

For a long time, only tradition and customs had important roles in limiting the scope and ambition of political power. Superstition and spiritual forces support requirements at war and even vestiges of the egalitarian organisation of the pre-Neolithic hunters and gatherers probably offered further contributions to the limitations. The main innovation is of religious origins, namely due to the emergence of monotheistic religions. The first form of institutionalised power-sharing was the idea that chiefs and kings were not omnipotent and were not constrained uniquely by unclear traditions and customs, but were limited by divine restraints. This was first an invention of the Jewish kingdoms. While they were of little significance in terms of state organisation, they first invented the notion of 'limited monarchy'. The Jewish monarchy is neither divine nor semi-divine and not even an intermediary between the community and God. The central event in Jewish history is that the entire community covenanted itself to God at Mount Sinai. For the first time, the people formed a *congregation*. The cult was not royal, not official, not priestly. It was *popular* and its essence was *participation*. The monarch was bound by an explicit, moral and partially written code imposed on him. And the code was in the possession of the entire congregation.[28]

In the post–Roman empire period, a plurality of institutional models survived. Antiquity left to the future a strong sense of the necessity of legislation and of its fitness to solve problems, with the memory of the ancient Greek constitutions and of the great Roman legislation. But the Roman legislation remained effective because it twinned with the cult of divine scriptures typical of the Judeo-Christian heritage. These reflected the idea that an authoritative book, whether the Bible or the *Corpus Juris*, could condense the rules for all individuals and society and that within it one could always find the solution to any problem. In addition, they also fostered the idea that the holder of power has the duty of new legislation, to create solutions to emerging problems not foreseen in the past.

The early Middle Ages were dominated by the dualism between ecclesiastical and secular authorities, the dualism between the emperor and the new Christian Church, particularly since in the West the emperor Graziano condemned pagan rites and immediately afterwards in the Orient the emperor Theodosius I proclaimed Christianity to be the state religion (Edict of Thessalonica, 380 CE). A crucial symbolic

---

[28] Finer, S. E. (1997), *The History of Government*, 3 vols, Oxford, Oxford University Press, pp. 238–9.

element of this dualism manifested immediately when Theodosius I was given a fine for the slaughter of Thessaloniki, ordered in a moment of anger (390 CE). The emperor was readmitted to the sacraments only after he had knelt down in front of the prestigious bishop of Milan, Sant'Ambrogio. In the first centuries of Christianity, religious authorities began to set rules of a general character such as those of the Universal Council of Nicaea (325 CE). The local synods produced rules slowly developed from specifically Christian '*consuetudini*' (customs), which were different to Roman law. Bishops, together with their pastoral powers, sacramental powers and disciplinary powers (including the fundamental power of excommunication), accumulated new public tasks formerly typical of secular powers, among which was the power to adjudicate (*episcopacies audientia*). In the West this was strengthened by the absence of the emperor (after the removal of Romulus Augustulus in 476) and the growing centrality of the bishop of Rome.

The papacy slowly became the scrupulous guardian of archives and tutor of ecclesiastical memory, with 'papal letters' sometimes going back to the fourth century. These had been preserved, informally collected and diffused because they contained teachings and solutions that could be exemplary and useful in other cases. This was the beginning of a unique repository of available precedents to reproduce, hand down and be thought about: the collection of the councils' '*canoni*' and papal letters (*Collezione Dionisiana*).

There was a crucial difference between the eastern and western parts of the empire. In the east, Caesaropapism prevailed, with the head of the secular power, the emperor (Caesar), in fact being the head of the Byzantine Church (pope). The Byzantine Church was more economically dependent on the state than the Roman Church, its rights were not formally defined, the appointment of the patriarch remained the prerogative of the emperor and the Byzantine clergy played a much smaller role in the state administration. In contrast, in the West the dualism persisted and was reinforced by more formal interpretations.

The long-lasting competing dualism between the two institutional orders, both legitimated to work for the collective good, persisted in the central Middle Ages and in the period of feudal fragmentation of the post-Carolingian Holy Roman empire and constituted a fertile ground for the specificity of Western institutions. A form of division of powers existed. The emperor managed the 'high politics' of the time (crusades, relationships with the territories of Latin Europe, internal peace and the safety of trade). The papacy (and its clergy) concentrated in its hands the power to settle controversies among the subjects concerning the most relevant aspects of life through canon law (marriage, the relationships among *familiae*, contractual relationships and public property). Other relationships concerning civil and penal controversies were managed by lords at the local level, often at more than one local level of the feudal pyramid.

4.5.2 Early Codification in the German Kingdoms

Next to the legacy of the empire and Roman law centred in the eastern part of the empire and of the new Christian authorities and Canonical Law centred in the new Rome, an additional source of normative production were the customs and traditions of the various German kingdoms installed in parts of the empire and efforts at their codification. Among these German populations, the Francs had special importance from the institutional point of view. Clovis I, the first Christian king, baptised by Bishop Remigius on Christmas night 496 with 3,000 of his men (he had been, perhaps, an officer in the Roman army), began to legislate the Salic law for his people, a source of subsequent legislation. The Normans in the kingdom of southern Italy issued the *Assise*, a code of norms of Norman origin (and in fact used in England too) showing the will of the government and their high conception of the royal office. The *proemio* made it clear that the new rules were necessary to eradicate bad customs. The Norman experience in England was so unitary from the beginning that a few years after the invasion it allowed the drafting of a complete list of people and goods (the Domesday Book), which indicates the king's preoccupation with knowing the exact scope of his patrimony. In Italy, the Lombards condensed their customs, which until then had been handed down in a non-codified way, in a book of codified rules in ungrammatical Latin, the *Edictum* (643). Although the *Edictum* was meant to be a codification of old customs, it was not without legislative innovations.[29]

---

[29] Significant examples are the replacement of the old right of revenge, the feud, with a flat pecuniary compensation for an offence and the use of the testament

At this stage, the early pluralism of the Middle Ages saw a source of normative production centred in Byzantium-Constantinople, one centred in the Church of Rome and the new institutions, slowly less customary and more codified, of the military aristocracy of German origins.[30] Nevertheless, in the context of the Middle Ages the idea that norms could be 'modified' and rules could be 'produced' was still weak. Rules/norms were rarely objects of 'decisions'. Neither their content nor their validity depended on politics. For a long time, politics remained the realm of *factual* developments, not of normative production; it was not meant to shape traditions or law, but rather to protect and restore them in cases of violation. An extensive public power active on a large scale was missing. There only existed single rights of imperialship, churchship or lordship distributed among many independent holders and often relating to a group of people, not a territory. The exercise of these rights 'did not constitute an autonomous and permanent function: their holders considered them rather as part of their social status … and did not feel the need for an administrative sub-structure explicitly finalised for the exercise of power'.[31]

4.5.3 The Emergence of Cities

The reality of new developing municipalities and city-states added a further element of pluralisation and changed the relationship between politics and normative production. Originally, the emergence of the power of cities, primarily in Italy, had to do with the transformation of customs into laws. For instance, the custom of collecting certain tolls and using them for the city without them being forfeited to the Earl for his own expenditure or sent to the kingdom's treasury became a right claim. The different relationships of the cities with the empire, the bishops and the local aristocracies let a complex situation emerge, which was diversified to the limit of chaos and progressively

---

against the old tradition of keeping heritages within the family. The *Edictum* also tried to eliminate the judicial duel (*pugna*) and the judgement of God or *ordalia*, but in this case traditions proved insurmountable.

[30] For these early institutional developments I rely on Gaudemet, L. (1993), *Les Sources du droit canonique (VIIIe–XXe siècles)*, Paris, Cerf and Caravale, M. (1994), *Ordinamenti giuridici dell'Europa Medioevale*, Bologna, Il Mulino.

[31] Grimm, *Diritto e politica*, p. 116 (my translation).

characterised by an unequal but colossal transfer of powers from the normative centres to single local realities.

In this phase, at about the beginning of the second millennium, a growing number of what we would today call public rights, from tax collection to the resolution of disputes to the delivery of military services, were incorporated in urban churches and abbeys or in territorial castles on the simple basis of continued exercise or the absence of contrary prescriptions by anybody. As these public powers were donated, definitively transferring some rights, so these same rights could be traded through private acts. Taxation rights and contributions of all kinds regarding castles, roads, harbours and so on were objects of donations, pledges, sales and successions. Slowly, lordships substituted the state, and made it redundant, unnecessary and costly. Cities began to accumulate these rights that were available on the market as they had lost their inherent 'public' nature. The 'usurping' and dispersion of public powers typical of the eleventh and twelfth centuries fostered the emergence of local powers with different modalities and this soon opened a new contraposition between the Holy Roman empire and the cities, which added to the already existing ones between the empire and the Church and the empire and the lords.

Official documents began to mention *communes* in the first decades of the 1100s, long after the institution de facto started existing. Communes were a self-sufficient reality which were not wanted by the empire or the legitimate local authorities, bishops, earls or marquises. They did not have an imposed, top-down ordering but a new autonomous order created from the bottom. Communes adopted the principle of self-legitimation, becoming de facto city-states. Local autonomy slowly transformed into political self-determination, including military adventures, even of a subversive nature (such as those of the Lombard League).

Imperial sovereignty could not be abolished or decay by desuetude. It was technically imprescriptible, notwithstanding its failure and the corresponding exercise of power by the communes and the papacy. From the point of view of the emperor, what the communes had acquired by custom on the public plane were bad customs to be weeded out. To regain them and to reaffirm that public power could only be exercised to the extent that it derived from the emperor was the failed programme of Frederick I (1122–90). The peace of Konstanz, which in 1183 provisionally, but with a definitive legal underpinning, ended the conflict between the emperor and the communes, left the cities feeling ready for self-governance and seeing the empire as an expensive, cumbersome and useless superstructure. However, many difficult passages and proofs were necessary to overcome it, in which the communes were often supported by the coincidence of their interests with those of the papacy.

The communes initiated the modern form of political institutions. Their statutes were an early constitution that the city ruler(s) – often a foreigner from a friendly city with a temporary contract – had to respect and implement. The corporations articulated intermediary bodies based on compulsory associations for professionals and collective responsibility for standards, debts and so on. The Captain of the People reintroduced the typical Roman Republic dualism at the top of the political institutions between the consuls and the tribunes of the plebians. Unlike the cities in other parts of Europe, which were generally free islands of merchants surrounded by vast agrarian-feudal territories, the central and northern Italian cities were soon constituted as chief towns dominant over the surrounding agrarian territories, even very large ones, and often degenerated into new principalities. The feudal monarchy remained the winning institution in most of the European peripheries but the European 'city belt',[32] running from central Italy to the Alps, to the Rhine river basin up to the low countries and the Hanseatic league of the North Sea, became the richest and most culturally advanced part of Europe, to be hard fought over by the emerging modern states on its eastern and western borders.

4.5.4 Institutions of Consensus in the Middle Ages

The populations in Europe were everywhere articulated into estates (*ceti, stands*) composed of earls, ministeriales and the free; the small nobility was composed of knights and squires, the two usually being enlisted under the nobility. Participation in the territorial diets extended at different stages to prelates, to cities and to merchants. Peasants were rarely included. Through its gentlemen's (*signorili*)

---

[32] For the crucial role of the central European 'city belt', see Rokkan, S. (1973), 'Cities, states, and nations: a dimensional model for the history of contrasts in development', in Eisenstadt, S. N. and S. Rokkan (eds.), *Building States & Nations*, vol. 2, New York, Sage, pp. 73–97, especially pp. 84–7; and Rokkan, S. (1999), *State Formation, Nation Building, and Mass Politics in Europe: The Theory of Stein Rokkan*, edited by P. Flora with S. Kuhnle and D. Urwin, Oxford, Oxford University Press, pp. 149–52.

estates, medieval society achieved access to the government of the territorial lord. The lord accepted this collaboration to the extent that the taxes he needed could only be provided by wealthy estates.[33] This inherent pluralism of the Middle Ages is at the root of the emergence and development of consultative and consensual political institutions.

Parliaments as seats tasked with taking decisions of collective interest were a typical Middle Ages institution. We can retrace their origin again in imperial, ecclesiastical, monastic and city-state developments. Diets were assemblies of the great, secular and ecclesiastic, summoned by the king to specific meetings to take or ratify political and military decisions and to legislate for necessary interventions. Their members intervened on a personal basis and formally only represented themselves. The ecclesiastical world used to meet and deliberate in councils and synods. The doctrine according to which the councils had powers superior to those of the Pope ('conciliarism') was widespread up to 1400, but the papacy eventually turned to absolutism by the middle of the century and the defects denounced by the councils were reproduced and aggravated by irresponsible nepotism.

We should not forget to add to this picture the monasticism movements starting in the sixth century. They all observed a 'rule', a complex of prescriptions. In particular, the Benedictine rule (*Regula Sancti Benedicti*, written in 516 by Benedict of Nursia) remains an extraordinary document for its longevity and institutional wisdom, an example of a 'constitution' for a community witnessing the Western vocation for writing rules and its anxiety about legality. Cluny, in opposition to the atomistic structure of the Benedictine monasteries, inaugurated a structure by 'orders', with a mother house to which many hierarchically dependent monasteries referred. This new type of organisation encouraged periodic meetings, 'general chapters', as a sort of parliament of the order. In the Benedictine Order the principle of the 'senior' or 'excellent' part prevailed, but in the middle of 1200 the idea of the 'major part', the majority principle, gained ascendancy in other orders, particularly among the Dominicans.[34]

---

[33] On estates as early forms of counter-powers, see Brunner, O. (1984 (1898)), *Land und Herrschaft: Grundfragen der territorialen Verfassungsgeschichte Österreichs im Mittelalter*, Darmstadt, Wissenschaftliche Buchgesellschaft, pp. 394–440.

[34] On the reinvention of the majority principle by monastic orders, see the introduction to Favre, P. (1976), *La décision de majorité*, Paris, Presses de la Fondation Nationale des Sciences Politiques.

Communal councils were modern decisional assemblies. The political councils and the justice councils of the lordships, princedoms and kingdoms were different to the communal ones in that they only had an advisory role. The historical parliaments were eventually recognised as such at a later stage, including well-known experiences. Only in England and in a few other countries far from the Carolingian core of Europe (Poland, the countries of Scandinavia, Hungary) were they bicameral. The continental rule was tripartition among the clergy, the nobility and what we would today call the bourgeoisie or burghers. What was particular to England was not the institution but its longevity and steady development. The general estates of France were similar but they never managed to acquire the contractual weight and the representativity of the English parliament because they were continually involved in conflicts with the provincial states. This also reflected the way in which France was formed, by successive acquisitions of regions that were included in the kingdom because of extinction of the local princeps dynasties.[35]

The plurality and the often-conflicting nature of normative sources (the papacy and the emperor, the cities and the lordships, the monastic orders and the Church) generated contrapositions and balancing between different powers and principles. This did not happen in any other part of the world at that time. These politico-institutional innovations were *factual* innovations that had to be reconciled, even when they challenged them, with the universal sources of the normative world. However, they were crucial in the Western experience. The potential of the medieval plural institutional structure deployed its effects on modern polities only when it was coupled with the somewhat contrasting force of the development of positive law. It was the combination of medieval embedded pluralism and differentiated legitimacy principles, on the one hand, and the development of a positive understanding of the normative dimension, on the other, that resulted in Western polyarchic development. The Middle Ages are often described as a 'dark age' but their contribution to the pluralism of Western political institutions is undervalued.

---

[35] See Blockmans, W. P. (1978), 'A typology of representative institutions in late Medieval Europe', *Journal of Medieval History*, 4: 189–215. For the difference between the early French and British assemblies, see Moore, B. (1966), *Social Origins of Democracy and Dictatorship: Lord and Peasant in the Making of the Modern World*, Boston, MA, Beacon Press, pp. 40–4.

4.5.5 The Crisis of Political Universalism

With the crisis of universalism represented by the decline of the two general principles of secular legitimacy (the empire) and religious legitimacy (the Church), accentuated by the new context of religious disunity, the institutional pluralism of the Middle Ages declined. We moved towards the system of early modern states. This was a long process of territorial retrenchment in the exercise of authority, but of concentration of its forms. If universal authorities such as the pope and the emperor became less relevant, the 'state' absorbed the lower-level authorities (communes, feuds and so on). In this new context in the eighteenth century a new legitimation principle emerged: sovereignty by representation.

The religious schism of the sixteenth century had challenged beliefs in a fundamental godly origin of law far more than the eleventh-century schism had done. The religious wars, which often became civil wars, progressively destroyed the idea of a unique content of godly will. The only solution to these fights was victory of one faction or the possibility that a neutral body could be raised above both fields, endowed with new powers and able to impose a new order on the contenders. The political system incarnated in the prince specialised and began to constitute the military, administrative and financial sub-structures. The birth of the modern state was possible to the extent that the new political power could emancipate itself from dependence on the pre-existing normative orders and widen its scope to the point of becoming an independent normative source 'producing' a new legal order.

The slow transformation from traditional representation in bodies with incompressible spheres of autonomy to the contemporary representation of citizens was in principle open to different interpretations, some of which were quite functional to a further concentration of power. New institutions and organisations were necessary to fill the widening gap between the individual citizen and public authority once most intermediary bodies had lost their prerogatives. In many ways, this meant a concentration of political power, in that the public authority was no longer conceived as a series of contracts among the governed and governors but as general norms increasingly emanating from the sovereign. Contractualism became less real and assumed the modern aspect of a philosophical justification of the rulers–ruled relationship.

In the political theory of the time, the power to issue rules soon obtained the meaning of a manifestation of public authority. Legislative activity (writing new norms) assumed growing importance, incorporating what was the *jurisdictio* and the *gubernaculum* of the Middle Ages. While the equilibria of the Middle Ages were equilibria among *different powers*, the early modern states consolidated their monopolistic control of destructive and coercive means over the territory. The monopoly of coercion was concentrated in territories narrower than those of the imperial scope. At the same time, the previous factual powers could only keep their grip and survive by fostering political institution differentiation. In other words, the territorial concentration of destructive power operated by the modern state meant that the previous equilibria among different factual powers (the Church, cities, lords, etc.) could only be preserved in the form of institutional power-sharing.

The theory of the separation of powers and of popular sovereignty slowly gained acceptance in this context. Locke's separation between executive, legislative and federative power never gained theoretical success, but the terminology of Montesquieu (executive, legislative and judiciary) spread. Sovereignty slowly slid down to the people. Once coercive means were concentrated, representation became the only institute through which the claims of the medieval dispersed powers could be preserved and, at the same time, the exercise of public authority could be legitimated. The late eighteenth-century Western revolutions put the seal on this process, which spread to all Western (and later world) states with different timing and modalities.

4.5.6 *The Differentiation of European Legal Systems*

The view of law as necessarily deriving from the state and resting on its monopoly of violence is a relatively recent phenomenon. Up to the seventeenth century and well into the eighteenth century, European jurists were still using a common legal grammar and they were still referring to a '*jus commune*', based on both the common Latin language and the Roman and Canon law heritage. The origins of this common grammar were the rediscovery of the Justinian *Corpus Juris Civilis* as it was taught at the University of Bologna during the eleventh century, when a teacher of rhetoric (Irnerius, 1060–1130) obtained a transcribed version of this sixth-century digest. This had disappeared from Italy and from European legal practice but had remained a prevailing source in the Byzantine empire. Prior to the rediscovery of the digest, some of its general principles had only existed as a form of vulgar law in a few parts of the former western Roman empire. After the rediscovery, the digest became the foundation of legal education in European universities. The main feature of this common legal culture and science was a formal rigour not dependent on a local context but on methodical disciplined reasoning.

With respect to this common heritage, which was neither ethno-culturally nor state-specific,[36] a process of legal territorial differentiation prevailed in the late eighteenth and nineteenth centuries. During this period, the 'territorial state' first and the 'nation-state' later emerged as the imagined a priori element of law and the legal system, accompanied by the necessary nationalisation of legal training. Legal education eventually was an element fostering loyalty to the nation-state. It regulated the opportunity to access knowledge, to be educated within its own frame of reference, to control credentials for practice and, by implication, to limit the territorial mobility of legally trained citizens. Elements of universalism continued to be upheld in some theories (among which Kant's 'Weltburger' and legal order for all humankind are the most noticeable), but the main trend was for the new entity of the state to legitimise its role, scope and reach by nationalising the legal system as much as possible. The sovereignty of states became absolute, as opposed to the idea of being bounded by universal legal principles. In the end, the idea that law can exist independently of the framework of the nation-state lost ground with respect to the idea that law can maintain itself and be realised only within the hierarchical structures of the state.[37]

The validity of norms/rules moved from being based on customs and transcendent orders to being based on decisions. These decisions were made within the political field. What was legally valid was determined by the political institution that produced it, and law could not have

---

[36] Neither the Roman empire nor the Roman Catholic Church had any national, ethnic or folk foundation.

[37] In passing, it is interesting to note that the recent debate about the end of territorial sovereignty is, therefore, a return to the past. It is a step towards legal territorial de-differentiation, with a re-emergence of a supra-national legal grammar that implies that state legislation is subordinate to more universal principles and legal rules.

a content independent of politics. A law produced by politics was no longer constrained by pre-established principles and did not offer any guarantee of conformity to justice ideals. This problem could no longer be solved by linking rules to non-positive norms that transcended the law, but only by guaranteeing the modifiability of law. This 'positivisation' of law was accompanied by an attempt to link law to higher-order principles and, given that godly revelation was now out of the question, these principles were sought in human nature. Natural law referred to the ideal way in which human beings would organise their coexistence in a hypothetical situation of absence of authority. Politics should be constrained by the natural law so identified. However, any reference to natural law as an ideal was in fact without a legal character and was, so to speak and paradoxically, a political argument. As such, it was subject to consensus and critique. As there are many ways to understand justice, it remained to be decided which one of these conceptions must be normative, which was also a political decision.

The same concept of 'political institutions' presupposes this process and incarnates it. The monarchic state claimed for itself a large decision-making capacity with respect to the social body, which was soon labelled with the new term 'sovereignty'. This term, without precedent in the Middle Ages, indicates the independence of the state with respect to external relationships with out-groups, but also the independence of the state as an absolute power with respect to in-groups. The prince could impose the law on the social body without being subject to constraints of any other type. With the strengthening of the modern state, the relationship between politics and law was radically modified. Law had become a production by people and an instrument to pursue goals which were political. The previous hierarchy between norms/rules and politics was inverted, with politics becoming over-ordinate rather than subordinate to them. Political institutions became the engine of normative production and modification. Their being unconstrained by higher universal principles generated concerns about their scope and pervasive nature and, therefore, new concerns about their organisation and design. Everything that we currently call sharing of powers, checks and balances, separation and/or limitation of powers cannot be fully grasped except in connection with the long process of positivisation of normative production.

In the absence of any other type of constraint, attempts to limit violence and coercion by political power have taken surprisingly

similar and limited forms in the few cases where this has been successful: the principle of the primacy of the law and of the equality of all
before the law; the idea of setting boundaries in certain fields of legislation (basic or human rights); the idea of splitting powers by norms of
competence (separation of powers); the idea of imposing procedural
norms and decisions reserved for specific organs; publicity of decisions;
the possibility of appeals (rule of law); the idea of setting rules concerning the distribution of public authority (alternation, elections); and the
idea of preventing limitation of certain freedoms (such as of opinion,
assembly).[38]

Through these mechanisms, political power was either dispersed or
equalised, creating the conditions for balanced political exchanges.
Eventually, the institutional balance resting on *institutional counter-
powers* (the differentiation of top political institutions) was the expression of *associative counter-powers* – that is, the values and the objective
interests of social and professional groups (the merchant community,
the clerical community, scientists, bankers, artisans, etc.) – and of *territorial counter-powers* – that is, competition among different territories
with their government levels. Each set of counter-powers had its own
pitfalls. Excessive institutional counter-powers may degenerate into
divided government, conflicts among qualified actors, competence deadlocks and conservative immobilism. Too strong associative counter-
powers may degenerate into corporatism and the corporatisation of
society, with rights usurped by social entities to the disadvantage of
individual options and opportunities. Too strong territorial counter-
powers could result in localist drives and a closure of territorial communities to innovations that threatened local identities, into competition
among different governmental levels, into exclusive drives for localism.
Hence, in different moments institutional differentiation took the form
of further balancing of the different varieties of counter-powers.

The Middle Ages had produced the early seeds of pluralism and
dispersion of factual powers; the modern state re-concentrated political
power in the hands of monarchs and established the principle of the
monopolisation of destructive means in any given territory. Medieval
pluralism and modern state monism jointly paved the way for differentiation of political institutions.

---

[38] Popitz, H. (1992), *Phaenomene der Macht*, Tübingen, Mohr-Siebeck, p. 65.

The six processes briefly reviewed in this section are crucial in the sense that each initiated factual developments of power-sharing that evolved into institutional forms. We do not observe them in any other parts of the world; not in the Byzantine (395–1453) or Ottoman empires (1299–1922);[39] or in the Empire of the Caliphate (570–1258); or that of Mamluk Egypt (1250–1517); or in the Ming (1368–1644); or in the Qing (1644–1912) Chinese empire; or in the Mongol empire (1206–1368); or in the Russian empire (from Ivan the Terrible (1533) to the Soviet revolution); or in Tokugava Japan (1600–1745).[40] There is no need to discuss here theories of oriental despotisms.[41] I simply note that these empires most often experienced a high concentration of coercive and destructive means but none had previously experienced a pluralisation of economic, symbolic and political forces and an institutionalisation of their relationships like that which slowly took place through the Middle Ages in Europe.

The difficulty in exporting power-sharing institutions to other parts of the world can be attributed to the absence of the aforementioned pluralisation experiences. Although power-sharing institutions are appreciated by political modernisers, many short-lived and rapidly deteriorating democratisation processes witness the huge difficulties in grafting political institution differentiation in unfavourable environments. Monopolisation of destructive and coercive means is a necessary condition for institutional differentiation. However, in many democratising polities the two processes of monopolisation of means of violence and pluralisation of socio-cultural and economic resources are unbalanced. The former is easier to imitate and quicker to establish with modern technologies and easily surpasses the equalisation process of economic and symbolic powers.

---

[39] The Ottoman empire millet system granted considerable autonomy to non-Muslim ethno-religious groups within the empire, but concerned almost exclusively civil and private matters with limited political offspring.

[40] My sources are Eisenstadt, S. (1963), *The Political Systems of Empires: The Rise and Fall of the Historical Bureaucratic Societies*, New York, The Free Press; Finer, *The History of Government*; Burbank, J. and F. Cooper (2011), *Empires in World History: Power and the Politics of Difference*, Princeton, NJ, Princeton University Press. I do not have enough information on the Indian Mughal empire (1526–1712).

[41] These originated in Aristotelian thought and remained alive in the West through the writings of Thomas Aquinas, Marsilio da Padova, Machiavelli, Bodin, Montesquieu, Hegel and up to Wittfogel's works.

5 | Meso-institutions
Political Institutes

In the past, there was enormous variation in the type of institutions with which government was organised. The specific Western experience was briefly recast in Chapter 4, arguing that power-sharing and decentralising institutions resulted from historical inventions in situations of factual relative balance among sets of power-resource holders. In the last two centuries, there has been an increasing process of imitation of the early institutional inventions, starting from Europe and then the USA and progressively expanding to other parts of the world. Today, the government structures of the existing states evidence highly isomorphic configurations. Even the most personalistic, sultanistic and dictatorial forms of government are likely to have a legislative body, executive roles, a court system, a constitution of some sort and a few other façade niceties that appear indispensable even to the most ruthless autocrat. So, the world has become more and more similar in appearance. Differences today concern the effectiveness of the political institutions that share similar names. Such differences regard the extent to which political power and the function of command is centralised or decentralised, shared or concentrated.

5.1 Political 'Institutes'

The four dimensions of the institutional differentiation of government discussed in Chapter 4 (circulation of elites; enlargement/restriction of relevant political actors; scope restraints; and implementation restraints) concretise over time and space in a very large set of norms/rules, so many that is hardly possible to account for them individually. Single rules/norms cannot be the basis for institutional analysis, as there are too many of them and they are disparate. Moreover, single norms/rules are shared by different bodies and organisations, political and non-political. For instance, the majority decisional rule exists in courts, bodies and assemblies of any kind, public and private. Similar rules/norms are present in different regimes. On the other side, broad regime configurations are too comprehensive to be the basis of institutional analysis and they are often only partially institutional (they also add other things).

Therefore, in the layering of institutions that range from single norms/rules up to entire institutional regimes, we need to identify a more limited set of *institutes*, as was suggested in Chapter 3 and Table 3.1. Political institutes are clusters of norms/rules that relate to the same functional problem within the framework of concentration/sharing of political power.[1] If we focus on the meso-level of institutes, we avoid becoming entangled in the myriad single rules/ norms, on the one hand, and in excessively aggregate political organisations (executives, parliaments and the like) or regimes on the other. In Table 5.1 I propose a parsimonious list of core political institutes.

Table 5.1 *Dimensions of power-concentration/sharing and the corresponding institutes*

Power-concentration/sharing dimensions	Institutes
Circulation of political elites	(1) Norms/rules of selection
	(2) Norms/rules of responsibility
Enlargement/reduction of politically relevant actors	(3) Norms/rules of inclusion/exclusion
	(4) Norms/rules of representation
	(5) Norms/rules of decision
Scope restraints	(6) Norms/rules of competence
	(7) Norms/rules of accountability
Implementation restraints	(8) Norms/rules of delegation
	(9) Norms/rules of redress

[1] Ostrom specifies the sets of rules that constitute the development of self-organisational arrangements for the management of the commons; Ostrom, E. (2010), 'Beyond markets and states: polycentric governance and complex economic systems', *American Economic Review*, 100: 1–33, 12. Some of these resemble my 'institutes' but others have nothing to do with them.

These nine institutes as clusters of norms/rules qualify the four dimensions of power-concentration/sharing discussed in Chapter 4. Some institutes are important in more than one dimension of power-sharing, most obviously competence norms/rules. Nevertheless, the institutes of selection and political responsibility mainly pertain to the dimension of the circulation of elites. The institutes of inclusion/exclusion, representation and decision substantiate the enlargement/reduction of relevant political actors. The clusters of norms/rules of competence and accountability concern the level of restraints on the scope of political power. The institutes of delegation and redress refer to implementation restraints or to their absence. The first two dimensions are more important. If the relevant political actors are few and the circulation of political elites is blocked, scope and implementation restraints are likely to be limited. However, these are empirical inductions. From the analytical point of view, the four dimensions and the relative institutes deserve to be treated independently.

In Table 5.2 the same institutes are presented not in terms of their reference to power-sharing but in their vertical layering. Moving from left to right, we go from micro-rules/norms to meso-institutes and to macro-regimes. Climbing the ladder of generality further, we can add a further column that includes institutional principles, such as 'rule of law', 'popular sovereignty', 'tradition', 'divine right', '*fuhrung*', 'constitutionalism' and other similar principles. Institutional principles imply a reference to sets of institutes but they are more abstract, more ideologically charged and more empirically indefectible, in the sense that they are not liable to defect and easily fail. As already mentioned, institutional principles are not discussed in this work.

The schemes of Tables 5.1 and 5.2 are analytical, not developmental. It is not suggested that the accumulation of micro-norms/rules resulted in institutes and then in regimes. It could be the other way round – institutes or regimes could have slowly modified through piecemeal, incremental changes. New general principles have emerged at critical junctures of major change and have slowly been substantiated later, with increasingly detailed new micro-norms/rules and institutes. Popular sovereignty emerged as a new institutional principle by the end of the eighteenth century and its specification and implementation has covered a long period, during which the institutes that composed it have become richer in normative detail. Single rules/norms and institutes

Table 5.2 *Norms/rules, institutes and institutional regimes*

Micro →	Meso	← Macro
Single rules/norms (examples)	Institutes	Regimes as inter-institute relations (examples)
Hereditary	Selection norms/rules	
Co-optation		
Nomination		
Election		
Confidence/censure	Responsibility norms/rules	
Dismissal/resignation		
Right to voice, organise, etc.	Inclusion/ exclusion norms/rules	Absolutism
Right to be consulted		
Citizenship		
Right to be represented	Representation norms/rules	Types of democracies
Right to vote		
Rules of representation		
Fairness of representation		
Hierarchy	Decision norms/rules	Constitutional monarchy
Voting		
Veto		
Negotiation		
Unanimity		
Legislation	Competence norms/rules	Electoral authoritarianism
Execution		
Inquiring		
Judicial		
Who is accountable	Accountability norms/rules	Totalitarianism
To whom		
For what		
Which evidence		
Which consequences		
Family or kinship	Delegation norms/rules	Parliamentarism
Clients		
Military		
Commissary		
Agencies		
Norms and rules to be heard	Redress norms/ rules	Etc.
Habeas corpus		
Precedents versus codes		
Constitutional review		

have appeared several times in different periods and parts of the world and they have decayed or have been rediscovered several times.

No institute alone can characterise more aggregate entities such as institutional regimes, which result from a specific combination of institutes. Absolutism, democracy and parliamentarism are not single rules/ norms and not even single institutes, but rather a combination of institutes. Sometimes, the dominance of a single institute may have negative effects on other institutes to the point of offending them. On the macro-side of Table 5.2, I simply provide exemplary references to more aggregative institutional concepts that result from the combination of institutes and their relative balancing. In the following sections, I discuss each institute separately.

5.2 Selection Norms/Rules

The selection institute is made up of the set of norm/rules concerning the selection of the top rulership positions.[2] Rulership positions often result from self-appointment by military conquering chiefs, rulers emerging victorious from internal strife or personalities acclaimed for their skills, qualifications or charismatic gifts. Selection norms/rules do not refer to these mere factual impositions of specific outcomes but to practices that have been accepted or at least not objected to over time.

Inheritance is already a norm/rule of succession. *Co-optation* by the incumbent ruler has also frequently been the selection norm. More sophisticated selection rules involve casting lots procedures, nomination procedures – in which the ruler is appointed by an authorised body following a decision rule – or election by a more or less extended college.

Classic Athenian democracy (about 400 BCE) believed that selection by election was not democratic enough, except for a few positions that demanded special skills (military commanders were elected). Magistrates, the executive arm of the council and assembly, including what we call the judiciary, were filled by casting lots. All positions had to be open to all citizens by rotation and nobody could serve as a member of the council more than twice. The same principle of selection by sortition or lot was introduced in the Florence Republic after

---

[2] The selection institute does not correspond to the selectorate theory of Bueno de Mesquita, B., A. Smith, R. M. Siverson and J. D. Morrow (2003), *The Logic of Political Survival*, Boston, MA, The MIT Press.

the short-lived reign of terror of Walter of Bienne, who was driven out in 1343. But the sortition was highly manipulated in the pre-selection of candidates. In imperial Rome, no regularised rule of succession existed. Co-optation by the incumbent emperor predominated, with the emperor designating his successor often after testing him in various command positions.

The hereditary principle of selection dominated the lives of the great empires with variations. At different times and in different dynasties, China selected the supreme ruler with a mix of inheritance and co-optation. Note that the true government was made up of a service nobility, rarely an aristocracy of blood. Government was entrusted to some 1,500 people, the pick of the nation's graduates in classical literature, who combined prestige, power and wealth. It is the only example of a meritocratic co-optation of a service aristocracy of literary talent. In the caliphate, the office of the caliph was hereditary but not reserved to direct lineage. The caliph designated a member of his family, usually but not necessarily a son. However, if he had not done this, then a self-appointed clique of court notables made the nomination, which had to be 'recognised' by the most influential governors. This generated continual challenges from groups in the empire, alimented by widespread scepticism about the legitimacy of the caliphal dynasties.

In the Byzantine empire few norms/rules guided selection. Succession was open and the doctrine maintained that whoever effectively held the throne did so by just and divine title, which provoked most damaging civil wars and rivalries over the throne. In the Ottoman empire the problem of succession was so acute that Sultan Mehmed II (1432–81) promulgated the famous 'law of fratricide', according to which the sultan may, for the welfare of the state, lawfully put his brothers to death – not a mere superficial rule if we consider that Murad III had his five brothers strangled and Mehmed III put to death sixteen brothers. Later, this rule was suspended and princes were only confined in the Topkapi palace. In the long run, the hereditary nature of the monarchy was the fortune of the Capetingians in the Frankish kingdom and of the Plantagenets in England, starting with Henry II (1154–89).

In the German territories and the Holy Roman empire, the selection principle was nomination by a few great electors in the case of a vacant seat. Electoral pacts, as they were called, conditioned the choice of the candidate. The imperial praxis foresaw first the tribute to the princes, then popular pronunciation (that is, of the 'bystanders') and finally the solemn feast. This solemn imperial ceremonial was unable to solve the decisive problem of the consolidation of dynastic succession. To give an idea of the complications that could develop during these phases, consider that it took Henry II thirteen years (1026–39) to get over it. Even the definition of the 'electors' was contested.[3] More complex procedures developed with the Swabians and successive dynasties, but the problem was never solved. The empire finally became hereditary only thanks to the de facto power of the Habsburgs, although it remained formally elective until its end in 1806. Even the Florentine Republic (around 1200) practised for a period the principle of nomination by an electoral college. The Podesta was a foreigner selected by the collegial body of the *Comune* who served for only one year. But the experience was short lived. The Roman Church always resorted to the electoral college of cardinals to elect the pope.

Given the extensive literature available, there is no need to linger on the contemporary practice of direct or indirect elective selection by a college that may extend to cover the entire adult citizenry. Elective selection is by now the rule in liberal polyarchies and it is used more and more as the legitimising device even in non-democratic regimes. Elective selection necessarily implies other rules/norms concerning the term limits of mandates (no limit, only one or two terms, multiple terms not in succession, etc.) and possible executive tenure violations.[4] Complex selection rules/norms preside over the appointment (and dismissal) by an electoral college (the parliament) of prime ministers in parliamentary systems.

The top ruling positions can be collegial, with more than one position filled at the same time. Weber discusses twelve types of historical collegiality and interprets them as institutional rules meant to inhibit and limit authority. In his view, collegiality is at odds with the principle of rational bureaucratic organisation and it obstructs promptness of decisions, unity of leadership and the clear (political) responsibility of individuals.[5] Nevertheless, collegiality of leadership selection survives.

[3] In the middle of the thirteenth century, there were seven electors (with the disagreement of Bavaria, which was excluded from the list): the archbishops of Köhl, Magonza and Trier and four laypeople: the Palatine earl of the Rhine, the margrave of Brandebourg, the duke of Sassy and the king of Bohemia.

[4] See Ginsburg, T., Z. Elkins and J. Melton (2012), 'Do executive term limits cause constitutional crises?', in Ginsburg, T. (ed.), *Comparative Constitutional Design*, Cambridge, Cambridge University Press, pp. 350–79.

[5] Weber, *Economy and Society*, vol. 1, pp. 271–82.

Examples include the Venetian Council of Elders, Roman magistrates, the eight *Priori* and the *Gonfaloniere della Giustizia* of the Florence Republican Constitution, the Politburo of the Communist Party of the Soviet Union (although this was a temporary situation while waiting for the predominance of a single leader),[6] the Yugoslav Federal Executive Council under Tito, the Uruguay collegial leadership in the period 1951–66, and the long-lived Swiss Federal Council.[7]

Extending the examples too much dilutes the concept of collegial selection, mixing it with collegiality in decision.[8] Decisional collegiality is a style of leadership in which decisions are arrived at in common without a voting mechanism and without individual dominance.[9] To avoid confusion, we should keep a clear distinction between selection collegiality (the concomitant selection of more than one executive position) and decision collegiality (a style of cooperation and negotiation in decision-making).

5.3 Responsibility Norms/Rules

The institute of political responsibility includes all those norms/rules that affect the tenure terms of political authority roles when they are at stake. These norms/rules are those with which one body or role retains the power to dismiss and revoke the top ruler, body or person. The term 'political' next to 'responsibility' is essential. It points to the fact that such competence is normatively, institutionally and legally unconstrained and

---

[6] Shapiro, L. (1969), 'Collective leadership as lack of leadership', *Survey*, Winter/Spring, pp. 193–200. Gilison argues, on the contrary, that collective leadership was strengthening in the post-Stalin period. Gilison, J. (1967), 'New factors of stability in Soviet collective leadership', *World Politics*, 19: 563–58.

[7] On the Swiss and Uruguayan experiences, see Altman, D. (2008), 'Collegiate executives and direct democracy in Switzerland and Uruguay: similar institutions, opposite political goals, distinct results', *Swiss Political Science Review*, 14: 483–520.

[8] See Baylis, H. T. (1980), 'Collegial leadership in advanced industrial societies: the relevance of the Swiss experience', *Polity*, 13: 33–56, 34–9. The article stretches the concept and the argument too much, making 'collegiality' pop up everywhere, in the Netherlands, Germany, Norway, Japan and even Great Britain.

[9] Collegiality can be plural if the selected executive members represent salient socio-cultural or political realities, or homogeneous if the background and interests are similar and group attachments are relatively unimportant. Plural collegiality normally operates under the collective bargaining principle, while homogeneous collegiality is based on the problem-solving principle. For the distinction between problem-solving and collective bargaining, see March, J. G. and H. A. Simon (1959), *Organizations*, New York, Wiley, pp. 129–32.

unappealable. In other words, it can be exercised with no need for justification and without any evidence or accountability basis. Only strictly political conditions and consequences may constrain it. Any time a sovereign revokes his ministers, a president changes his administration, a prime minister reshuffles her cabinet or an assembly censures and denies confidence to a prime minister, it does so because of a mere trust and confidence relationship. In all these cases, the norms/rules invoked refer to the political responsibility of one body/role towards another body/role.[10]

Even if some reasons are advanced to argue the end of the confidence relationship, they are not meant to pass any test and there is in fact no third party or referee that can judge the validity of the decision. The reasons for the change could be the most different: incompetence, moral indignity, scandals, personal antipathy, attempts to gain a new public image, the need to find a scapegoat for some negative event, the need to rebalance the gender or partisan composition, and so on. The motivations, the judgements and their valid application to individual cases (are they really responsible?) are unimportant. The sanction may be applied even in the absence of any accurate reporting and oversight or any accountability mechanism. Perceptions, sometimes vague ones, may be the basis for a total disallowance of leaders. The discretionary nature of the act of the superior role is evident when one considers that major breakings of the rules or clear evidence of incompetence which can be ascertained by neutral observers or political adversaries can easily be ignored or attributed limited importance. On the contrary, respect for legality, competence, honesty and effectiveness cannot be invoked by the responsible role against the decision of the superior one. Only questions of political opportunity in terms of costs and advantages affect the decision and its ex-post evaluation.

Strictly speaking, even the final act of any representation linkage, the election of candidates and their confirmation or revocation belong to this institutional genus. When voters at fixed times are asked to confirm and revoke a representative, the judgement on which the eventual result rests is unjudiciable, unchallengeable and substantively undefinable. It is a decline in trust, of which practitioners, observers and experts may elaborate more or less credible interpretations.

---

[10] Therefore, the impeachment rules concerning presidents are not instances of the institute of political responsibility. They are shaped as a trial in front of a jury and require evidence of specific guilt.

Political responsibility rules/norms are therefore extremely simple rules/ norms but crucial to the life of any executive and fundamental for the circulation of political elites. The absence of the responsibility institute for the top political roles sets the demarcation line between polyarchic and monocratic forms of government. Political responsibility towards the nomination procedure is a powerful mechanism affecting the politician's life but a poor mechanism for providing accountability. We should not confuse, therefore, accountability mechanisms with political responsibility mechanisms (see Section 5.8).[11] Contemporary liberal polyarchies are profoundly dependent on this blind mechanism of political responsibility.[12]

5.4 Inclusion/Exclusion Norms/Rules

Rules and norms of inclusion/exclusion determine which individuals and which categories of individuals can take part in the political process and thereby influence its outcomes. More precisely, these rules/norms define the extent to which new claimants, individuals and groups can express grievances and complaints and seek redress without suffering unbearable costs. People who shape political institutions define their membership and their boundaries in more inclusive or exclusive ways. Historically, political institutions were better at exclusion than inclusion, and inclusion was often hard fought for.[13] One can gain inclusion through one's own means and actions, usually collectively, but one is always excluded by somebody and from something, which is the pre-existing departure point

---

[11] The use of the two terms interchangeably is diffuse. See Bingham Powell, G. (1989), 'Constitutional design and citizen electoral control', *Journal of Theoretical Politics*, 1: 107–30; and Strøm, K. (2000), 'Delegation and accountability in parliamentary democracies', *European Journal of Political Research*, 37: 261–89.

[12] On strictly individual ministerial accountability, see the descriptive works by Marshall, G. (ed.) (1989), *Ministerial Responsibility*, Oxford, Oxford University Press; and Woodhouse, D. (1994), *Ministers and Parliament: Accountability in Theory and Practice*, Oxford, Clarendon Press, covering British and New Zealand practices. Similar works exist in all languages and national experiences but comparative appreciations are rare. See Strøm, K., W. C. Müller and T. Bergman (eds.) (2006), *Delegation and Accountability in Parliamentary Democracies*, Oxford, Oxford University Press.

[13] Holden, M. (2006), 'Exclusion, inclusion and political institutions', in Rhodes, Binder and Rockman (eds.), *The Oxford Handbook of Political Institutions*, pp. 163–90.

of reference. Gender, race, residence, ethnicity, social status, religion, education, income and age have been and still are institutionalised criteria for exclusion from the political process.[14]

However, inclusion/exclusion reflects not only formal individual or collective rights but also factual obstacles that rules/norms may set to prevent individuals and groups from being incorporated in the functioning and decision-making of the polity. The history of political participation is constellated by direct repression and harassment. Territorial dominant groups have limited the freedoms to talk, write, associate, organise and protest, and have effectively used state/territorial institutions and their administrative and policing machines against new claimants.[15] Recent literature has emphasised the importance of state traditions and their role in the process of repression and harassment, linking them to types of alliances among key social groups, to the sources of revolutions and their outcomes, to the process of social group formation and to collective action.[16] The interest focusses on the territory/state as a set of resources to which dominant groups could resort in their attempts to obstruct emerging claims and demands. The calculation of the cost of internal repression or tolerance made by dominant groups depends primarily on the availability of the means of repression; that is, on the availability of a bureaucratic tradition and machinery to oppose new movements. It depends only secondarily on the incompatibility of interests between dominant groups and new claimants. Therefore, the nature of the territory/state (external challenges, boundary consolidation, centralisation, the development of policing and administrative apparatuses and the army, etc.) influences the costs of tolerance and repression of new claimants' voices. Levels of

[14] In ancient polities, the entire population was often made up of subjects. In the often-idealised Greek polis and Roman Republic the political rights associated with citizenship did not extend to women, slaves and aliens, which on average meant three-fifths of the adult population.

[15] On the obstacles to inclusion, see the institutional thresholds discussed in Rokkan, S. (1970), 'Nation building, cleavage formation and the structuring of mass politics', in *Citizens, Elections, Parties: Approaches to the Comparative Study of the Process of Development*, Oslo, Universitetsforlaget, pp. 79–82.

[16] Moore, *Social origins of democracy*; Skocpol, T. (1979), *States and Social Revolutions: A Comparative Analysis of France, Russia and China*, Cambridge, Cambridge University Press; Katnelson, I. and A. R. Zolberg (eds.) (1986), *Working Class Formation in Western Europe and the United State*, Princeton, NJ, Princeton University Press; Birnbaum, P. (1988), *State and Collective Action: The European Experience*, Cambridge, Cambridge University Press.

administrative and legal harassment are, therefore, linked to *stateness*.[17] Where stateness is weak, a repressive strategy is not available or is likely to be very costly; where it is strong, such a strategy is available, even if other variables may impinge on the willingness of the established elite to resort to it.[18]

Beyond forms of direct harassment, repression, censorship and so on, exclusion may be determined by the unfairness of election rules that exclude or limit the capacity to be represented in bodies to which one is in principle admitted. Elective elites have a higher propensity than monarchs, bureaucrats, lords and the military to see the conflicts and requests coming from new claimants as political opportunities rather than political threats. When electoral mobilisation and electioneering occur, they become elements in the transformation of social influence into politico-administrative influence. However, dis-representative devices can prevent and delay the fair representation of political movements in elective assemblies for a long time. A restricted franchise is the most obvious example, but even when suffrage was extended, diverting mechanisms were often devised or retained to ensure that the suffrage had a limited impact on the political process by increasing the cost to newcomers of votes and/or seats.

These mechanisms persisted throughout the nineteenth century, distorting the free and direct expression of the voter's choice. Non-secrecy through oral voting and the showing of hands greatly facilitated pressure and manipulation by government officials and the local elite alike, particularly in non-urban settings. Indirect voting meant that the ballot was cast not for legislative candidates but for grand electors, introducing a filter against 'dangerous' candidates and an additional barrier for new movements and for parties that could not rely on an established and visible social elite. Plural voting and curia/estate voting hindered the fair transformation of electoral strength into parliamentary strength. The curia and estate systems assigned a disproportionate number of seats to the upper estates, generally representing aristocratic and wealthy families

---

[17] The level of stateness should be assessed independently of the nature of the institutional and political regime. See Nettl, P. J. (1968), 'The state as a conceptual variable', *World Politics*, 20: 560–92.

[18] Mann, M. (1993), *The Sources of Social Power*, vol. 2: *The Rise of Classes and Nation-States, 1760–1914*, Cambridge, Cambridge University Press, pp. 358–95 provides several tables of data about the 'size' of the state and discusses this dimension to some extent.

and the clergy, while formally giving the right to vote to everybody. The practice of plural voting – that is, the attribution of extra votes to wealthy and/or well-educated citizens or to representatives of special institutions (churches, universities, etc.) – had the direct effect of bureaucratically separating citizens into voting categories based on class criteria.[19]

Exclusion from political institutions also means the incapacity of peoples, groups and organisations outside the inner circles of the territorial institution to exert a degree of control over the actions and decisions of the top rulers. Exclusion in this case refers to the extent to which top ruling roles are shielded from pressure. The process that extends and finally grants control by elective representatives over the formation, personnel, duration and legislative activities of executives is historically long and contested.[20] Executive roles may be appointed and dismissed by forces outside the control of elective assemblies. Cabinets might be dependent on the support of elected assemblies for their continued existence, but their ministerial personnel might be freely chosen by other bodies such as the monarchy or a non-elected first chamber. Cabinets depending on the support of a chamber to be installed may still be forced to resign by forces other than those in such a chamber. Cabinets may continue to face considerable legislative conflicts with other non-representative bodies, such as a first chamber or dynastic bureaucracy milieus. All these mechanisms prevent the political responsibility of the executive (see Section 5.3) in the face of elected bodies. In short, exclusionary norms/rules affect formal individual rights, collective organised action, representation fairness and the eventual capacity of these elements to affect the executive branch of government and its commands.

The comparative politics literature generally agrees on the following propositions concerning the pervasiveness and persistence of exclusionary norms/rules of this type:

(1) If a legal order and a consolidated boundary predate the formation of a strong central bureaucracy, exclusionary and repressive

---

[19] For a detailed discussion of all these devices with reference to the European experience, see Bartolini, S. (2000), *The Electoral Mobilisation of the European Left: The Class Cleavage 1880–1980*, Cambridge, Cambridge University Press, pp. 348–58.

[20] For an account of early institutional developments in Europe, see Anderson, E. N. and P. R. Anderson (1967), *Political Institutions and Social Change in Continental Europe in the Nineteenth Century*, Berkeley, University of California Press.

norms/rules remain independent of the requests and direct control of the executive;

(2) If the consolidation of the state's basic institutions is uncontested or only relatively so, pressure for exclusionary norms/rules through a centralised administration of law and order will be weaker and the legal tradition is less likely to be state-centred;

(3) If the creation and consolidation of state structures does not involve processes of large-scale political mobilisation or violent popular resistance, exclusionary apparatuses are likely to be less politicised and their repressive means to be more responsible to local judicial bodies;

(4) If central bureaucracy never consolidates or if it consolidates after representative institutions have been introduced, the state apparatuses do not constitute an available resource for the exclusionary repression of newcomers.[21]

5.5 Representation Norms/Rules

Norms/rules of representation concern the modalities with which individual, collective, corporate or institutional actors allowed to have a say in the political process connect to the wider population. As was discussed in Chapter 4, representation was unknown in the Greek/Roman age and was invented in the Middle Ages. Institutes of representation emerged from contact between the empire and the barbarian population who had installed themselves in its western territories. These populations were organised in groups and sub-groups with a variety of habits, customs and rights. The slow fusion of the different Germanic and Latin characteristics and institutions fostered the tendency of these internally homogeneous groups to organise themselves as political bodies with different degrees of autonomy and with at least partial sovereignty. These groups slowly developed the figure of

---

[21] These propositions are widely discussed in the literature on state formation and political development. See Dahl, R. A. (1971), *Poliarchy, Participation and Opposition*, New Haven, CT, Yale University Press; the articles in Tilly, C. (ed.) (1975), *The Formation of National States in Western Europe*, Princeton, NJ, Princeton University Press; and Daalder, H. (1995), 'Paths towards state formation in Europe: democratization, bureaucratization and politicization', in Chehabi, H. E. and A. Stephan (eds.), *Politics, Society, and Democracy: Comparative Studies*, Boulder, CO, Westview Press, pp. 113–30.

a 'mandatary', an individual or collective body that could act in their stead whenever and on those matters on which the group could not decide by itself. Slowly these mandataries became organised in various forms as feuds, communes, territories, lordships and so on, following the lines of pluralisation of medieval society. Later on, the estates (*stand, ceti*) of lordships, the nobility, the clergy and other groups acquired rights to be 'represented' as a body in the variety of councils, diets, curiae, assemblies and parliaments that constituted the institutes of consensus of the time, with the different names *parliaments* (England, Ireland, Scotland, Sicily, the papal state, the Kingdom of Naples), *cortes* (in the Iberian peninsula), *estates* or *general estates* (in France and the Low Countries), *rigsdag* (in Denmark and Norway), *riksdag* (in Sweden), *sejm* (in Poland) and *Landtage* (in Germany). They varied considerably in their mandate limits, powers and structure but they all were regular, not ad hoc, assemblies. They all embodied a radically new principle, namely that a part in these bodies was 'standing for' a totality outside the body.[22]

Estates, boroughs, cities and corporations linked to their respective 'representatives' via a true delegation of a private nature. Representatives were bound to represent the interests, desires and requests of their groups to the ruler, king or emperor. The representative and the represented were linked by the obligation of the mandatary towards the mandator, the precise instructions of the latter to the former (the *cahiers de doléance*), the need of the mandatary to ask his mandators for instructions when confronted with unforeseen circumstances (the '*mandati ad audiendum et referendum*'), the revocability of the conferred mandate, and its onerousness. All these elements certify the privatistic derivation of this representation.[23]

In the modern age and with the consolidation of state institutions, the institute of political representation has evolved in the context of the bounds of a common tradition, language, ethnic group and territory, and later always more in the context of nationality. It has articulated itself in relation to large groups of citizens in front of a sovereign who has acquired absolutist powers, while strengthening national cohesion,

---

[22] Lord, R. H. (1930), 'The parliaments of the Middle Ages and the Early Modern period', *Catholic Historical Review*, 16: 125–8.

[23] On this fundamental point, see Nocilla, D. and L. Ciaurro (1987), 'Rappresentanza politica', in *Enciclopedia del diritto*, vol. 38, Milan, Giuffrè, pp. 543–609.

enlarging the state functions and concentrating public powers. This happened first and more thoroughly in England – where from the beginning the crown was a rather powerful territorial institution (since the Norman king William I conquered England in 1066) – and only later on the continent, where the monarchical element remained weaker for a long time because of the feudal fractioning of the post-Carolingian empire, and where the key enemy was often not the local monarch but a different nearby powerful territorial group. On the continent, social groups remained embedded in the monarchical element for longer and only at a later stage did their coalitions against absolutist power initiate the transformation of absolute monarchy into constitutional and representative monarchy.

The essential point here is that in the modern age representation lost its early character derived from private law and acquired a publicist nature. This was witnessed by a change in the obligation of the representative to the mandator, the absence of any precise instruction by the latter to the former, the autonomy of the former in unforeseen circumstances, the repudiation of any imperative mandate, and eventually in the principle, formalised in the French Constitution of 1791, that 'the representatives nominated in the districts do not represent a particular district, but the entire nation'.

The medieval representative bodies were intermediary bodies between the mandators and the sovereign; they represented somebody in front of somebody else. When the role and power of the assemblies increased, they ceased to represent the citizens to the sovereign who governed them; they began to govern themselves. A representative body inserted in the state needed the autonomy to work as one of its main governing bodies, if not the main one. Representative assemblies could not acquire the new governing functions without affecting the previous representative functions.

There is a paradoxical element in this change because the representative bodies ended up representing somebody (groups, the people or the nation) in front of themselves. The third actor towards which the representatives should represent the people disappeared.[24] The thorny problems and the inconsistencies of the elusive concept of political representation in contemporary liberal democracies lie in this transformation. The theory of representation as mandate refers to the

---

[24] Sartori, G. (1963), *Democrazia e definizioni*, Bologna, Il Mulino, pp. 352–75.

medieval understanding and it is not sustainable outside the precincts of private law. In the contemporary notion of representation, representatives are not agents or delegates who follow instructions, and the idea of the mandate and of the delegation cannot be entertained. In politics, agents (the members of representative assemblies) represent the principal in front of themselves, and I find it confusing and misleading to use the term 'delegation' or the jargon of principal–agent theories to identify the contemporary representative link (see Section 5.9).

As is amply discussed in the literature, we cannot associate the notion of representation with that of representativeness in the sense of social similarity or resemblance. The groups whose existential characteristics deserve to be represented cannot be defined a priori and are subject to continual redefinition. It is excluded that contemporary representation can be imbibed with social similarity.[25] Similarly, if representation concerns 'interests' – as is often assumed – we need to think that such interests can be defined by the representative. In the case of interests understood as the subjective will of the represented, the problem is how so many wills can be aggregated: 'The more numerous the people that one wants to represent, and the more extended the ambit in which one tries to represent them, the less the word represented maintains a meaning amenable to the effective will of real people different from the will of those same people designed to represent them'.[26] Pitkin notes that:

A political representative ... has a constituency rather than a single principal; and that raises problems about whether such an unorganised group can even have an interest for him to pursue, let alone a will to which he could be responsive, or an opinion before which he could attempt to justify what he has done ... while it may be difficult to determine the interest or wishes of a single individual, it is infinitely more difficult to do so for a constituency of thousands. On many issues a constituency may not have any interest, or its members may have several conflicting interests.[27]

---

[25] Representation as social resemblance persists in the case of gender or ethnic representation understood as 'balance' or reserved seats.

[26] Leoni, B. (1961), *Freedom and the Law*, Indianapolis, IN, Liberty Fund. Italian version: (1994), *La libertà e la legge*, Macerata, Liberilibri di AMA, p. 152 (my translation).

[27] Pitkin, H. (1967), *The Concept of Representation*, Berkeley, The University of California Press, pp. 215 and 219–20.

In the end, it is impossible to decide what the representatives should represent: social groups, interests, values, ideas or territory, and so on.[28] Moreover, there are no standards for assessing how well a representative behaves and there are serious doubts that this performance is linked to a sanction or to success in being reconfirmed in office. There is nothing that links representation to so-called accountability (see Section 5.8) but an eventual final failure to be reconfirmed. However, the deterrence of failed confirmation can hardly be defined as the constituency's punishment for failing to act in accordance with its wishes. Its wishes (like interests, etc.) are unknown before and after and they cannot be deliberately expressed in the act of voting (any word referring to them in a ballot makes it invalid).

Moreover, representation cannot be delegation or a mandate in principal/agent terms whenever those who are elected actually owe their election more to their parties than to the voters; when parties are organised in ways which are not themselves democratic in selecting their candidates; the more parties become more generalist, catch-all, de-ideologised and with vague and undifferentiated platforms; and if parties collude or large numbers of voters fluctuate greatly on numerous changing issues.[29]

A person can be represented, 'made present again', by another person only in terms of rather general ideas. But even in this case one can only represent if one feels the expectations of those one represents, and feels them as normatively binding expectations. The normative precept has a moral character for which the sanction of missed reconfirmation is a poor and easily circumvented incitement. In short, political representation cannot be precisely defined but only in terms of the fact that representatives are periodically subject to the unchallengeable judgement of the voters, whose judgemental bases are not defined or prescribed institutionally. In my view, this conclusion is independent of whether representatives perceive themselves as trustees or delegates, the distinction being somewhat immaterial.[30]

---

[28] This is the reason why no form of 'corporative' representation ever worked and gained legitimacy.

[29] See Casey, G. (2009), 'The indefensibility of political representation', a talk given at the Austrian Scholars Conference on 13 March 2009.

[30] On the delegate and trustee understanding of representation, see Pitkin, *The Concept of Representation*, pp. 191–2.

For these reasons, contemporary political theorists focus on the formal procedures that define representation; that is, the procedures through which a representative obtains his standing, status, position or office. One can merely assess whether a representative legitimately holds her position. Representation norms/rules, therefore, do not define the basis or the standards for assessing the quality of representation. They define nothing other than its fairness and correctness in procedural terms. The focus switches, therefore, to the institutional obstacles set up to impede the free and fair selection of representatives (some of which were discussed in Section 5.4).

5.6 Decision Norms/Rules

Decision norms/rules constitute a vast political institute which includes two dimensions that are difficult to separate: (1) how many decide and (2) what rules aggregate the preferences of those who decide.

For a membership or territorial group, political decisions can be *collective* or *collectivised*. Collective decisions are taken by the same group to which they apply. They generate few legitimacy problems but, depending on the decision rule that applies, relevant problems of negative externalities emerge for groups different to those who prevail. In general, however, collective decisions need to be 'instituted' by other bodies and this usually reduces their potential negative externalities. Collectivised decisions are taken by a smaller group sample of the entire group. They are more or less easy to achieve depending on the number of deciders involved. By reducing the number of deciders, collectivised decisions reduce problems of coordination among them. However, they potentially create higher external costs for those not participating in the decision. Therefore, the problem with collectivised decisions is the trade-off between the internal and external costs of decisions.[31] If only one person decides, internal decision costs are minimal, but external costs may be preposterous. If many decide, decision costs grow exponentially to unbearable levels, with the potential external costs of decisions declining in parallel. The predicament of collectivised

---

[31] Buchanan, J. M. and G. Tullock (1962), *The Calculus of Consent: Logical Foundations of Constitutional Democracy*, Ann Arbor, The University of Michigan Press, pp. 63–84; Sartori, G. (1987), *The Theory of Democracy Revisited, Part One: The Contemporary Debate*, Chatham, Chatham House Publishers, pp. 214–23.

decisions is how far to reduce the number of deciders in view of reducing the transaction decision costs implied by the aggregation of their preferences, on the one hand, and making sure that the reduction of decision costs does not come at the price of growing external costs on the other.

In politics, most decisions are collectivised and the realm of true collective decisions is procedurally and substantially restricted. Therefore, the specific decision norms/rules applied are crucial for the trade-off between internal and external costs and for the legitimacy implications of potential redistribution and welfare outcomes.

5.6.1 Hierarchy

Hierarchy is a decision rule in which the ego can define the alter's choices. The legitimacy of hierarchy is based on tradition, charisma, formal legality or simply profound factual asymmetries in the control of crucial resources. Hierarchy is a mechanism of differentiation and integration. It differentiates because in a system of roles it recognises the role of 'head' or 'chief' and the role of subordinate; it integrates because the hierarchy constitutes the mechanism though which the head coordinates the activity of subordinates. Hierarchical decision rules and conflict resolution can be regarded as more efficient than other decision rules because they enormously reduce internal decisional costs. Hierarchical decisions can overcome the Pareto optimality principle and impose solutions that imply losses for B that can be compensated for by the gains of A. However, hierarchy can also impose welfare-inefficient solutions in which the advantages of A are inferior to the losses imposed on B. Finally, hierarchical decisions may also be exploitative in the sense that the hierarchy is also able to impose losses on both A and B only to its own advantage.[32]

Therefore, for hierarchy to be welfare-beneficial, the assumption must exist that hierarchical authority will aim at some sort of collective welfare or distributive justice and not at its own interests. This also implies that the hierarchy will have all the relevant information to operate welfare-maximising or distributive-justice decisions. Both assumptions are very problematic. For these reasons, absolute

[32] Scharpf, F. (1997), *Games Real Actors Play: Actor-Centered Institutionalism in Policy Research*, New York, Westview Press, pp. 171–83.

hierarchy is rarely found. Even military and bureaucratic organisations practise it with some prudence. However, there are historical cases that fit the type: the prototype is the absolute and direct rule of the Assyrian emperor, much before Frederick the Great of Prussia, Philip II of Spain, Louis XIV of France and Joseph II of Austria aspired to run their states in person and managed to do so.

5.6.2 Voting

Voting is an old principle of classic republican institutions that was rediscovered and readapted by medieval monks.[33] It is a decision rule in which the composition of preferences is finally ascertained by some rule of counting that sets the threshold for the effective decision. This counting rule may require unanimity, a qualified majority, an absolute majority or a relative majority. When the term 'majority' is used in connection with decisions, a reference to precise counting criteria is inherent. However, some understandings of the term 'majority' refer to a reality that exists beyond any problem of procedure and counting, such as 'popular majority' or 'silent majority'. In these cases, the majority principle includes more things than I want to discuss here under the label of the majority rule as a voting device.[34]

The more the counting rule departs from unanimity, the more internal decisional costs decrease and external decisional costs rise. Outcomes under majority rules have redistributive capacity and may solve distributive conflicts more efficiently than under unanimity or negotiated agreements. However, in the presence of cohesive majorities, voting turns out to be a game between two actors, one of which has

---

[33] On the historical origins of the majority principle, see the appendix in Favre, *La décision de majorité* and Ruffini, A. (1976 (1927)), *Il principio maggioritario: profilo storico*, Milan, Adelphi.

[34] The term 'principle' appears in French (*principe de majorité*), German (*Majoritatsprinzip*) and Italian (*principio di maggioranza*) works. See Gierke, O. von (2004 (1913)), 'Uber die Geschichte des Majoritatsprinzips', in Vinogradoff, P. (ed.), *Essays in Legal History*, Oxford, Oxford University Press, pp. 312–35; and Ruffini, *Il principio maggioritario: profilo storico*. The term 'rule' appears frequently in English-language texts. The expression 'majority decision' appears almost exclusively in the American literature on the theory of decision: May, K. (1952), 'A set of independent necessary and sufficient conditions for simple majority decisions', *Econometrica*, October, pp. 680–4; and Sen, A. (1964), 'Preferences, votes and the transitivity of majority decisions', *Review of Economic Studies*, 31: 163–5.

dictatorial powers. If the majority is assumed to be self-interested, it may pursue policies that inflict damages on the minority that are greater than the advantage for the majority and which are therefore welfare losses (or unfair in distributive terms). For these reasons, voting rules generate three types of problems crucial for their legitimacy: problems of authenticity (under which conditions does the decision express the authentic will of the group?), of eligibility (who has the right to participate in majority decisions?) and of effectiveness (in which fields and under which conditions are majority decisions effective?).[35]

5.6.2.1 Authenticity

A group may produce a majority decision that does not reproduce the authentic will of the group majority (1) because of paradoxes of voting that generate cyclical instability and outcomes that depend on the order of the votes among alternatives; (2) because the procedures that institute the majority decision constrain freedom of choice to the point that they only allow the registration of decisions taken outside it; and (3) because the group that resorts to majority decisions is preliminarily constituted in such a way as to predefine the decision it will take. An 'authentic' majority decision is, therefore, a decision taking place in the absence of the aforementioned limitations.

The instability and cyclical nature of voting outcomes deriving from the Condorcet paradox under assumptions about the motivations of the actors has obsessed the rational choice literature on voting. However, the paradox of voting – which I do not discuss here in substance – materialises when the voting is done in isolation and it is not seen within the context of other political institutes. In fact, other rules and norms are explicitly devised to avoid the cyclical majority problem and the irrationality of outcomes. Rules/norms may exist that delegitimise voting and move the issue to a hierarchical decision. Other powers may intervene to substitute voters unable to produce stable outcomes, as when assemblies are dissolved. Conference committees in bicameral legislatures and agenda setting have the power to decide take-it-or-leave-it solutions. Two-party or two-coalition legislatures and high-party and coalition discipline do not face these problems

---

[35] Bartolini, S. (1988), 'Principio di maggioranza, regola di maggioranza e decisione di maggioranza', introduction to Favre, P., *La Decisione di Maggioranza*, Milan, Giuffré, pp. 2–27; and Sartori, G. (1974), 'Tecniche decisionali e sistema dei comitati', *Rivista Italiana di Scienza Politica*, 4: 5–42.

and electoral rules may foster this concentration of actors. There is abundant political science and constitutional law evidence to solve the problem generated by abstract assumptions.

Critiques of the authenticity of majority decisions include elitist theories, for which majority voting is only a legitimising principle to the extent that the majority is dispossessed by the elite in the execution acts of the decisions. In the tradition of Marxist thinking, the majority decision enjoys more consideration, but even in this case its authenticity is challenged by the conditions of its implementation in a class society. The majority itself is mystified by factors extrinsic to the decisional process. The authenticity of majority decisions is also questioned when confronted with ex-ante or ex-post institutionalised exchanges and negotiations. In the contraposition between vote decisional channels and corporative-bureaucratic channels of exchange and resource bargaining, an expansion of the latter deprives the former of relevance and of binding nature. The problem of the authenticity of majority decisions presupposes the study of its process of institution, during which the decisional alternatives can be drastically reduced, altered and reshaped by forces not reducible to the majority decision that will follow.

5.6.2.2 Eligibility

Specific institutional bodies and committees and prevalent rules/norms of inclusion/exclusion usually solve the issue of who has a right to participate in majority decision-making. Nevertheless, eligibility problems always loom behind any solution. Representative democracy has solved the issue of eligibility through generalised voting rights. However, the resort to the majority decision as a legitimate form of determination enlarges to ever-wider ambits: from school councils to the decision to strike, from local choices concerning services and productive activities to referenda and to party primaries for leaders and candidates. This exacerbates traditional eligibility problems. The question of who has a right to participate in majority decisions concerning, for instance, the location of an energy plant, of an army barracks or closure to traffic of a city centre is practically impossible to decide through voting to the extent that who is eligible to decide, in most cases, determines the decision that is made.

In the central politico-decisional process, rules that define the admissibility of majority decisions have been progressively defined and the 'decision against the majority' exists. The potential dictatorial powers of majorities can only be limited by other institutional rules/norms.

However, in new and often unforeseen ambits of application, this is less the case. Political citizenship is challenged by tendencies that do not dismiss primary political rights but produce what we may call local and functional 'secondary political citizenship' conflicting with them.

5.6.2.3 Effectiveness

Although voting may be presented as a short-cut technique for decision-making, its effectiveness rests on several non-technical elements. Voting cannot avoid the legitimacy predicament of politics: why should people that have not participated in the voting decision or those who have participated in the decision and seen their preference defeated respect the decision reached? The expectation that decisions will be abided by requires belief in the fairness of the rules for arriving at decisions but also in the restricted range of these decisions. Majority voting in a collectivity requires a minimum level of collective identity that defines the members of the group for which the voting results are valid and binding. Voting can hardly be considered an effective decision rule whenever the membership predicament is not solved as an initial condition.

Collective identities exist psychologically at the level of primary groups, kinship groups, clans, tribes, the village community and so on. Collective identities beyond primary ones can depend on nationalism, religious proselytising or cultural stigmata. Supranational or humankind-wide identities would be necessary for the effective application of majority voting for world collective goods such as antipollution measures. In short, without some element of bounding, the resort to voting is unlikely to be legitimated and effective, which implies that majority voting cannot be a self-legitimising technique. However, while a level of collective identity seems to be required for effective majority decisions, too much identity makes them unviable. If identities become too strong and encapsulated, majority rules cannot be applied across them. The divisions between segmented communities may make majority decisions non-viable.[36]

---

[36] See Lijphart, A. (1968), *The Politics of Accommodation: Pluralism and Democracy in the Netherlands*, Berkeley, University of California Press; Daalder, H. (1971), 'On building consociational nations: the case of the Netherlands and Switzerland', *International Social Science Journal*, 23: 355–70; Daalder, H. (1984), 'On the origins of the consociational model', *Acta Politica*, 19: 97–116; Nordlinger, A. (1972), *Conflict Regulation in Divided Societies*, Cambridge, MA, Harvard University Press.

In conclusion, conditions need to be met to make voting effective. (1) The 'scope' of majority decisions must be substantively limited. Certain decisions need to be protected from majority voting in the sense of being excluded from it.[37] (2) There must be an expectation that at a different time on a different issue the majority may be different and that activities orientated to the modification of the existing majority have a chance of being successful. (3) The issues involved should not concern the fundamental state-territorial institution. It is hard to submit to majority decisions issues concerning the dismembering of an existing territorial state. In discussion of the confining conditions for its effectiveness, majority voting loses the status of being an inspiring principle of democracy that historically derived from classic theories that emerged in the fight against absolutism.

5.6.3 Negotiations

Negotiations are attempts to obtain gains from cooperation when no fallback rules of hierarchy or counting can be invoked. Negotiated decisions are ubiquitous in the political process and take place in all types of institutional settings. In the process of negotiation, communication takes place in which each actor advances threats, promises and symbolic elaborations concerning facts and beliefs with the intention of achieving the best terms of the exchange. In principle, it is possible for actors to withdraw their resources from the exchange so that the relationship falls into deadlock or slides into conflict; that is, into the reciprocal withdrawal of advantages (confrontation) or the deliberate generation of damages (fights).[38]

Negotiations are characterised by different degrees of institutionalisation. In contexts with no norms/rules that facilitate the achievement of an agreement, negotiations are likely to succeed only when agreements are self-executing and implementation is not a problem. Otherwise, implementation entails prohibitive transaction costs if all the details must be foreseen. In dealing with negotiation as a decision norm/rule, we usually refer to negotiations taking place within a framework of

---

[37] Dahl, R. (1956), *A Preface to Democratic Theory*, Chicago, IL, The University of Chicago Press; Bobbio, N. (1981), 'La regola di maggioranza: limiti e aporie', in Bobbio, N., C. Offe and S. Lombardini (eds.), *Democrazia, maggioranza e minoranze*, Bologna, Il Mulino, pp. 33–72.

[38] Stoppino, *Potere e teoria politica*, p. 196.

other rules and norms, in which some sanctions exist to reduce unilateral action or withdrawal, the uncertainty of the future and the risk of opportunism. This situation identifies cases of *joint production*, in which cooperation is institutionally prescribed and benefits cannot be produced unless players join forces to produce them. Therefore, complex negotiated agreements depend on more demanding institutional settings. A semi-permanent relation of exchange within a range of organisational actors (such as political parties in coalition formation or a legislative decision process) generates 'structures' of voluntarist but frequent interactions that facilitate negotiation outcomes, although the option of exit is always available in principle.

Most of the time, policy choices derive from negotiations among key associations or organisations with the government overseeing or participating as a negotiating partner. Negotiation in the shadow of a governmental hierarchy is what allows the achievement of equilibria that would not otherwise be possible under conditions of mere unilateral action or voting. The adding of the bargaining power of the third party, the government and its formal hierarchy corrects the limitations of negotiation systems and makes them serve better public purposes. These types of negotiations imply that each partner is obliged to modify its original goals during the negotiation. Through the negotiation interaction partners need to develop a common interpretation of the situation to use as a basis to look for the compromise solution.[39]

Rules/norms specify the set of actors that explicitly undertake to respect certain interest positions of the other parties, to pursue certain substantive goals and to follow certain procedures in their future interactions. Examples could include governmental coalition alliances among political parties, framework agreements among neighbouring regions or regions and governments, and neo-corporatist concertation among governments and interest organisations. In these negotiations, there is always a need to reduce the number of collective or corporate actors capable of representing the aggregate preferences of their members.

The most productive negotiation context is one in which (1) parties are unable to reach their purpose through unilateral action, (2) joint production depends on unanimous or nearly unanimous agreement,

---

[39] On negotiation, see Scharpf, F. (1995), 'Essai sur la démocratie dans les systèmes de négotiation', in Telò, M. (ed.), *Démocratie et construction européenne*, Brussels, Editions de L'université de Bruxelles, pp. 145–69 (in particular on this point see pp. 161–2).

(3) legal protection of core interest positions of the actors is provided and (4) the negotiated agreements have binding force. Therefore, these forced or compulsory *joint decision systems*[40] can also be described as voting under the quasi-unanimity rule of a restricted set of licensed actors. Joint decision systems pervade the entire structure of inter-institutional relationships in any regime: the relationships between executives and legislatures, between cabinets and their majorities, between majorities and minorities, between central powers and federal powers and so on. In bicameral systems joint decisions require both chambers to approve equal legislation; in federal systems joint decisions require the consent of sub-federal entities in the deliberative and/or implementation phase. In presidential systems and in separation of powers, joint decisions require agreement between the presidential executive and the chambers. In all these cases, actors are able to oppose solutions they dislike but they have no alternative option for unilateral action, and different institutional configurations may foster or reduce deadlocks. In this type of negotiation, the focus is on value production rather than on distributive bargaining. In any case, negotiated decisions imply that actors accept only those agreements that are better than the outcome expected without agreement. In no other interaction mode (not in unilateral action, voting or hierarchy) can the same claim be advanced.

If the negotiation is not one shot but reiterated, then a strategy of rewarding cooperation and punishing defection could achieve stable cooperation. Identification of the best solution is facilitated by mutual trust, good communications, skills and expertise. Bargaining through issue linkage (of unrelated issues), package deals and logrolling may permit successful negotiations involving losses for one of the involved and affected actors. The condition is the presence of actors that are able and authorised to enter negotiations spreading over several policy areas. Deadlock points emerge when all sides prefer mutual defection to cooperation, a situation that is fostered by the increasing visibility of deals (as when elections are approaching and when parties in a coalition prefer individual visibility over cooperation).

Concerns about reaching an agreement and future problems of implementation must be endogenised in the agreement and this increases the costs of decision. Such costs can be reduced only in situations in which a qualified institutional actor (the agenda setter,

---

[40] Scharpf, *Games Real Actors Play*, pp. 141–3.

the central staff, the president or another) is able to explore the limits of solutions that are more acceptable or reach near unanimity. In these cases, consensus instead of unanimity is the decision rule; that is, a rule under which discussion continues until no one insists on opposing a proposed solution but under which in the face of continued obstruction it is still possible to resort to non-unanimous decisions.[41]

When negotiated agreements involve decisions about how costs and benefits will ultimately be shared and distributed, the beneficiaries of the status quo have an advantage as they may obstruct change by exponentially increasing the transaction costs. The cost of non-agreement is not the same for all actors, depending on the availability of alternative options and of credible threats. Normally the distribution of relative gains and losses depends on the relative cost for each actor of non-agreement.

5.6.4 Vetoes

Vetoes can also be discussed under competence norms/rules (see Section 5.7), and it is debatable whether to consider them a decisional rule. However, vetoes affect the final decision in a negative sense, preventing it, which is a decisional rule. The norm/rule simply grants one body or institutional role the capacity to block decisions reached by other bodies or roles.

The paradise, so to say, of veto powers was undoubtedly the Roman Republic's constitution before the senatorial domination following the formal collapse of the 133 BCE constitution. Numerous magistracies of different prestige and powers were elected in couple (one-year rotation) by the assemblies (the senate was at that time a purely consultative body).[42] The general principle was that any superior magistrate could veto the actions of a more junior magistrate (e.g. consul over quaestor over aediles) and of co-equal colleagues.[43] Considering the presence of three assemblies with different legislative competences and about twenty magistracies with

---

[41] Scharpf, *Games Real Actors Play*, p. 144.
[42] The most significant magistrates included two *Consuls* (the highest offices with *imperium*); *Praetors*, inferior in rank to the consuls and auxiliary to them; and *Aediles*, *Questors* and the *Tribunes of the Plebs*, with considerable rights to veto, including the counter-veto of the other tribune. Only the two *Censors*, more prestigious than powerful, were elected for five years.
[43] Note that the Athenian order was more monistic: magistrates rotated annually, either by lot or vote, the Council prepared matters for the assembly and the assembly debated and decided the main issues.

veto powers, the system seems an unworkable constitution, which, surprisingly, performed quite well in republican times.

To the best of my knowledge, formal (not de facto) veto powers then disappeared, to reappear in North America first and then in almost all presidential and semi-presidential systems. In a presidential system with its separation of legislative and executive powers, the veto represents a way to fuse legislative and executive powers 'without too much loss on either the executive or the parliamentary side of the ledger'.[44] In this reading, presidential veto power represents the presidential defence against parliamentary trespassing and presents itself in three variants: pocket veto power (the decision to refuse to sign a bill that cannot be overridden); partial veto (which partially deletes, cancelling single provisions); and the package veto (the power to reject a bill in its entirety, which can be overridden, usually by a super-majority). The use of veto powers becomes an extremely powerful instrument in all those situations in which the president enjoys considerable leverage on legislation directly, as in many Latin American cases, or indirectly, as in semi-presidential systems.

5.7 Competence Norms/Rules

Norms/rules of competence concern the allocation of authority and are at the core of norms/rules of conferral. They confer public powers on individuals and bodies. They define what pertains to the chief and what to the shaman, to consuls and the senate, to the king and the cities, to the pope and the emperor. I have already discussed key competencies under different rubrics. The competence to nominate and revoke, given its paramount importance in the world of politics, was discussed as a separate institute – that of political responsibility. Competences to harmonise competence conflicts among different bodies are usually reserved for special courts and are discussed in Section 5.10. Therefore, the remaining conferral norms/rules that distribute core competences concern primarily what pertains to executive bodies and roles and to legislative assemblies, and consist of:

(1) the competence to draft/amend legislation or to delegate legislative powers, usually entrusted to assemblies;

---

[44] Sartori, G. (1997), *The Paradox of Governing by Legislating*, in *Comparative Constitutional Engineering*, New York, New York University Press, pp. 161–172, p. 161.

(2) the competence to legislate under delegation and to implement and enforce legislation, decrees, executive orders and regulations, usually entrusted to executive bodies and roles;
(3) the competence to inquire and to force to release information about management, decisions, careers, authorities and agencies, usually entrusted to assemblies.

It is difficult to clearly attribute even core competences to a specific body or role because their interdependence is high. Many ancient and modern political systems, and particularly contemporary liberal polyarchies, explicitly and intentionally disperse competencies and attribute them to different bodies/roles. Some conferral norms/rules reserve competencies for a body/role, such as judicial review, which usually ends in a special court, or the case of precisely enumerated competences of federal/regional systems. Nevertheless, competences fully and exclusively reserved for a single body/role and complete separation of competencies are rare, and are usually limited to historical and geographical cases in which the distance and difference are large and the dependence is low. Otherwise, a considerable proportion of competences is apportioned to different bodies/roles and, therefore, requires additional norms/rules to harmonise potential conflicts of competence. In these cases, norms/rules of conferral define competencies that are *shared, overlapping* or *concurring*.

A *shared* competence entails different decision-makers enjoying the autonomous right to decide on the matter, as in the case of legislation in a perfect bicameral system. *Concurring* competencies imply undertaking joint action and joint obligations vis-à-vis third parties, as when local authorities take part in the implementation of decisions made at the national level. *Overlapping* competences may best be described as a vast grey area of superposition of different bodies' competences, for which the norms/rules of conferral require ex-post or ex-ante review and validation by other bodies of decisions taken by a body. Examples may include the treaty-making power competence of the US president, linked to advice and consent of two-thirds of the senators,[45] the case of

---

[45] Note, however, that it has become common practice for the president to bypass the consent of the senate by entering into sole-executive agreements that eventually have the same functional effect as treaties. The Supreme Court has de facto approved this practice by refusing to rule on the matter. The norm, in this case, repudiates and substitutes the rule. See Tomain, J. P. (1973), 'Executive agreements and the bypassing of Congress', *The Journal of International Law and Economics*, 8: 129–32.

delegated legislation and emergency powers, the European Union/
member states' relationships in many fields of policymaking, and,
simply, when a mayor has the competence to approve a building licence
but only after the approval of the technical office. In these cases,
competence conferral norms/rules establish the conditions under
which conferral can be validly exercised.

All forms of modern democratic government are to some degree compound governments in which different centres of power exist and enter in
relations of competition, cooperation, negotiation and occasionally
conflict.[46] The essence of the distinction between forms of government is
the quantity, autonomy and interdependence among these centres.
Sharing, overlapping and concurring can take place along a vertical
dimension (the connection between vertical jurisdictions in a *multi-
layered* system of government) and a horizontal dimension (the connection between horizontal jurisdictions in a *multi-centred* system of
government).

Vertical apportionment of competencies between central government
and sub-territorial governments implies costs of harmonisation. The harmonisation may aim at preventing or reducing the lower-level government's advantage or disadvantage. It may also prevent lower-level units
from competing among themselves to attract individuals and resources
through policy differentiation. Vertical harmonisation is facilitated by
the presence of some general rule that offers a special defence to one of
the institutional bodies, such as the pre-emption doctrine in US
federalism[47] and the so-called German *Copperworking* clause[48] in
the case of concurring competences between the federal and *Länder*
governments.

The horizontal interconnectedness among the competencies of several
bodies or institutional roles that are not territorially layered is not
qualitatively different to the vertical competence layering between state

---

[46] Fabbrini, S. (2010), *Compound Democracies: Why the United States and
Europe Are Becoming Similar*, Oxford, Oxford University Press.

[47] Pre-emption indicates the capacity of a higher-level government to remove one
or more legislative, executive and/or administrative powers of a lower-level
government. Complete pre-emption is envisaged in Section 10 of Article I of the
US Constitution that prevents any state from entering any treaty, alliance,
coining money and so on. Contingent pre-emption implies that a state power can
be superseded only if certain conditions exist. See *Maryland v. Louisiana*, 451
U.S. 725, 746 (1981).

[48] According to art. 72 II of the German *Grund Gesetz* as amended in 1990–4.

and sub-state-territorial units. The most important and complex inter-connectedness of norms/rules of conferral concerns the interaction between executive and legislative bodies. The complexity of these inter-actions depends, on the one hand, on the specific competence powers of presidents, cabinets and assemblies that define the nature of the regime but also, on the other hand, on the norms and traditions of domination or balance among the same bodies, the two dimensions being somewhat independent. They together define what we usually call a system of checks and balances, where the checks and balances are simply shared, concurring or overlapping competence powers.

The interconnections among norms/rules of competence are very much case-specific. Therefore, norms/rules of competence are often regrouped to identify 'regimes' with shortcuts such as parliamentarism, presidentialism and semi-presidentialism (or mixed) or federalised, decentralised and centralised systems. However, these shortcuts pre-sent pitfalls. These classes are often neither exclusive (cases belong to more than one class) nor inclusive (cases are left out of the classes). Grey areas and ambiguous and hybrid cases exist at the boundary between classes. In part this is unavoidable because there are more things in heaven and on earth than are dreamt of in our philosophy. In part, however, this is also due to the difficulty in distinguishing the specific features of the *institutional regime* (the connection among the institutes discussed in this chapter) and the *political regime*, for which other political structures are added next to the institutional design. On the distinction between institutional and political regimes, more fol-lows in the next chapter. Here it is enough to state that institutional analysis should be primarily concerned with institutions as norms/rules of conferral and should try to separate the institutional design from the specific political structures that derive from behavioural interactions among actors (such as the party system, the cleavage structure, coali-tion patterns, the interest intermediation system, the elite's political culture). The combination of these additional political structures often blurs the institutional design resulting from the rules of conferral.

5.8 Accountability Norms/Rules

Accountability is defined by agency theory using two criteria: an agent is accountable to the principal if: (1) she is obliged to act on the latter's behalf; and (2) the principal has the power to reward or punish the agent for her performance.[49] This definition rests on meagre conditions. The first implies an unspecified obligation towards a principal (moral, legal, political?). The second implies rewards and punishment for the agent. On close inspection, what is missed is exactly accountability mechanisms; that is, the specific rules/norms that link the obligation to act to the reward/punishment. I have argued before that a power of reward/punishment simply identifies a 'political responsibility'. If this power is supposed to depend on accountability, we must specify the rules/norms of accounting.

A more complete definition is that 'accountability is a relationship between an actor and a forum in which the actor has an obligation to explain and to justify his or her conduct, the forum can pose questions and pass judgement, and the actor may face consequences'.[50] The relationship between actor and forum concerns the question of *to whom* the account is to be rendered. Forums are of different types: legal, administrative, professional, social, political. Accountability relationships also define *who* shall account: individuals, groups, corporate entities and so on. A third dimension concerns *what* the actor is compelled to account for – what the nature of the obligation is. There are obligations arising from hierarchy, contract and formal delegation acts. There are also diagonal accountabilities (administrative, ombudsmen, inspectorates, supervisory, audit offices, etc.) and horizontal accountabilities (social, towards the general public). Fourth, accountability mechanisms need to identify what sort of explanations and justifications are required to whom accounts and whether the forum can require monitoring and supervision materials, ask questions, express judgements and contest evidence. Fifth, accountability requires specifying which aspect of conduct is accountable. There are procedural, programmatic and financial but also ethical accountabilities. A total accountability covering every type of behaviour is inconceivable (but, as I argue later, it is exactly the kind of responsibility that is called 'political'). Finally, accountability should generate specific consequences for the actor.

---

[49] Strøm, 'Delegation and accountability in parliamentary democracies', pp. 261–89.
[50] Bovens, 'Analysing and assessing accountability: a conceptual framework', p. 450.

Therefore, a precise definition of accountability rules/norms requires these six elements: *who* is accountable, *to whom* are they accountable, *what is the nature* of the obligation, *for what* are they accountable, *what evidence* is the basis for evaluation and *what consequences* may follow.

Accountability mechanisms exist in various inquiring bodies that explicitly go through the accountability steps. They apply to executive members in front of inquiring parliamentary committees and top administrators in front of their political superiors or committees of inquiry, special grand juries of various types, ombudsman institutions controlling administrative practices and bodies that oversee the activities and performance of independent agencies, and so on. In general, therefore, *true accountability rules/norms prevail in the connection between political and administrative institutions* and focus on administrative performance and the correctness of specific roles. Accountability and oversight processes take the form of reporting requirements, detailed definitions of the instruments and means of the bureaucratic (or political) structure, and the possibility of appealing to courts. Accountability rules/norms are more effective in endowing politicians with more effective mechanisms to check bureaucratic and agency behaviours when the forum to which one has to account is restricted, more informed and more competent, the evidence is wider and the sanctions are specific and more easily assigned to individuals.

The term 'accountability' has recently spread into the language of politics. It is often argued that members of parliament (MPs) are accountable to voters, executives are accountable to MPs, bureaucrats are accountable to ministers, and so forth. This usage of the term is improper. The problem is that in politics it is the supposedly accountable agent who defines the preferences and interests of the principal. Therefore, the principal cannot 'oblige' the agent to act on his behalf. This would require a different process in which the preference of the principal can be ascertained independently of the agent. It is also difficult to establish to whom the agent should account: her own voters? The entire constituency, including those who did not vote for the agent? The entire electorate? The nature of the obligation is also undefined. For what should politicians be accountable? For effective problem-solving or for overall policies, for personal behaviour (moral or sexual, for instance), for detailed legislative activity or for their public image or linguistic and dialectic capabilities? And what is the proportion of blame or prize to be given to the individual representatives or to the collective body to which they belong (the cabinet, the assembly, the party)?

Furthermore, it is unclear what sort of explanation and justification can be required from the politician and what sort of evidence should be the proper basis for accountability. Monitoring evidence, supervision materials, questions and answers are left to ideological-political debates. No specific kind of explanation or justification is explicitly required. How can ordinary people manage the structural difficulties and ambiguities involved in the interpretation of mandates and their implementation? Policies pass through too many hands to be a basis for evaluation. Unanticipated effects are likely to be as widespread as errors simply because we do not have a fully specified model of which factors will affect the outcomes.[51] Finally, one can doubt the eventual sanctioning implied in the accountability concept. Retrospective sanctioning is left to the powerful but blind renewal/non-renewal at the end of the term for those incumbents who decide to run again.

It can be argued that other forces (the media, interest groups, opponents) may act to objectify the basis for accountability judgement by offering more information for evaluation. But all these forces in politics are subject to heavy selective emphasis, profound differences of opinion on the relevance and gravity of misbehaviours, politically biased media coverage, and the like. And politicians' attempts to anticipate the reactions of their presumed principals are not only constrained by huge cognitive difficulties but are also characterised by explicit attempts to mould and fake public opinion.[52] Accountability reports and oversight are mediated by the same political forces that should be subject to it.

None of the analogies of 'acting for others' satisfactorily explain the relationship between a political representative and her supposed principal. She is neither agent nor trustee, nor deputy, nor commissioner; she acts for a group of people without a single interest, most of whom have difficulties in forming an explicit will on political questions.[53] The political obligation is indefinable, as is the political accountability of the agent.

---

[51] Schedler, A. (1994), *Taking Electoral Promises Seriously: Reflections on the Content of Procedural Democracy*, IPSA, Berlin, August 1994, p. 27.

[52] Pierson, P. (2000), 'The limits of design: explaining institutional origins and change', *Governance: An International Journal of Policy and Administration*, 13: 475–99, 483.

[53] Pitkin, *The Concept of Representation*, p. 221.

This is why in politics there can be political representation and political responsibility but little accountability. The institute of political responsibility does not offer the wonderful gifts pledged by political accountability. It simply gives one body the right to withdraw at any moment or at fixed intervals their confidence in a different body to which certain tasks have been assigned. Political responsibility is blindly general and every voter is able and authorised to use whatever criteria may lead to removal of their support. Political responsibility does not rest either on specific skills or characters of the agent, on rational evaluation of performance, on objective facts or benchmarks, or on administrative mismanagement. The relationship between voters and elected officials in parliamentary assemblies is not one of accountability but one of representation and responsibility.

What is at stake here is not merely conceptual clarity. Accountability is mentioned as a key feature of democracy, enhancing citizens' control of office holders and legitimacy.[54] It is often presented as the essence of democracy. However, if proper accountability mechanisms work very poorly in politics, we are setting our standards too high for the normative theory of democracy. We raise expectations and generate hopes about democratic institutions that cannot be fulfilled and may, on the contrary, generate disappointments and mistrust. To state that top politicians are 'accountable' is a conceptual mistake that turns into a mystification. We sell a fashionable but damaged good and we renounce from educating citizens on the virtues of representative democracy, among which political representation and responsibility, although limited in scope, are prominent, while political accountability, forceful in its promises, is virtually inexistent.

5.9 Delegation Norms/Rules

Persons or bodies that cannot accomplish a specific task or action can delegate somebody else, a person or body, to accomplish it on their behalf. Delegation is one of the oldest political institutes because it concerns one primordial problem of rulership: to whom to delegate territorial political power and how to make subordinates responsible and loyal. The problem is both a problem of information about local

---

[54] See Olsen, J. (2013), 'The institutional basis of democratic accountability', *West European Politics*, 36: 447–73.

conditions and a problem of concrete territorial control of rebellious behaviour with poor communication technologies. Simply put, the problem was avoiding brutal sergeants, incompetent colonels and disloyal subordinates.

The early form of delegation probably reproduced a segmentary hierarchy system through the appointment of family or kinship relatives as territorial (or functional) delegates, supplemented later with *clientes* (with a relationship of personal dependence on the patron), military commanders and eventually appointed commissaries. The tendency to distribute power in accordance with the control of lethal weapons was widespread. However, this threatened central ruling authorities, for the military might be more loyal to their own military leaders than the latter were to the central rulers. Alternatively, executive operations in distant parts of the polity could be left to a governor appointed by the central government as a revocable 'delegate'. One way to gain a degree of hold on local governors was to assign them a part of the revenues of the landed estates, as the central ruler could block a recalcitrant governor with the threat of dispossessing him.[55] Finally, local functions could be entrusted to a grand official, a provincial plenipotentiary. If a stranger was appointed, the local magnates could exercise their influence to frustrate his efforts unless he accommodated their entrenched privileges. If an influential local lord was appointed, the risks were even worse.

Central rulers adopted all sorts of expedients to make their resident officials compliant: rotating them from one area to another before they could strengthen local roots; distributing local functions among several co-equal officers; appointing kinsmen; and sending special commissioners to report or interfere. Nevertheless, the frequency of revolts by satraps, governors, strategisers and *amirs* witnesses that control was always a problem.

During the Han empire, China was the first to develop what today we would call a bureaucratic caste of appointed officials (the *shou*) characterised by uniformity, symmetry and limited autonomy. They were civil servants in local secondment, indoctrinated in a special ideology and esprit de corps, Confucianism, and were shifted around frequently.[56] Another common solution was to reserve delegated

---

[55] A solution that Weber labelled 'prebendian feudalism'. Weber, *Economy and Society*, vol. 1, pp. 259–62.

[56] In the T'Ang empire (about 500 to 900 CE), the growth in the number of imperial wives reached the ridiculous figure of 40,000; the suspicion is that

government for special kinds of aliens, often slave aliens. Eunuchs were extensively used in Assyria, Babylonia, the Byzantium empire and above all the Persian empire. Slave soldiers in Abbasid Egypt (1200–1500), the *Mamluks*, had a similar role. In the Ottoman empire, territorial control was guaranteed by the alien (non-Turk) slave institution of *Janissaries* and *Sipahis*, recruited through a typical Ottoman institution, the *devshirme*, a levy of infant males from Christian families brought to the capital, raised as Muslims and trained as civil servants or soldiers. As Xenophon suggests,[57] alien eunuchs without children, wives or relatives could not pass on their privileges to descendants. Being generally shunned by others, they directed their affection to those who had made them rich and powerful.

In Japan, the problem proved less acute. The emperor, not ruling by divine mandate but being divine and therefore absolutely absolute, delegated rule to the Shoguns (from 1600), who in turn delegated authority to their vassals. The latter, despite being appointed on a hereditary basis, were in a state of total subjection in the no-exit context of an isolated and homogeneous country that in 1638 still forbade every Japanese from leaving the country, executed all those who returned, decided that no ocean-going vessels might be built and only allowed a few Dutch traders to reside on a tiny island off Nagasaki.

Formalisation of the delegation relationship emerged as a Roman imperial and then Roman Catholic institution. Roman territory outside Italy was subdivided into provinces, which were ruled by governors of senatorial rank, usually former consuls or praetors.[58] The control mechanism was based on socialisation as the governors were drawn from prominent Roman *gens* and had previously served in the public life of the Republic. Notwithstanding this, the problem of their loyalty continued to plague the Republic given that governors had control of the local army. Therefore, the first emperor, Augustus, made himself governor of almost all the provinces with legions and used *legati* to rule them.[59] The term

---

marriage was a way of consolidating ties between the emperor and prominent local families.

[57] Xenophon (317 BCE (1914)), *Cyropaedia*, 7 vols, translated by W. Miller, Cambridge, MA, Harvard University Press, vol. 5, p. 60 and following.

[58] An exception was the province of Egypt after the death of Cleopatra, which was ruled by a governor of only equestrian rank, perhaps to discourage senatorial ambition.

[59] The rest of the empire was governed by proconsuls (former praetors made *legati Augusti pro praetore*), appointed typically for twelve or thirty-six months. In

delegate/delegation comes from the term *legatus*, literally 'tied up', 'bound'. The institution of the *legatus* made its way into canon law. In the Roman Catholic Church, a *legatus* is a cleric sent on an ecclesiastical or diplomatic mission by the pope as his personal representative to exercise control over distant territories: *legatus a latere* (a legate from the pope's side); apostolic delegates (representatives to the Church in a region); and papal judge delegates (appointed to decide a case appealed to the papal court).

In the Middle Ages, the institution of delegation lost its grip and was substituted with more personal linkages between rulers and their territorial representatives, as in the institution of vassalage, which diffused in the Carolingian kingdoms. A formal and solemn oath of loyalty constituted a bilateral relationship based on reciprocal commitments: protection and maintenance for the senior and support and help for the vassal. The different institution of the 'feud' implied the king renouncing the government of entire territories governed by hereditary families. The hereditary nature of the feud transformed a relationship based on personal confidence and grounded in the quality of the vassal into an impersonal relationship which was automatic and independent of individual characteristics.

During the early modern period, the Holy Roman empire was divided into imperial circles,[60] administrative units with the task of organising defence and collecting imperial taxes. These territorial administrations often appealed to the principle of refusing to recognise any superior authority (*superiorem non recognoscens*).[61] For a weak elected emperor,

less important provinces, prefects (i.e. knights) were appointed. The best-known example is Pontius Pilate, who governed Judaea, an annex to Syria. Only with the stabilisation of the Pax Romana after the mid-first century CE were prefects gradually replaced by procurators, the latter not being military but fiscal officials.

[60] From 1512 until the collapse of the Holy Roman empire in the Napoleonic era, there were ten imperial circles. The Crown of Bohemia, the Swiss Confederacy and Italy remained unencircled, as did various minor territories that held imperial immediacy. Although the empire lost several western territories after the secession of the Seven United Netherlands in 1581 and during the French annexations of 1679 (Peace of Nijmegen), the ten circles remained largely unchanged until the French revolutionary armies radically altered the political map of Europe.

[61] The principle was first invoked in the First Crusade. The group of armed warriors and almost unarmed pilgrims who invaded Jerusalem on 15 July 1099 exterminated almost entirely the Muslin and Jewish populations, repopulated the city with eastern Christians, Syriacs and Armenians and set to deciding who

the question was not so much one of making sure that the lower authority would act in the interest of the superior authority as it was of ensuring any formally devolved authority would not autonomise itself totally and refuse to recognise the superior authority.

It is an interesting question whether the companies founded by the Dutch and English/British governments at the beginning of the seventeenth century can be regarded as forms of political delegation. While Spanish and Portuguese trade with overseas colonies and territories was shaped as and remained a monopoly of the king, and therefore the state, the Dutch East and West India companies and the English/British East India Company were mega-corporations founded by the government as purely commercial enterprises amalgamating several trading companies. They were private joint stock companies to which trade was monopolistically delegated. However, the Dutch companies in particular – the British only at a later stage and in the case of India – rapidly moved to direct territorial control to compete with the rival Portuguese, French and Spanish companies. At this stage, not only trade but also the powers of government were delegated to private companies.

Territorial control via delegation had a distinctive top-down vertical dimension and was a primordial political concern for all sorts of rulers. It is no longer so in most modern states. The age of nation-building and nationalism split the territories of large empires and radically reduced incentives for secession, fostering a more uniform culture uniting citizens and rulers. Finally, when the principle of elective selection of both central and local rulers expanded, centre–periphery relations were constitutionalised. Territorial delegation was less problematic, also thanks to the bureaucratic professionalisation of personnel and to its combination with elements of political decentralisation of decision-making (regionalism, federalism).

should rule the new territory. Eventually, the military leaders appointed Gottfried of Bouillon, Duc of Lower Lorrain, as king of the Kingdom of Jerusalem. This rule could not be legitimated either by the Byzantine emperor (to whom Palestine had belonged until it was conquered by the Arabs in 638), by the Roman Church pope (who was intent on trying to solve the eastern schism and unwilling to create further problems with Jerusalem) or by the Roman-Germanic emperor (who was weak and far away). The crusade kingdom was therefore born as a result of the revolutionary principle, in that time, of the absence of any superior authority.

Delegation retains a territorial dimension in a few cases, primarily in federalised states. In Spain, the term is used in a strict sense to designate the administration of some provinces on behalf of the central authority, be it the king or the parliament. An additional domain that presents some of the early territorial characteristics is the growing delegation of once national competencies to supranational or multilateral bodies and organisations. In this latter case, delegation is bottom-up rather than top-down, as in the historical cases.

Today, therefore, the historical problem of delegation is almost exclusively reformulated as *functional delegation of a horizontal nature*. The delegation institute is reserved to three main domains: delegation between executives and legislative bodies, delegation to bureaucratic bodies and delegation to specialised technical agencies. In most parliamentary democracies explicit norms foresee the circumstances and procedures through which the legislative assemblies can delegate some competences to the cabinet, usually within the framework of general law.[62] In US constitutional law, the transfer of a specific authority by one of the three branches of government (executive, legislative and judicial) to another branch or to an independent agency is not the object of specific rules but of one that prohibits it. The non-delegation doctrine is the principle that the Congress of the United States, being vested with 'all legislative powers' by Article 1, Section 1 of the Constitution, cannot delegate that power to anyone else. When in the mid-1930s several new agencies were created to fight the Depression, the Supreme Court found these delegations violated the separation of powers and struck down several pieces of New Deal legislation, only to slowly change its mind in the following period.[63]

[62] European Union delegation is a specific form of secondary legislation. A legislative act, such as a Directive or Regulation, can delegate power to the Commission to adopt acts to supplement or amend non-essential elements of the legislative act [Article 290 TFEU]. See Pollac, M. (1997), 'Delegation, agency and agenda-setting in the European community', *International Organization* 51: 99–134; Kassim, H. and A. Menon (2003), 'The principal-agent approach and the study of European Union: promise unfulfilled?' *Journal of European Public Policy*, 10: 121–39; Hawkins, D., D. A. Lake, D. Nielson and M. J. Tierney (2006), *Delegation Under Anarchy: Principals, Agents, and International Organizations*, Cambridge, Cambridge University Press.

[63] The question has become that of the capacity of the Congress to sufficiently direct the agency through the delegation law to limit its actions to those that would not violate the separation of powers. The judiciary, on the other hand, reviews the question of whether the statute provides enough guidance for the

Competences are delegated to bodies of experts, bureaucratic or special agencies, whose major qualification is specialised knowledge. In principle, these are *both* accountable and responsible to the executives or assemblies and they can be sanctioned or removed. To solve problems of information impoverishment and/or overload at the centre of the hierarchy, organisational and transaction cost theory suggests that superiors should limit their directives to matters that must be handled at their own organisational level, while leaving everything else to lower agents (subsidiarity principle). Considerable work has gone into specifying the conditions under which a hierarchy may work at multiple levels without ignoring pertinent local information and without overtaxing the limited capacity of hierarchical superiors to process information and solve conflicts among sub-units. In the case of excessive hierarchical control, conflicts, centralisation and poorly informed decisions may follow. If the hierarchy dilutes, lower-level actors are left to sort out policy conflicts among themselves.

Economic, legal and social theories offer contributions to guarantee an effective delegation relationship. Principal–agent models are an analytic expression of the agency relationship in which one party, the principal, considers entering into a contractual agreement with another, the agent, in the expectation that the agent will subsequently choose actions that produce outcomes desired by the principal. Difficulties arise from the asymmetric distribution of information (including moral hazard and adverse selection) that favours the agent and allows her to engage in opportunistic behaviour which is difficult to detect (shirking). However, while rules of delegation are extensive and quite sophisticated in private law, they are somewhat meagre and unspecified in public law and even more so in politics. Legal doctrine discusses in detail the potential consequences of relationships in which one person acts with the assent of another in the name of or on behalf of that person and subject to a level of control. The doctrine precisely specifies the nature of agency relationships, fiduciary duty, the rights and means of control by the principal, and so on. From the sociological point of view, social devices to limit agency costs include 'professionalisation', embeddedness and personal familiarity, trusted social networks, track records and reputation, and fiduciary relationships in cases in which the asymmetries

court to review the agency's actions to ensure that they comply with
Congressional intent (the 'intelligible principle' test).

are so big that the principal cannot claim control of the agent (disabled people, etc.). Legal and sociological approaches also discuss the problem of the agent serving many principals and having to face conflicts of interest among sometimes incommensurably different interests.[64]

Attempts to transfer the economic, legal and social underpinning of delegation relationships into politics face additional problems already discussed in Section 5.8. When politicians, bureaucrats and experts disagree on how to pursue an outcome or on which outcome to pursue, either politicians are willing to pay the cost of writing detailed statutes that limit discretion or politicians set up strong ex-post accountability mechanisms to ensure desirable bureaucratic and agency actions. Otherwise, granting large discretion to bureaucrats, experts and independent agencies is essentially abdicating policy-making authority to them. Delegation slides into disempowerment.

Notwithstanding these problems, the concept of 'delegation' is often applied to a whole variety of political institutes. It is argued that voters 'delegate' parliamentary representatives or elected heads, parliamentary representatives delegate the chief executive, the latter in turn delegates individual ministers and each minister delegates further down to bureaucrats, agencies and so on.[65] So put, the problem of democracy is making sure that the delegated follow the wishes of the delegating and one can describe the political system at large as a series of delegative acts under the label of principal–agent theory.[66] The challenge is to create a 'perfect contract design' that ensures agent compliance through incentive structures and

[64] Kiser, E. (1999), 'Comparing varieties of agency theory in economics, political science, and sociology: an illustration from state policy implementation', *Sociological Theory*, 17: 146–70; and Shapiro, S. P. (2005), 'Agency theory', *Annual Review of Sociology* 31 (August 2005): 263–84.

[65] Huber, J. D. and C. R. Shipan (2009), 'Politics, delegation, and bureaucracy', in Goodin, R. E. (ed.), *The Oxford Handbook of Political Science*, Oxford, Oxford University Press, pp. 849–65; McCubbins, M. D., R. Noll and B. Weingast (1998), 'Political control of the bureaucracy', in Newman, P. (ed.), *The New Palgrave Dictionary of Economics and Law*, London, Palgrave, pp. 50–5.

[66] Particularly useful is Stiglitz, J. (1987), 'Principal and agent', in *The New Palgrave: A Dictionary of Economics*, 6 vols, London, Palgrave Macmillan, vol. 3, pp. 966–71; and Williamson, O. E. (2002), 'The theory of the firm as governance structure: from choice to contract', *Journal of Economic Perspectives*, 16: 171–95. For a critical review see Moe, T. M. (1984), 'The new economics of organization', *American Journal of Political Science*, 28: 739–77.

performance monitoring mechanisms that minimise agency loss and avoid slippages.

Transferring the jargon of delegation contracts to the whole set of political relations is problematic. In politics, delegation is not a contract but a specific political relationship that cannot be fully specified ex ante in contractual terms. The principal–agent relationship assumes the existence of the wills or preferences of those who delegate and opposes them to the selfish compulsion of those who receive the delegation. This line of thought falls short of specifying what is 'delegated' in these imaginary contracts: wills, preferences, ideas, interests? Furthermore, in replicating the principal–agent model for any relation from voters to administrators we quickly get to an unmanageable level of complication. We become entrapped in an endless game of multiple and interchanging principals and agents and it is doubtful that a proper system of incentives can be designed in politics that ensures the adherence of delegates to the preferences of the delegating, even if we were to know them.[67]

We should not, therefore, abuse the term delegation with its own precise sense of a mandate expressed as commitment by the agent to execute the will of the principal. We should reserve it for those situations in which the will or preference of the principal can be reasonably ascertained, the mandate defined and the behaviour of the agent properly checked in relation to the mandate. These are conditions which are difficult to meet in core political processes, as I already argued in the discussion of the accountability institute (Section 5.8), which, most of the time, goes together with the delegation idea.

5.10 Redress Norms/Rules

Redress rules/norms concern the mechanisms that allow appeals against and remedies for undesirable or unfair decisions by rulers. Since ancient times, norms and rules have existed that set torts and redress damages at the request of a party, together with ones protecting from infringements that are regarded as inimical or dangerous for the entire community and which are prosecuted even in the absence of claims by a party. Rules of redress against political and administrative

[67] De Jouvenel (1992 (1959)), 'Authority: the efficient imperative', in *The Nature of Politics: Selected Essays of Bertrand de Jouvenel*, edited by D. Hale and M. Landy, New Brunswick, NJ, Transaction, pp. 84–93.

decisions by rulers or their territorial agents are different. For a long time they were less developed and formalised. Usually a subject could only seek redress by a superior authority against decisions of an inferior authority. Going beyond this general norm was a historical revolution that we owe most clearly to Roman law: 'the principle of being able to sue the authorities was and would in the future of Europe come to be of overriding importance, and it represents the greatest, most durable, and far reaching of all Roman contributions to the history of government'.[68] Nowadays, redress against decisions stemming from political authorities can be sought in two domains: those of *constitutional* and *administrative justice*. Both involve procedures through which political authorities allow their decisions to be challenged and possibly overruled.

Not all countries have special constitutional jurisdictions and courts, but most foresee a possibility of legislative or executive overrule. First, in forms of right-based constitutionalism (a justiciable bill of rights), the list of rights generally embodies the liberal precept that the state should not infringe on a few matters and should remain neutral in the face of certain kinds of issues. Frequently, religious beliefs and issues are 'privatised' thanks to declarations that render political rulers impartial among different religious doctrines and faiths and liable if they violate this impartiality. Similarly, it may be possible to ensure this political neutrality concerning questions of race and ethnicity, language, educational schools and traditions and so on. Right-based constitutionalism is a safeguard against ruling authorities' ambitions to issue commands in these reserved areas. The instigations of groups and individuals remain outside the sphere of the political. Indeed, they remain competing instigations and not conflicting instigations to be reduced to unity through commands.

Second, to the extent that the state is not a monocratic body but a multi-centre set of interacting bodies, a further body is necessary to settle controversies about the competences of such bodies and to solve conflicts among them. In this second function, the role of constitutional justice appears more uncontroversially political. But in both types of functions – protecting rights and settling controversies among political bodies – the courts and a Supreme Court act at the political core of the polity.

Constitutional justice is part of the judicial system and as such it is shielded to some extent form political influences. However, the subject matter it deals with makes it nearer to politics than normal

[68] Finer, *A History of Government*, p. 604.

jurisdictional activities. Constitutional norms are far less detailed than ordinary norms. Being at the source of the entire legal system, they have the character of general principles. They leave, therefore, a larger margin of interpretation. This is balanced by the fact that these rules are more difficult to change and require a broad consensus to do so. Constitutional jurisdiction cannot be modified by ordinary law but only by constitutional revisions, which are not easy to adopt in view of solving very controversial political matters.

The presence of a constitutional court and of a constitutional jurisdiction strengthen the enforcement capacity of constitutional rules. If the protection of certain rights is without organised sanctioning through the constitutional jurisdiction, the procedures for political decisions and issues of constitutional legitimacy are left to political majorities, the balance among political forces and the checking control of public opinion.

Although subjective influences can be limited, there is no binding interpretative method or one that can be imposed by the legislator. Therefore, it is unavoidable that constitutional justice will present elements of political discretion and that judicial power is also to a certain extent political power. However, constitutional jurisdictional activity remains characterised by decisions taken within the sphere of the law, which is unlikely to pursue political goals of its own, is able to offer higher guarantees of impartiality, is independent of political support and consent, and is not obliged to take on board factors and considerations external to the norms to be applied.

These ambiguities have fostered different interpretations. Constitutional justice is seen as judicial by Kelsen and, on the contrary, as political by Schmitt. This double and ambiguous character has been extensively discussed when focussing on the problem of the democratic legitimacy of constitutional justice. Habermas has proposed reserving it for special parliamentary bodies and not judicial bodies.[69] Rawls, in contrast, defends the thesis that the legitimacy of constitutional justice depends eventually on the argumentative capacity of the court itself.[70] Constitutional justice remains a grey area between the judicial and the political.

---

[69] Habermas, J. (1996), *Between Facts and Norms: Contributions to a Discursive Theory of Law and Democracy*, Boston, MA, Polity Press.
[70] Rawls, J. (2005), *Political Liberalism*, New York, Columbia University Press.

The separation of politics and law is no easier in the second component of redress norms/rules: the field of application of law through *administrative justice*. The separation between politics and law in this field of application does not guarantee that the judicial procedure is politically neutral; that is, without margins of interpretation and innovative decisions. Total political neutrality within this jurisdictional function would require the legal order to be without gaps, contradictions and linguistic ambiguities and, more importantly, totally independent and impermeable to social pressures and changes.

Paradoxically, one might even think that 'administrative law' is the most political of all jurisdictions. Normal or special courts, according to national traditions, decide on the validity of the action of other political bodies when challenged by a private actor. In this case, the state distributes behavioural compliance with its own decisions, including appeals against them. Administrative bodies adjudicate on requests for behavioural compliance advanced by political authorities and do so with reference to other rights or institutions.[71]

In constitutional and administrative justice, the courts are decision-makers. However, they remain courts in that they depend on other private or public bodies to invoke their powers. They cannot self-activate. Judicial proceedings remain essentially bipolar, and tend to resolve disputes in terms of the interests and claims of the parties represented and on the basis of materials presented by the parties. One can think that if the problem requires the consideration of other parties not present in front of the court and not involved in the dispute, then the court is not the ideal body to resolve the dispute.

5.11 Conclusion

Many things have been left out in this list of core political institutes. Some of them will be discussed in the next chapter as macro-institutions – regimes as the upper layer of institutional analysis. Other items frequently enrolled in the rank of political institutions are in fact 'political structures', specific configurations of actors without normative content

---

[71] On the connection between legal and political studies, see Drewry, 'Political institutions: legal perspectives', in Goodin, R. E. and H.-D. Klingeman (eds.), *A New Handbook of Political Science*, pp. 191–204, mainly dealing with the USA and UK.

(for instance, 'competition', 'party systems', etc.). However, I have not covered certain items which are often regarded as political institutions.

Human rights often appear in the list of core political institutions. Human rights, like many other kinds of rights – social rights, property rights, religious rights, gender rights and so on – may appear in codified texts and embody a normative claim: they must be respected and special redress institutes may watch over their realisation. They may be more or less extended in different acts or constitutional texts in different countries and different times. However, they are commitments towards outcomes which are strengthened by their codification and by the specific jurisdictional defence that ensues. Although they confer private powers in the form of rights, they do not confer public powers. They are not norms/rules that transform a set of competing or contradictory instigations into a single command valid for a membership or territorial group. They do not regulate and discipline the struggle for political power; that is, for the position of institutional roles of authority. They confer prerogatives and powers in the form of guaranteed individual powers (the rights to . . .), but not in the form of collective powers. As was argued in Chapter 4, political institutions should not be confused with the powers they confer but identified as the norms/rules that concede those powers. For all these reasons it seems to me that rights of this kind should not be considered political institutions, no more than a right to exercise a profession or to move freely on a territory should.

The rule of law is often listed among core political institutions. In large part what we label the rule of law appears in my list of institutes under the rubric of redress norms/rules: a constitutional jurisdiction, the political independence of the judiciary, the presence of administrative rules of redress and so on. But the rule of law is also the result of the entire institutional configuration of the regime and of additional non-institutional features (such as the independence of the media, the reactions of groups and movements to infringements). If we make it an independent core political institute, then it will force us to discuss it in conjunction with many other core institutes that substantiate the rule of law. I prefer to see the rule of law as an institutional complex principle that requires going beyond strict institutional analysis.

Finally, for practically all political organisations such as legislatures, executives and courts, there are many detailed and complex rules of procedure that technically define the validity of their acts and are decisive for the rule of law. Rules of procedure too could be seen as a separate political institute. Although occasionally some of the procedural rules become very important, I have opted to exclude them as a separate item because their number is too high. Therefore, the more important rules of procedure are listed under the various institutes, while more detailed procedural rules and norms are excluded from the discussion.

6 | Macro-Institutions
Territories, Constitutions and Regimes

I have moved from a discussion of the nature of political institutions *as single norms/rules* to a discussion of more complex institutional sets defined as *institutes*. In this chapter I climb further along the layering of political institutions and deal with macro-institutions. The contributions of Western medieval pluralism and of modern state monism discussed at the end of Chapter 4 are reflected in two fundamental macro-institutions. One has to do with the necessary precondition for power-sharing, which is the monopolisation of destructive resources and of 'legitimate' violence over a territorial space: the 'territorial institution'. The second refers to the general framework of power-sharing taking place within a territory in which destructive means have been successfully monopolised and there are no challenges to the ruling function. This is the 'fundamental norm' or 'constitution'. Both elements delineate the shape of the prevailing *institutional regime*, which is the third macro-institution considered in this chapter. The territory, the constitution and the institutional regime are macro-institutions that are located at the highest level in the vertical layering of institutions and are constituted by complex combinations of single norms/rules and institutes. At the same time, like all macro-phenomena, they are characterised by emerging properties that cannot exclusively be reduced to lower-level institutions. In this chapter I discuss their particularities.

6.1 The Territorial Institution

The 'state' is sometimes regarded as a political institution or as the synthesis of all political institutions. However, a set of highly inter-related bureaucratic organisations make up the state, each with its own internal institutional ordering. The category is too broad for any further elaboration in institutional terms. Moreover, if we stick to the understanding of institutions in this work, the state as such can hardly be defined in terms of norms/rules of conduct, recognition or conferral.

Nevertheless, one dimension of the state is associated with a clear normative claim and a norm/rule of conferral. The state's existence rests on the necessary condition of an exclusive territory. The attribute that distinguishes the state from all other entities is territorial possession. All states impinge on a territory and have a primary commitment to its defence. There is no state that does not consider the undermining of its territory an offensive behaviour. Therefore, the defence of the territory is a normative commitment that supersedes all others. One can say that at any given moment the individuals or groups that control the territory are normatively identified with the obligation to care for and defend it.[1]

States are founded or extinguish themselves, are enlarged or become reduced, as a result of either territorial conquest or secession. At war, all other institutions may be sacrificed to the needs of territorial defence. Territory and rulership are inextricably linked. Throughout recorded history there are no examples of territories without a ruler of some sort. The early solutions used to be patrimonial in the sense that the territory, the entire land, belonged nominally to the ruler, king, prince or emperor. In this sense, *territorial safeguarding is a primordial political institution independent of the state's level of infrastructural differentiation and bureaucratic development.* The territorial institution exists independently of whatever other forms political institutions take and it is a necessary condition for them. It precedes any fundamental law, none of which can be envisaged without a safe territory for its application.

Although territoriality was of great importance even for nomadic groups of hunter-gatherers, considering the importance of the territorial prey, game and vegetation, territory became a dominant political institution with standing establishments. In the distant past, we were born as members of a group without any alternative option. Today, we are born as members of a territorial institution without any choice. However, this institution is difficult to define, it usually escapes attention, it is taken for granted and it is often concealed by other legitimising devices such as society, community and government. This

---

[1] On the territorial institution, see de Fina, S. (1974), *Diritto e società*, Milan, Giuffrè.

territorial institution becomes fully visible only when it is challenged and risks collapsing, sliding into the mere fight for territorial control.

In contemporary political thinking, territoriality is somewhat downgraded. It is debated whether the traditional territoriality of state politics can be overcome, is going to be overcome or is already overcome. It is argued that rulership does not need to be territorial, as for instance in systems demarcated by kingship or in nomadic groups. Finally, it is argued that territorial and fixed systems of rule do not need to entail mutual exclusion, citing the historical example of medieval overlapping jurisdictions or more recent private or public trans-territorial regimes.[2] Sovereignty that is somehow linked to the territorial institution is seen as mere hypocrisy[3] and, in the post-sovereignty era, polycentric, multi-layered, multi-level forms of governance of territorial units are no longer what they used to be.[4] The argument is that new political forms prevail nowadays and that in the modern horizontal world, territory is no longer the main reference, neither for the issuing of commands nor for the production and distribution of behavioural compliance.

These arguments point to concrete developments, but I find them exaggerated. The examples are too limited, marginal and unstable to lead to the conclusion that systems of rule no longer differentiate subjects into territorially defined, fixed and mutually exclusive enclaves of domination. Be that as it may, if territoriality were really to dissipate in the contemporary or future world, then this dissipation would also profoundly affect what we call political institutions. The territory and its monopolisation by a specific group are still the preconditions for the development of any fundamental norm located at the top of the pyramid as a legitimate source of contro-grade normativity.

To argue this thesis, my first point is that the territorial institution is a *purely political institution* and not a social, economic or legal one. It is a meta-institution; that is, an institution that stays beyond the other institutions and is a precondition for their possibility.[5] The territorial

---

[2] Ruggie, J. G. (1993), 'Territoriality and beyond: problematising modernity in international relations', *International Organization*, 47: 138–74.

[3] Krasner, D. (1999), *Sovereignty: Organized Hypocrisy*, Princeton, NJ, Princeton University Press.

[4] Hooghe, L. and G. Marks (2003), 'Unraveling the central state but how? Types of multi-level governance', *American Political Science Review*, 97: 223–43.

[5] On the concept of 'meta-institution', see Lorini, G. (2014), 'Meta-institutional concepts: a new category for social ontology', *Rivista di Estetica*, 56: 127–39.

institution cannot be assimilated to the legal order because oppositions of fundamental territorial groups cannot be composed by legal and juridical mechanisms. The legal order only emerges as institutions imposed by the original territorial ruler or group in command. Whenever politics concerns the composition of the territorial group, the definitions of the rules on ruling and the acceptance of undesired outcomes, the legal order loses its capacity to frame politics. Therefore, the essential political conflict is that between the original territorial group – which defends the existing legal order – and any possible anti-territorial group that opposes it or wants to modify it. From the point of view of the former, law is consensus as it is produced following defined procedures. For the latter, law is dissent to the extent that the legal order is territorially produced and it is alien to it. For supporters of the territorial institution, law is freedom even if it reflects an associational option which is not possible to refuse; for others, law is subjection to the extent that it punishes and discriminates a dissociative option regarded as unimaginable.

Therefore, the normal political dynamics of opposition and conflict, cooperation and competition between socio-economic and political groups is possible only *within* the territorial legal order. When the latter is at stake, then inevitably opposing groups resort to extra-juridical means, and cooperation and coexistence become impossible in mere juridical terms. The dialectic of the socio-economic and political conflicts within the territorial institution is only an intra-legal dialectic, to the extent that such conflicts and interests originate within the legal order and can only be composed within it. Once constituted, the legal order limits these problems, but it cannot exclude them from politics without reducing politics to one of its variants: politics within the territorial institution – that is, politics within a legal order.

Neither can the territorial institution be assimilated to social ties and identities or economic transactions and interdependencies. Cooperation, solidarity, altruism and other orientations that belong to the patrimonies of humankind are forces with a limited scope of action that depend on the building of group identity, within which alone they are effective. They are a weak force, working at a relatively small social distance, which rapidly fades when the distance increases. In the political domain, such forces manifest themselves as ingredients of sub-aggregates, strengthening their internal unity and cohesion but similarly increasing inter-group animosity and hostility. When politics concerns the constitutive predicaments mentioned above, they cannot be solved by these social ties and identities or by economic interdependencies. These predicaments are only solved by the territorial institution as a de facto, not de jure, confinement of people in a coercive and involuntary form of living together. Human societies emerge from a process of synthesis among spontaneous antagonistic forces that eventually can only be constrained by a rigorous territorial authority.

My second point follows directly from the first, of which it is a specification. The territorial institution is not associational. Every organised group (company, society, guild, club, union, league, partnership or fellowship) has an order that reflects its functional existence and is an internal element of the association, its internal constitution. However, the order of these spontaneous associations does not generate any external order. True associations qualify as such because they are the expressions of spontaneous actions by the members concerning their formation and conservation, consensus and solidarity, based on voluntary adhesion and sharing of aims and resources. Although the internal order activates the group as a unitary actor, it nevertheless creates nothing outside itself in associational terms.

The territorial institution is often portrayed as an association among all citizens endowed with – like any association – a specific statute, a specific government and a specific membership similar and isomorphic to (and sometimes deriving from) other associations. It seems that the territorial institution is designed by the dictate of a given fundamental norm. It is described as if the citizens effectively belong to an association that is self-governing and self-sufficient and within which the powers of those governing and the rights and duties of those who are governed correspond to specific associational positions within the group.

However, the territorial institution constitutes an artificially bonded and forced association, for which the associative form is only a disguise of the exercise of power through which it was achieved. In fact, the territorial legal order does not constitute an associational order. Its juridicity is not equivalent to the institutionality of a true association because the society in it and under it does not constitute a true voluntarily constituted social group. In this fictitious association, we are enrolled involuntarily and independently of a will to be part of it. This forced aggregation cannot be framed within the experience of normal non-territorial social groups.

Authentic (voluntary) associations do not and cannot create external authoritative orders able to impose themselves on the unwilling. The presence of a legal order able to combine groups that cannot be assimilated without force and violence testifies a discontinuity and a qualitative difference to ordinary social groups. This also explains efforts by territorially dominant groups to generate their own associations via symbolic production, the creation of identities and enemies, and so on in attempts to dissimulate the non-associational nature of the original formation. A society constituted by mere socio-cultural and economic relationships does not exist in the absence of a monopolised territory on which to impinge. It is not conceivable that society builds the monopolising territory that most suits its goals, or constitutes itself in such a way as to exclude the territorial institution (as anarchist theory would put it). Government, bureaucracy, armed forces, police, judiciary, bodies of local government, parliamentary assemblies and state organisations are hardly imaginable without the territorial monopolisation institution. History does not provide a single example of a social group that dominates outside or against the territorial institution. Eventually, the territorial institution is the indefectible condition of any other social phenomenon. Apart from primordial identity codes (ethnicity, religion),[6] no other system (property, contracts, associations, rights, civil society, etc.) can be defined independently of the territorial institution.

From the above follows my third point: that the territorial institution should not be confused or identified with 'government'. Government employs its force apparatuses (police, judiciary, administration, etc.) to administer the law. However, whenever government is at stake, it becomes the target of attacks that are irreconcilable according to the law. This means that the legitimate monopoly of force presupposes the unchallenged functioning of the territorial institution but goes into crisis when an attack is directed against it. In these situations, both the territory and the state apparatuses – police, military and so on – tend to fractionalise and dissolve. Military and revolutionary subversion may be regarded (by Western observers after World War II) as an extraordinary event, but it is exactly that which qualifies and witnesses

---

[6] For the different codes of identity, see Eisenstadt, S. N. and B. Giesen (1995), 'The construction of collective identity', *Archives Européennes de Sociologie*, 36: 72–104.

the true nature of the territorial institution and the difficulty in reconciling it with the government as a legal entity and its instruments as legitimate, though violent, means. Government action rarely has territorial implications. The government does not need to test its political power if it enacts welfare provisions, energy-saving regulations or urban planning laws. However, the situation is different if the territorial integrity, private property or military alignments are at stake. The territorial institution represents the maximum concentration of political violence, which, between the alternatives of life or death, in a more or less impelling way smoulders in any territorially defined group.

My fourth point is that, outside the potential antagonism referred to above, the territorial legal order can be permissive and characterised by different political values. A territorial institution constituted by any new territorially dominant group, after a certain period in which it continues to function as a coercion institution derived from its original nature as a conquering army, develops into a form of provisional government. It calls for groups of citizens to participate in it to select the political class charged with its defence. There are dominant groups, but also many other groups, each engaged in an attempt to influence government decisions.

The territorial institution domesticates through a number of developments: through the assumption of a consensual and spontaneous associational pact among the members of the territory that resembles that of any authentic association; through formal and customary solidifying of the fundamental principles of the legal order to guarantee a degree of unchangeability of the law by the government; through subordination of the government to popular or electoral investiture; through the assumption of a transfer of power from the original territorial institution to the global community of members; and through the view of government as an instrument of the will of the citizens, their deliberations, their majorities, their representatives and so on. In this way, the order is legitimated and violence is excluded and substituted by the participation of the members of the community.

This legitimation process assumes the validity of the past for all those who will get the status of members by birth. Violence does not disappear, as the government must react to disobedience, but presents itself in qualitatively different terms. Coercion appears as an auto-punishment to the extent that the citizens inflict on themselves a punishment that the government achieves by applying a law that they themselves have chosen. However, this negotiated society excludes a unilateral rejection of the fictitious contract; it excludes the possibility that anyone could refuse the underwriting. The political institutions of the territory are not violence but consensus, while the territorial institution is violence against its enemies. This excludes the territorial institution being able to entirely dissolve itself within the legal order. However, the way in which this transformation is operated when successful is the preparation of a fundamental norm, of a constitution.

6.2 The Fundamental Norm

From the historical point of view, there is no original territorial group that does not prepare the ground before triggering the electoral and plebiscitary mechanisms of legitimation of the new fictitious political association. In all these cases the provisional government is crucial in this preparation, usually through repressive and purging operations meant to expel people hostile or unloyal to the new legal order from the army, the judiciary, the police and political groups. The passing of power from the provisional government to the legal government always takes place after the political landscape has been sanitised. Through these processes, the original territorial power dissolves in the constitution of the formal government and, eventually, in a popular selection of rulers. So, power-sharing devices generally begin to unfold when the role of the anti-territorial opposition has been limited or eradicated.

Therefore, even if the new legal order emerges as a forced association imposed by the original territorial power group, its normative content (principles, rights and obligations, form of government, etc.) and the selection of the people to govern result from the will of the citizens and from overcoming the original power acquired by some of those people because of conquest. This participation results in tangible political advantages for most citizens. And this is more possible the more the proportion and the resources of the citizens who remain alien and opposed to the new legal order are small and shrinking. New antagonisms among political groups which have emerged as associations within the legal order express themselves in the terms and means of the legal order itself.

In the new framework, members are not asked to make a choice between opposing territorial groups and orders. The territorial institution rarely leaves its future to be decided through electoral mechanisms. People may be asked to ratify the fundamental norm that will be the basis of the new legal order, of any conferral of public power, of any violation and of any newly devised rule of conduct. When the process of drafting a fundamental law is at least temporarily successful, the territorial institution identifies with this fundamental norm or constitutional text.

From the point of view of the allocation of public powers, which is what interests us here, constitutions can be defined as 'codes of rules which aspire to regulate the allocation of functions, powers and duties among the various agencies and offices of government, and define the relationships between these and the public'.[7] This definition is functional for a discussion of political institutions and excludes rules of personal conduct for the citizens to follow and a list of rights (minimum wages, rights to education and welfare, etc.). Constitutions identify authority as the ultimate source of the normative production from which all other sources derive.

The constitution is a normative text that is valid because it is produced and approved by some type of 'constituent body'. This constituent assembly is a simple extra-juridical political assembly. It ceases to be so and becomes a constituent assembly thanks to the fiction determined by its deliberation of the fundamental norm. It writes a constitution because it is constituent and it is constituent because it writes a constitution.[8] The constituent assembly has the function of hiding the fact that the law emerges from non-law. It helps this crucial passage. The fundamental norm is a fiction that guarantees the apparent anteriority of the juridical to the political, while it is in fact exactly the contrary.[9] The desired limitation of the power of political forces can be achieved only with norms the status of which is supra-ordered with respect to ordinary legal norms produced by politics, and the solution cannot but be the constitution.

---

[7] Finer, S. E. (1979), *Five Constitutions*, London, Penguin, p. 15.

[8] How the constituent assembly is composed, works and adopts procedures can affect the outcome in terms of stability, conflict resolution and public participation. See Ginsburg, T., Z. Elkins and J. Blount (2009), 'Does the process of constitution making matter?', *Annual Review of Law and Social Science*, 5: 201–29.

[9] Raz, J. (1970), *The Concept of a Legal System*, Oxford, Clarendon Press, pp. 128–39.

A constitution is part of positive law. However, with the adoption of a constitution, positive law becomes 'reflexive'. Two sets of norms differentiate. One, the constitution, regulates the condition of validity of the other. In this way, the production of rules is regulated by rules. Political power maintains its faculty to impose rules on society but no longer possesses the latitude of action of absolute rule. It is subject to legal constraints activated by procedural rules, rights to be respected and the interactions between political organisations made possible by these same rules.

A constitution generates the distinction between political decisions and the general criteria that preside over their formation. This separation allows politics to free itself from continually searching for and discussing principles, increasing its decisional capacity. It also facilitates the acceptance of decisions by those who had been on the losing side. Constitutions set procedural limits to the ways to arrive at decisions, and substantial limits to the area in which to make decisions. They may require a special consensus procedure for amendments, establish restrictions concerning subject matters that cannot be amended and disable the procedure of amendment in emergency situations.[10] Codified constitutions may be very specific in their content (like the Dutch, Swiss and Mexican constitutions) or, on the contrary, be written as a general framework model of constitutional generality (the US example).

Constitutions usually set a clear separation between the setting of law and the application of law. Once law is decided, it becomes independent of its political origins. Political power continues to exercise its decisional capacity on the law in the sense that it can repeal or modify it, but it cannot control its application. If rulers are authorised to give an authentic interpretation of the law they emanate and can call back to themselves any jurisdictional act, or interpret the rule in individual cases, then the capacity of law to generate security and trust in social behaviour is affected.

Constitutions are often distinguished as either 'codified' or 'uncodified' (because all constitutions are, in one way or another, 'written', including the British one). The practice of resorting to a fundamental

[10] For details and concrete examples, see Rasch, B. E. and R. D. Congleton (2006), 'Amendment procedures and constitutional stability', in Congleton, R. D. and B. Swedenborg (eds.), *Democratic Constitutional Design and Public Policy*, Boston, MA, MIT Press, pp. 319–42.

norm has a relatively recent but successful history. The British, American and French constitutions have had a lasting influence, generating a set of constitutional families that have spread around the world:

(1) British and dominions or Westminster-type constitutions (Canada, South Africa, etc.);
(2) American presidentialism with federalism, which has influenced most Latin American republics and, partly, the Chinese constitution of 1912, which never came into force;
(3) French 'revolutionary' constitutions with a strong ideological impact, influencing the Spanish 1812 constitution and, through this, the Spanish American republics and the Portuguese constitution of 1822;
(4) the family of constitutional monarchy constitutions with non-responsible cabinet government: Germany, 1867; Austria-Hungary, 1867; the Japanese constitution of 1889 modelled on the German one; Russia, 1905; and the Balkans after the collapse of the Ottoman empire.
(5) early French, Belgian, Dutch and Piedmont parliamentary constitutions and the Turkish 1908 constitution, shaped on the west European cabinet pattern;
(6) the post-1945 wholesaling of constitutions in Africa and Asia along colonial lines with hybrid forms.

There have been few true innovations. The two new constitutional models were the soviet and the corporatist/fascist ones. Both proved fake and the latter also short lived. On the contrary, the French post–World War II semi-presidential system has had a considerable impact in eastern Europe and other parts of the world, notwithstanding the negative precedents of the Weimar Republic and the second Spanish Republic.

Although rules are dominant in written constitutions, norms are no less relevant for constitutions than they are for all other institutions.[11] However, they are more fluid in terms of clarity, certainty and enforceability. No matter how specific a constitution may be, it will be incomplete and over time this may foster constitutional norms, given that

---

[11] For the opposite thesis, see Ridley, F. F. (1975), 'Political institutions: the script not the play', *Political Studies*, 23: 365–80. This author excludes political norms (or informal institutions, if one prefers) from the realm of political institutions.

constitutional changes are usually difficult. Almost inevitably norms develop to supplement or to put into practical effect provisions of the written constitution. Special statutes or extra canonical norms, like administrative regulations and practices, may become so important that they achieve the status of constitutional norms. Constitutional norms may arise from political practice and exert a compelling force on political actors. They establish new interpretations that in fact complement, add or remove part of the constitutional text without any formal amendment. These changes are usually seen as 'constitutional conventions', which develop when there are precedents, when political actors feel bound by the precedents and when reasons are developed in favour of respecting the precedents.[12] These conventions modify the specified allocation of public powers foreseen by the texts when, over time, they are acquiesced with or not objected to by actors that could raise a claim against them.

The United States presidential democracy is not only a product of the rules laid out in the constitution but is also rooted in norms such as gracious losing, the underuse of certain formal prerogatives and bipartisan consensus on critical issues. In this case, political norms help to explain how rules work. The two-term presidential norm in the USA is a case. The 1789 constitution was silent on the issue of presidential re-eligibility. However, since George Washington retired in 1796 after two terms, for almost 150 years a convention operated to limit the term to two mandates. In 1951, the twenty-second amendment formally entrenched the two-term limit in the constitution, triggered by the fourth consecutive election of F. D. Roosevelt in 1944.

The complex interplay between political norms and rules is evident in the debate on semi-presidentialism, which, through norm variations, sometimes operates like a parliamentary system (e.g. Austria, Ireland), as an example of dramatic dual-executive conflict (the Weimar Republic and the second Spanish Republic) or a hyper-presidential system (France and many eastern European countries). The cultural environment, particular historical experiences and the roles of powerful leaders are invoked to explain the different modalities.

---

[12] On constitutional conventions, see Marshall, G. (1984), *Constitutional Conventions: The Rules and Forms of Political Accountability*, Oxford, Oxford University Press.

Some Latin American countries offer striking examples of how norms and political practices can change the functioning of the constitution. In some cases, they have deliberately adopted constitutional norms and practices that result from agreements among political actors to overcome perceived problems in the constitutional text (in this case, a purely presidential one). In Uruguay, the fact that the party winning the presidency had no majority in the two houses of congress after elections in the 1980s led to special agreements known as 'National Intonation' and 'National Coincidence', in which the winning presidents (Sanguinetti and Lacalle) broadened the parliamentary support base of their presidencies. This reflected a coalition government logic that was alien to the presidential constitution.[13] In Bolivia in the 1980s, pure presidentialism was modified and made more like parliamentary practice. The fragmented electoral record of presidential elections and the constitution requirement (art 90, 1967 constitution) that in this case the congress should choose among the three best-placed candidates twice resulted in the candidate with the most votes not winning the presidency. The system was formally presidential because, once elected, the president held office for a fixed term without depending on the confidence of the congress, but the congressional election resulted in patterns of parliamentary coalitions that made the system work very differently from a presidential one.[14]

A similar case of norms changing the rules is offered by the Netherlands. Since the 1970s, it has become a somewhat established practice that no new coalition can be formed during a legislature and a cabinet cannot be replaced by a new one without the legitimation of a new vote, although, as in all parliamentary systems, there is no Dutch constitutional rule that prohibits this. In the Swiss Federal Council, the only constitutional requirement is that no single canton can have more than one councillor. 'Proporz' norms have developed which in 1959 led to the establishment of a 2,2,2,1 formula (two liberals, socialists and Christian democrats – formerly Catholic-Conservatives – and one member of the Swiss People's Party – formerly the Farmers' Party). In the British case, the flexible and uncodified constitution offers a great

---

[13] Although the resulting cabinets did not include the leaders of the parties involved and were not formally responsible to the houses.

[14] Linz, J. J. (1994), 'Presidential and parliamentary democracy: does it make a difference?', in Linz, J. J. and A. Valenzuela (eds.), *The Failure of Presidential Democracy*, Baltimore, MD, The Johns Hopkins University Press, pp. 34–9.

number of political institutions that are norms and customary practices. It is enough to say that the powerful office of the prime minister
has no statutory definition, with legal power being vested in the various
ministries, while in practice ministers are responsible to the prime
minister. Finally, consider how many times in parliamentary systems
prime ministers resign in the absence of any explicit no-confidence vote,
but instead because of vague norms that define declining support for
the existing cabinet. There are examples from multiple countries and
times.

In any context, the competent scholar can identify constitutional
norms and conventions with relative ease, yet the connection between
constitutional rules and norms requires careful handling because it may
involve some of the most fundamental political changes. New norms
may be merely additional and specify changes; in other cases, they
imply a fundamental reworking of the whole framework. The question
is the extent to which constitutional conventions affect core institutes
(such as responsibility, decision, competence, accountability) and
excessively damage the congruence between texts and practice. If
pushed to the extreme, constitutional changes resulting from the
incorporation of new norms or the repudiation of existing norms
may allow political actors to act in ways that are far from what the
codified constitution prescribes or permits. The disjuncture between
the constitutional text and official conduct may become so wide as to
qualify a constitutional text as nominal or even fake.[15] The boundary
between norms that modify the text in a compatible way and norms
that make it nominal or fake is sometimes difficult to draw. Hybrid
cases often result from these ambiguities (see Section 6.3 on regimes).

In conclusion, the connection between codified texts and norms or
practices separates *working constitutions*, made up of dominant written rules supplemented by norms which are congruent with the basic
institutional principles, from *façade constitutions*, in cases in which
practices and norms contradict the codified text, and from *fake constitutions*, where political institutions are replaced with personalistic
practices and arbitrary decisions. To judge this issue of working versus
façade versus fake constitutions, we may ask whether any of the
founding political institutes is profoundly offended by the changes

[15] Albert, R. (2015), 'How unwritten constitutional norms change written
constitutions', *Dublin University Law Journal*, 38: 387–418.

and whether the balance among institutes is completely destroyed. I will return to this later in this chapter.

The territory and the constitution are somewhat encompassing entities if analysed as institutions. The territorial institution is primordial. It exists even with minimal or fake political institutions. It is antecedent to any constitutionalised order and it persists in the background of any. The constitution defines a large part, although not the entirety, of the political institutes and cannot be dealt with as a single institution without redundancies, as I discussed in Chapter 5. However, the combination of specific institutes and their relationships define the macro-institution that we usually label the 'institutional regime'.

6.3 Institutional Regimes

Some analyses take a *holistic approach* to regimes, conceptualising them as whole entities that include more factors beyond the institutional regime delineated by the fundamental norms: parties and party system configurations, political values and principles, the nature of the political elite and so on. Although these additional elements improve the characterisation of the type of regime, they somewhat blur the precise institutional configuration. Here I focus on *institutional regimes*, distinguishing them as much as possible from *political regimes*, to which I dedicate a note at the end of the chapter. This is not to deny that a two- or a multi-party system, an adversarial or consensual culture, simple or complex cultural infrastructure, the variety of capitalist economy, fragmented or corporatist interest representation, and a cross-cutting or reinforcing cleavage structure affect the functioning of the institutional regime. However, the constellations and structures of these factors are *not institutionally prescribed*. They may have affected the genesis of the institutional design, its present working and its changes. They may be yardsticks to evaluate the compatibility of a given institutional regime with a given social-political structure and culture. Nevertheless, these considerations assume we have the capacity to analytically differentiate the institutional configuration of the regime from its socio-political structure/culture.[16]

---

[16] Easton, D. (1990), *The Analysis of Political Structures*, London, Routledge, p. 14 defends a holistic approach to regimes. Duverger's idea of seeing an institutional regime as a constellation of institutions, where the institutions are the single stars, is more in line with my argument. Duverger, M. (1960, 5th

An analytical approach that separates the institutional design of the regime from its socio-cultural underpinning has its pitfalls. The most important of these is its potential endogeneity. It can be argued that the institutional regime is artificial because it is endogenous to the configurations and preferences of actors.[17] However, as was previously argued (Section 3.1.7), the institutional regime's endogeneity is no different from the endogeneity of the structure of actors or of their preferences. A two- versus multi-party system reflects the institutional constraints on inclusion/exclusion and on the representation norms/rules (electoral system) as much as it reflects the socio-cultural determinants of actors' preferences. The latter, in turn, are historically shaped by institutional configurations and political offers. Much depends on where we put the independent variable because in social reality nothing is ontologically exogenous unless we make it so by assumption. The only way to overcome the endogeneity problem that affects all human affairs is to study institutions, actors, preferences and socio-cultural determinants together. Both holistic and analytical approaches to the regime have some advantages and some pitfalls, and here I vindicate the possibility of studying political institutions independently of possible endogenous effects. The analytical approach is a methodological choice and does not reflect any ontological assumption. I investigate what an institutional theory of regimes should look like.

Following this idea, an institutional regime is defined by the specific configuration of institutes and their relationships. Regimes are characterised by the inter-institute rules and norms that define their balancing principle. The logic of each institute is to realise itself at its maximum possible value. However, when this happens, it is usually at the expense of other institutes. The possibility exists of an insufficient realisation below the acceptable minimum, and of an excessive realisation becoming injurious to other institutes. Therefore, in a balanced realisation of an institutional regime that embodies elements of power-sharing, political institutes must be adequately realised without unnecessarily offending the others.

Institutional regimes can therefore be characterised by the proportion of safeguards and the realisation of fundamental power-sharing

edition), *Institutions Politiques et Droit Constitutionnel*, Paris, Presses Universitaires de France, p. 13.

[17] Przeworski, 'Institutions matter?'.

institutes. There are different historical and geographical balances of the nine core institutes discussed in Chapter 5. There are different balances in times of peace and war. There is unbalancing that generates different types of institutional regimes. The balancing between different institutes can be analytically represented with indifference curves that yield different combinations of the different institutes without any of them falling below the minimum point at which they become unbalanced. When this happens, the institutional regime changes its nature. We can imagine these curves as in Figure 6.1, as a combination of institutes that yields the same utility for the entire community until the point is reached when the denial of the institutes identifies a qualitative jump into a different type of regime.

In democratic institutional regimes special courts (constitutional or supreme) are responsible for rules of recognition that oversee the balancing in such a way that the measure of institute A shall never be injurious to institute B beyond what is necessary in the specific circumstance. The difficulty is to define the point X beyond which the realisation of institute A offends institute B to the point of making it ineffective. Perhaps courts can define the minimum below which

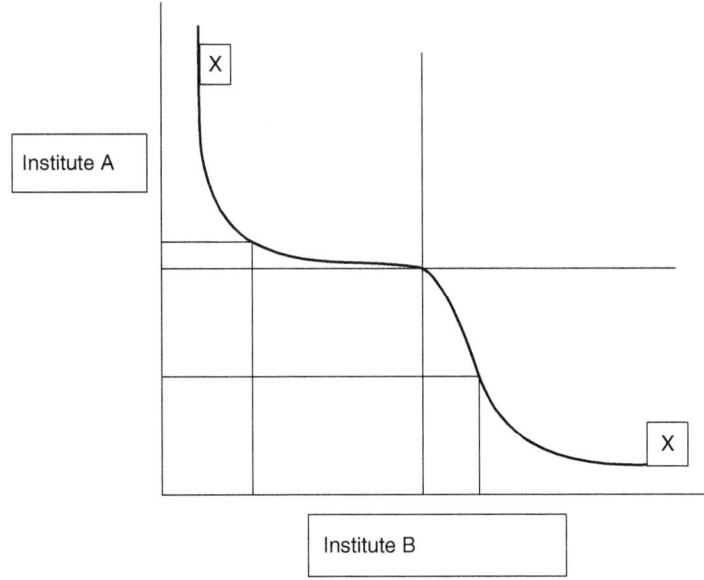

Figure 6.1 Balancing political institutes.

a political institute ceases to exist and is injured by other political rules. It is doubtful, however, that a constitutional court can decide in each circumstance which combination of institutions is adequate and this is inevitably left to the balance of political forces.[18]

This idea of balancing among essential core institutes is inspired by the classic political philosophers' anchoring of their preferred conception in the empirical world to a specific balancing of values, from which they try to deduce or derive the conditionality of other values. Kant takes as his fundamental normative value the concept of 'freedom', from which he deductively derives the principle of 'autonomy' and, at the empirical level, its preference for the rights of liberty and equality.[19] For Spinoza, the supreme value is internal order guaranteed by the state combined with the value of autonomy. Individuals will only respect obligations to other individuals if the state manages to guarantee security, from which he derives a preference for the republican model.[20] For Hobbes, the supreme value is peace and personal security, from which he opts for the absolutist model as the only one able to guarantee them. These are the conditions for consensus on the obligation among individuals.[21] For Locke, the supreme value is political freedom joined with the principle of autonomy, from which he derives a strong preference for liberal institutions. Consent to law is conditional on these laws safeguarding liberty and property.[22] For Rousseau, the supreme value is equality. This value combines with the usual principle of autonomy and through the medium of the general will leads to a preference for direct democracy and a sort of assembly

---

[18] In a 2017 ruling (sentence 35/2017), the Italian Constitutional Court declared an electoral reform (approved by law no. 52 of 5 May 2016) unconstitutional because it introduced a double-ballot majority prize, the disproportionality of which *excessively* offended the representation principles embedded in the constitution. The Court, however, did not discuss, and was unequipped to discuss, whether the offence to the representation principle was balanced by gains in other institutes such as the selection rules for the prime minister or the cabinet's visibility and political responsibility.

[19] Kant, I. (1958 (1797)), *Groundwork of the Methaphisic of Morals*, New York, Harper Torchbooks.

[20] Spinoza, B. (1991 (1670)), *Theologico-Political Treatise*, Indianapolis, IN, Hackett Publishing Company.

[21] Hobbes, T. (2012 (1651)), *Leviathan or The Matter, Forme and Power of a Commonwealth Ecclesiastical and Civil*, Oxford, Oxford University Press.

[22] Locke, J. (1988 (1689)), *Two Treaties of Government*, Cambridge, Cambridge University Press.

regime, with no reference to the liberal values of the separation of powers.[23] These political philosophers 'balance' values or principles, not institutes. Nevertheless, through a deductive or derivative argument they come to concrete institutional arrangements seen as ideal balancing of the values. We can follow a similar logic by starting from the core institutes and characterise types of regimes in this way.

Totalitarian and dictatorial rulers either do not create political institutions or they reduce them to fake and façade institutes. Self-appointed tyrants and appointed leaders turned dictators rule without significant constraints on their personal leadership. The hierarchical norms of decisions prevail over any other institute and reduce it to a façade. Every type of authoritarian regime excludes certain political actors unfriendly to the regime through manipulation of selection and representation rules/norms and fraudulent voting procedures to the advantage of the ruling coalition, and manipulates voters through controlled information. In the context of the sacrifice of the inclusion, representation and responsibility institutes, all other institutes become façades.

Variations may involve the extent to which decisions are hierarchical or open to other decisional rules: veto rules allow the ruling leader and coalition to override any possible undesired decisions and practices, purely nominal competence norms/rules, and accountability and redress institutes lacking independence. Recent scholarship argues that authoritarian regimes without any form of power-sharing institute don't last as long, on average, as those that have at least some of them.[24] This is the reason why a growing number of regimes have let other bodies such as legislative assemblies enjoy a level of autonomy in at least some areas[25] and allow a limited inclusion of groups or parties not closely aligned with the ruler and ruling coalition to contest controlled and manipulated elections. The latter are useful to provide the

---

[23] Rousseau, J. J. (2012 (1762)), *The Social Contract*, London, Penguin.

[24] Gandhi, J. and A. Przeworski (2007), 'Authoritarian institutions and the survival of autocrats', *Comparative Political Studies*, 40: 1279–1301; Geddes, B., J. Wright and E. Frantz (2014), 'Autocratic breakdown and regime transitions: a new data set', *Perspectives on Politics*, 12: 313–31; Miller, M. K. (2015), 'Democratic pieces: autocratic elections and democratic development since 1815', *British Journal of Political Science*, 45: 501–30.

[25] See Krol, G. (2020), 'Legislating parliaments in authoritarian regimes: Eurasian legislatures and presidents compared', Florence, European University Institute, PhD dissertation.

regime with at least a modicum of information about the environment, facilitating its survival through adaptation.

Constitutional monarchies in continental Europe in the nineteenth and early twentieth centuries included many balancing institutes and had high levels of inclusion, but were characterised by a lack of political responsibility of the executive authorities to anybody except the monarch, which offended representation and inclusion. More balanced power-sharing institutes characterise polyarchies. However, different types of institutional polyarchies can be described by different balances of the various institutes.

6.3.1 Presidentialism

Pure presidentialism rests on the balancing of three institutes: the mode of popular selection of the top executive; the absence of a responsibility institute between the executive and the legislature; and a (quasi-) monopoly of legislative competence of the chambers. Presidentialism sacrifices the institute of political responsibility and rests on two *institutionally unconnected* top bodies. This is the core balancing principle from which most other features of the institutional regime derive. Presidents and chambers can, therefore, be in an incongruent political fit and this usually requires a negotiation relationship between them.

In presidential institutional regimes of this type, the question becomes how 'governing' and 'legislating' can be fused without too much loss on either the executive or the legislative side of the ledger.[26] The institute of veto powers against the assembly and the initiative, emergency and decree powers of the presidency (endemic in Latin American presidentialism) balance the legislative competences of the assemblies. They represent the presidential defence against parliamentary trespass. To a large extent, the interaction among presidents and assemblies imposes joint action, which requires negotiation agreements to achieve the non-veto of the president and agreement between the houses. It is a *compulsory negotiation system* in which inter-organisational unanimity/consensus is often the decision rule for new legislation. A high degree of agreement advantages the status quo as any of the key actors may delay or block change by increasing the transaction costs. Possible deadlocks are overcome by negotiations that allow moving from formal unanimity to

[26] Sartori, *The Paradox of Governing by Legislating*.

consensus decision rules. A strong agenda setter may explore the limits of solutions which are more acceptable or reach near unanimity. 'Checks and balances' is therefore an expression that should be reserved for this institutional configuration in which the absence of a responsibility institute obliges core bodies to check and influence each other's positions in view of a compromise.

6.3.2 Hyper-Presidentialism in Latin America

Latin American presidential systems are unique in their dominance of the presidential institution. While early constitutions in the region tended to follow the US presidency model, subsequent constitutions evolved away from this in favour of giving the president more authority in law-making.[27] These regimes, despite resting on the absence of the responsibility institute, do not put the legislature and the executive on the same level but sacrifice the checks and balances principle so that neither the assembly nor the judiciary have the capacity to force the president into a compulsory negotiation system.

In some systems, the president has the power to dissolve the chambers before a general election (as in Uruguay, Venezuela and Chile) and also has important legislative initiative, decree and veto power, which can be overridden by an absolute majority of the legislature (Brazil and Colombia) or, in some cases, by a two-thirds majority (Argentina and Chile). Using his veto power, which is a reactive instrument, the president can stop any attempt to change existing legislation. On the contrary, using his decree power, which is a proactive law-making power, he can promote significant legislative changes. In contrast to bills passed by the chambers, presidential decrees have immediate force of law. Some constitutions allow a delegation of legislative power to the president. Moreover, presidents can circumvent the parliamentary agenda by presenting numerous decrees and determining the priority of decrees to be examined by the parliament. This often makes the legislative process increasingly difficult and, consequently, strengthens the presidential power over the legislative function. In short, the system does not foresee any institute of responsibility of one body to another, and if it does, it is to favour the

---

[27] Cheibub, J. A., J. Elkins and T. Ginsburg (2010), 'Latin American presidentialism in comparative and historical perspective', *Texas Law Review*, 89: 170–3.

presidential capacity to dissolve the assemblies. On the other side, hyper-presidentialism does not balance presidential rule by forcing it into a joint negotiation decisional rule typical of the pure presidential system.

6.3.3 Parliamentarism

All parliamentary systems are characterised by the predominance of the political responsibility institute: the power of the assembly to censure the executive and force its resignation. In principle, the political responsibility institute makes the assembly predominate over the executive, and in an assembly type of parliamentarism this is unbalanced by other rules/norms. However, the triangular relationship among the head of state, the executive and the assembly/ies is anchored to the responsibility institute in the sense that each body has some capacity to appoint/remove the others. The head of state (alone or in conjunction with the premier) often has the power to dissolve the assembly in political circumstances in which she judges it incapable of supporting any executive.

The often-mentioned second feature of parliamentary regimes is the institute of indirect parliamentary selection of the top executive positions (both the prime minister and the head of state). However, this difference is less decisive as there are and have been cases of prime ministers being popularly elected, of cabinets not directly appointed by the assembly and of parliamentary heads of state being directly elected. Therefore, the link between the assembly/ies and its specialised committee that is in charge of the daily executing and governing functions is the cornerstone of the institutional regime, from which the balance with the other institutes derives. This link generates specific problems typical of the parliamentary system.

In the case of bicameral parliamentary structures, the decision rules require forms of inter-organisational negotiation, which become more complex the more the two chambers have symmetric powers, reflect different principles of representation and are elected with different electoral systems. To avoid the situation of a joint decision trap, the solution is to resort to unicameralism or to asymmetries of competence rules between the two chambers that introduce a predominance of one of them (through veto or overriding).[28] If control over the executive

---

[28] Sartori, G. (1997), 'Problems with parliamentary systems', in *Comparative Constitutional Engineering*, pp. 185–9.

through investiture, confidence and censure votes (the political responsibility of the cabinet) and the mechanisms of legislative overriding are not reserved for a single chamber, inter-organisational negotiations affect not only legislative production but also the governability of the system. In other words, under the predominance of the responsibility institute legislative decision rules inevitably affect the life, stability and effectiveness of the cabinet.

Under the institute of the executive's political responsibility, legislative and executive activities are linked by a complex set of institutional norms/rules. Parliamentary group cohesion is usually enhanced by the executive responsibility institute (imposed by the need to support/ oppose the cabinet) but it also requires high levels of enforced (by headquarters) or spontaneous (ideological) discipline. These in part derive from the selection institute for MPs (the electoral system can force the discipline of parliamentary groups) and partly from the procedural rules of the assemblies (affecting the possibility of defectors splitting and joining other parliamentary groups).[29] However, they also reflect non-institutional features of a political and cultural nature (e.g. the strength of party organisation, party and candidate financing rules, and the normative acceptability of defection by members of parliament and of cabinets changing cap during the legislature).

Gridlocks can occur in the capacity of the assembly/ies to provide stable support for the cabinet. Therefore, the balance between executive and legislative powers depends on stabilisation of this support. Constructive votes of confidence make it difficult to withdraw support from an executive. Forms of 'rationalised parliamentarism' (like the French package vote and the French and British guillotine) basically aim to reduce or limit the legislature encroaching on the executive. They functionally resemble the veto powers of the president under presidentialism.

In short, the pre-eminence of the responsibility institute extends the problem of legislative efficiency to that of the stability of the executive cabinet through that of the discipline of groups of members of parliament. This can be seen in two opposite ways. A strong institutional link between the assembly majority and the cabinet may be an efficient device to increase the scope, speed and coherence of legislation. On

---

[29] See Volpi, E. (2019), 'The politics of turning coat: a comparative and historical analysis of party switching', Florence, European University Institute, PhD dissertation, ch. 5.

the other hand, in cases of weak or no discipline, coalitions and a symmetrical bicameral structure, the same link may produce exactly the opposite effects of unstable executives, gridlocks between chambers and delayed or failed legislation. Deadlocks occur in parliamentary regimes because party and coalition discipline are not derived exclusively from the institutional requirement to support the cabinet.[30]

Many other institutional features are important, but secondary, in parliamentary systems. The parliament may elect the executive (Ireland, Germany, Switzerland[31]); the head of state appoints the cabinet but this can only enter office by receiving a formal vote of confidence (Belgium, Italy); or ministers accede to office without receiving any formal endorsement from parliament in the absence of explicit non-confidence (the Netherlands, Denmark, Norway, Sweden, Finland, Iceland). There might be considerable differences in the extent to which the cabinet or the assembly controls legislative initiatives.[32] These variations, although important, are not crucial as none decisively offend the cornerstone of the political responsibility institute.

6.3.4 Semi-Presidentialism

Many countries in western Europe, in post-Soviet eastern states, in Latin America and in other parts of the world[33] adopt the institutional

---

[30] Cheibub, J. A. and F. Limogi (2002), 'Democratic institutions and regime survival: parliamentary and presidential democracies reconsidered', *Annual Review of Political Science*, 5: 151–79.

[31] Mentioning Switzerland in a discussion of parliamentarism may be contested. The cabinet cannot be deposed during a legislative term and there is no vote of confidence between elections, and therefore the principle of political responsibility is absent or muted. If we follow this line, the Swiss case becomes an unclassifiable platypus, a unique case. However, although the *collective responsibility* of the Federal Council is not formalised, its members remain *individually responsible* and can be forced to resign (the last time this happened was the case of Elisabeth Kopp in the 1980s). Moreover, I much doubt that a Federal Council could remain in charge against the will of the parliamentary majority, were this to be the case. It has never been the case so far. I suspect that this fact owes more to Swiss political culture than to the institutional rules.

[32] Polsby, N. W. (1975), 'Legislatures', in Greenstein, F. I. and N. W. Polsby (eds.), *The Handbook of Political Science*, Reading, Addison-Wesley, vol. 5, pp. 277–91.

[33] An incomplete list includes the historical cases of the Weimar Republic and the second Spanish Republic and the contemporary cases of Iceland, Austria, Ireland, Portugal, France and Finland in western Europe; Lithuania, Romania, Poland, Bulgaria, Slovakia, Croatia, Serbia, Macedonia, Russia and Ukraine

configuration labelled 'semi-presidentialism'.[34] The institutional configuration of 'semi-presidential' systems has a momentous particularity. It combines and tries to maximise two institutes that are largely incompatible: the institute of the direct popular selection of the president as head of state and the institute of the cabinet executive's political responsibility to the assembly/ies. These two institutes are incompatible in the sense that their potential cannot be maximised at the same time in the decisional institutes. Neither does a clear principle exist that establishes the predominance of one institute over the other. The fact is that no decisional rule can simultaneously satisfy the institute of direct selection and that of executive responsibility. In practice, one must be sacrificed. We could say that semi-presidentialism is not anchored either to the institute of political responsibility or to the institutional non-connectedness of top political bodies. In a different reading, semi-presidential systems are anchored to both institutes simultaneously. The president–prime minister dualism is without an unquestioned principle of hierarchy. At the same time, it does not force these positions into permanent negotiation made necessary by their mutual independence.[35]

An improvement of classification comes from a further differentiation of semi-presidential regimes into two sub-types: the *premier-presidentialism* type – in which the president has significant powers but the cabinet is truly responsible to the assembly – and the *president-parliamentary* type, in which the institute of responsibility of the cabinet is shared between the president and the assembly, with a predominance of the former.[36] These sub-types correctly portray two predominant equilibria defined by differences in rules that are

(since 2014 and previously between 2006 and 2010) in post-communist Europe; Peru in Latin America; and Burkina Faso, Cape Verde, East Timor, Madagascar, Mali, Mongolia, Niger, São Tomé and Príncipe, Sri Lanka and Guinea-Bissau, Mozambique, Namibia, Senegal, Taiwan and Georgia (between 2004 and 2013) in other parts of the world.

34 The label was coined in Duverger, M. (1980), 'A new political system model: semi-presidential government', *European Journal of Political Research*, 8: 165–87.

35 See Bahro, H., B. Bayerlein and E. Veser (1998), 'Duverger's concept: semi-presidential government revisited', *European Journal of Political Research*, 34: 201–24.

36 Shugart, M. S. and J. M. Carey (1992), *Presidents and Assemblies: Constitutional Design and Electoral Dynamics*, Cambridge, Cambridge University Press, pp. 1–27.

usually quite clearly established in constitutions. Therefore, the two sub-types define more homogeneous sets of regimes.

The premier-presidentialism type tends to produce a more stable institutional configuration as it establishes a hierarchy between the two institutes to the advantage of cabinet responsibility in front of the assembly. On the contrary, the president-parliamentary type makes a less clear-cut choice and lets the cabinet's responsibility be shared between the president and the assembly. The resulting tension between the two institutes is left unresolved and the system is difficult to harmonise as its way of working depends less on competence rules than on the relation between parliamentary and presidential majorities. Therefore, the president-parliamentary type of regime is freer to evolve depending on political circumstances, traditions, special events and personalities. It can either slide into forms of hyper-presidentialism or into forms of premier-presidentialism without significant constitutional revision of the main institutes, but merely because of new configurations of political actors that modify practices and norms. In the language of political institute analysis, the difference is simply that in the first sub-type the institute of political responsibility in front of the assembly prevails, while in the second it enters into contrast with the powers of the directly elected president, with the result that one institute is offended in a decisive way.

In general, semi-presidential regimes have a propensity to expose the institutional rules to institutional norm deviation in practice, and this explains the enormous variety of cases that fall in this category. The result is a bewildering variety of special arrangements that range along the continuum of the indifference curve that goes from offending the institute of parliamentary responsibility to offending the institute of direct selection for the top leadership position. Intermediate positions are possible, determined by traditions and precedents, the vagaries of political events, personalities, the composition of the parliamentary majority and the position of the president in relation to this majority. While any configuration of institutes always leaves much to be specified to describe real practices, semi-presidentialism is simply the Mecca of such indeterminacy.

There is a general point to be highlighted in cases of semi-presidentialism. Although it may work and develop in different directions and sacrifice one institute to the advantage of another, unapplied and idle institutes should not be regarded as non-institutions. These hibernated institutes may reactivate in different circumstances. This does not only work for semi-presidentialism, of course. Hitler destroyed any alternative authority except his own. Mussolini left untouched the Albertino Statute of 1856 and the monarchy, which he had to regret on 25 July 1943, when both reactivated after a long period of dormancy. This is a reminder that, unlike institutions such as social norms, role expectations and so on, which cannot be defined irrespective of their effective operation, political institutions that are in desuetude or unapplied should not be regarded as non-institutes or non-rules.

6.3.5 *Divided Government*

It is often argued that presidentialism and semi-presidentialism may generate 'divided government'. Divided government in non-intentional power-sharing rests on the absence of the institute of responsibility. It results from different partisan orientations of different bodies and can only occur when such bodies are 'separated' and 'irresponsible' to one another, as in pure presidentialism. However, presidential regimes explicitly foresee this possibility and usually have other institutional mechanisms to handle the forced negotiation system that derives from divided government. In contrast, in semi-presidential systems, and particularly in their *president-parliamentary* variant, the divided government category is translated into 'cohabitation' periods in which the two institutes of direct selection of the president and of cabinet responsibility are in opposition, and usually one prevails over the other.

The concept of divided government is often broadened to all cases in which the executive fails to be supported by a legislative majority.[37] This implies that there is divided government in all cases of an absence of majority in the assembly. In this version, the concept of divided government also applies to parliamentary systems in cases of minority, caretaker or technical cabinets that do not enjoy majority support in the legislature. I disagree with this extension of the divided government concept. Divided government is a normal possibility in systems with

---

[37] Other versions identify divided government with political divisiveness, even within similar majorities or within coalition governments in parliamentary regimes. Elgie rightly dismisses these extreme conceptualisations. Elgie, R. (ed.) (2001), *Divided Government in Comparative Perspective*, Oxford, Oxford University Press, pp. 1–20.

unrelated executives and legislatures. In contrast, with the predominance of the responsibility institute, any cabinet, either majority, minority, caretaker or other, can survive only thanks to the at least implicit
support of the assembly and can be brought down any moment this
fails. In practice, the result may be accentuated negotiation decision-
making between the executive and the legislature. In this case, we see
the advantage of separating institutional analysis from broader political factors. From the institutional point of view, divided government is
a specific configuration that can only result from the separate election
of the chief executive office and of the legislative chamber(s), made
more likely by differences in the electoral rules and by the absence of
concurrent elections of the two bodies.

6.3.6 Federalism

Even federalism can be described as a specific combination of different
political institutes, whether we understand it in a restricted way, as
constitutive federalism, or in a more extended way, as a form of ex-post
federalisation or regionalisation.[38] Federalism is usually discussed in
connection with issues such as the size of the country, bicameralism,
efficient provision of public services, ethnic heterogeneity, liberal democracy, the protection of individual rights, the viability of other lower-
level state institutions, the size of government and inbuilt pro-status
quo bias. Here I only focus on the characterisation of federalism in
terms of the core political institutes discussed in this chapter.
Federalism is defined by specific values of four political institutes:
inclusion, representation, decision and competence.

From the point of view of *inclusion rules*, federalism compounds
government by explicitly recognising the right of inclusion of sub-state-
territorial units in various aspects of the political process. The form of
association varies, but all federal states recognise territories as constitutive elements of the polity under the neat epigram 'self-rule plus
shared rule'. The US and Australian federal constitutions focus more
on federal competencies since states already existed with their own
constitutions. The Swiss constitution is the most explicit in securing

---

[38] Riker, W. H. (1975), 'Federalism', in Greenstein, E. L. and N. W. Polsby (eds.),
Handbook of Political Science, vol. 5, pp. 93–172, 101 and Elazar, D. E. (1987),
Exploring Federalism, Tuscaloosa, University of Alabama Press, p. 12.

the role of the cantons to protect their linguistic diversity.[39] Although more centralist in its original design, the Canadian constitution recognises the role of the provinces. The German Basic Law adopted in 1949 gives a more comprehensive account of the interdependent roles of federal and *Länder* governments. The essence of federalism is a presence of two spheres of government, neither of which is sovereign but each of which has some constrained powers.

As a mode of the *representation institute*, federalism combines and balances individual representation with representation of territories and a specific legislative body dedicated to representing them. Although bicameralism is not an exclusive property of federalism, it takes a strong asymmetric character in it. In this sense, federalism affects constraints and opportunities for social organisation, often offering different sets of choices for voters, parties and groups.[40]

As a form of the *competence norms/rules*, federalism affects the vertical division of public powers. However, central government institutions often include the federalist dimension within their institutional design, and federal institutions, therefore, are not limited to the vertical dimension of the division of powers.[41] On the issue of the division of competences, the constitution can enumerate federal powers and guarantee the remaining ones to the states (US model) or alternatively can enumerate both sets of powers and sometimes also engage in defining the intermediate grey area of concurrent competences. In some cases, implementation is shared; in others, it is reserved for the states. For this,

---

[39] For a general review of variants of federalism, see Galligan, B. (2006), 'Comparative federalism', in Rhodes, R. A. W., S. A. Binder and B. A. Rockman (eds.), *The Oxford Handbook of Political Institutions*, pp. 261–80.

[40] Tuschhoff, C. (1999), 'The compounding effect: the impact of federalism on the concept of representation', *West European Politics*, 22: 16–33 emphasises federalism as a form of representation.

[41] Loewenstein, K. (1965), *Political Power and the Governmental Process*, Chicago, IL, University of Chicago Press distinguishes between interstate federalism and intrastate federalism in the sense indicated in the text. For Braun, 'Canada epitomises interstate federalism with Canadian provinces having no direct say in federal legislation or implementation, but being relatively autonomous in their own legislative powers. Germany, on the contrary, has intrastate federalism with the Lander having a direct say in national legislation, through representation in the Bundesrat, and the main responsibility in its implementation.' Braun, D. (2004), 'Intergovernmental relationships and fiscal policymaking in federal countries', in Imbeau, L. M. and F. Petry (eds.), *Politics, Institutions, and Fiscal Policy: Deficits and Surpluses in Federated States*, London, Lexington Books, pp. 21–48, 47.

federalism requires a redress institute to deal with potential conflicts of competence. In federal systems the constitutional jurisdiction and legislative overrule by the courts is enhanced and complicated by the institutionalised plurality of normative sources.

Finally, as a form of *decision rule*, federalism fosters forms of inter-organisational negotiation modes of decisions. These can take the form of inter-chamber negotiations, as the different chambers represent truly different interests and concerns. However, this is not the case when the state chamber is ineffective in this function. Because Australian parties are dominant and well integrated across the national and state spheres, senators represent party interests that are national rather than state-focussed. In Canada, the state chamber's ineffectiveness in representing the states' interests is due to the appointment of senators by the national government on political and patronage grounds.

As was argued in the previous chapter, the delegation institute is no longer applicable to vertical intergovernmental relations. These are no longer two sets of separate cross-cutting machinery.[42] A steady growth in public policy responsibilities has forced all types of government to resort to at least some form of decentralisation, enhancing the independent role of local-level governments and generating a large grey area of competence overlap. In this way, the notion of federalism has extended to include not only constitutive federalism but also other forms of differently decentralised regionalism. These developments have fostered the integration of different theories of federalism, regionalisation and decentralisation under the general hat of 'multi-level governance' seen as different arrangements of supply and demand for jurisdictions.

A part of the literature challenges the efficiency of monopolistic, territorially fixed and nested governments, stating that dispersion of governance across multiple jurisdictions is more flexible than concentration of governance in just one. Other scholars argue that efficiency and redistribution are better served by amalgamating numerous and overlapping jurisdictions into a limited number of municipal governments. Beyond the bedrock agreement that flexible governance must be multi-level, these is no consensus on whether jurisdictions should be

---

[42] To the point that in the United States, 'public administration and the processes of federalism have merged to a nearly indistinguishable point'. Agranolf, R. M. and M. McGuire (2001), 'American federalism and the search for models of management', *Public Administration Review*, 61: 671–81, 671.

designed around particular communities or functional and policy problems. Should jurisdictions bundle competencies or should they be functionally specific? Should jurisdictions be limited in number or should they proliferate? The debate focusses much on efficiency considerations in the provision of public goods and leaves backstage the question of power-sharing among levels of government.[43] The chief benefit of multi-level governance lies in its scale flexibility. Its chief cost lies in the transaction costs of coordinating multiple jurisdictions. Marks and Hooghe rightly point out that territorial jurisdictions are more auspicious to citizens' voice structures, while functional jurisdictions rest on a valorisation of exit options.[44]

It is interesting to explore the issue of whether multi-level governance can be regarded as a new or additional political institute that has evolved from complexification of the connection between territorial and functional jurisdictions. However, in this case some work needs to be done on more clearly defining the norms and rules that constitute the institute and its different modalities.

6.4 Inter-institutional Links

The concise discussion of the shortcuts that define different types of regimes in the previous section was meant to show that, *from the institutional point of view*, these regimes and their potential variations can be described in terms of predominant and subordinate institutes and of balancing among institutes. It was necessarily a concise treatment, but a promising one. Perhaps we should altogether avoid identifying different institutional designs with shortcuts such as presidentialism, parliamentarism, semi-presidentialism, unicameral and multi-cameral systems. Instead, the latter should be defined starting with the types of institutes that define their core feature. A limited set of institutes and their relationships with other institutes define these regimes precisely. Variations can be identified by adding other institutes, and design inconsistencies are clearly identified by the

---

[43] This is not the case of Casella, A. and B. R. Weingast (1995), 'Elements of a theory of jurisdictional change', in Eichengreen, B., J. Frieden and J. von Hagen (eds.), *Politics and Institutions in an Integrated Europe*, New York, Springer, pp. 11–41.

[44] Hooghe and Marks, 'Unraveling the central state, but how?'. An excellent summary of these debates, on which I draw.

concomitant presence of institutes that are incompatible or difficult to harmonise. Let us discuss some of the advantages of this strategy of institutional regime analysis.

A structural discussion in terms of one or more chambers is sometimes insufficient or misleading, while the apportionment of conferral norms/rules better identifies the variety of solutions. In the USA, the presidential veto powers have led to the institutional design being described as a tricameral system. In Belgium, there are five legislative assemblies with differentiated competences but also increasingly overlapping ones. The great variety of multi-cameralisms are usually arranged in terms of the 'congruence' of the representative principle[45] and the 'symmetry' (or similarity) of power/competences.[46] Nowadays, at least one chamber is 'representative' of the whole citizenship, while the other(s) may represent different constituencies: a historical nobility second chamber; a federal senate indirectly elected with a territorial base (French senate); representatives of state governments (the German Federal Republic); guild/corporate second chambers (only Ireland); an appointed upper chamber (former British colonies); cultural community chambers (Belgium); forum model second chambers (Japan, Australia, contemporary United Kingdom?); identical or quasi-identical chambers (Italy, Romania).[47]

The differentiation of assemblies generates potential differences of preferences and brings to the forefront the competence to mediate and harmonise between them in cases of dissent. These competence rules are key to asymmetries between chambers because mechanisms of reconciliation mark their difference in status. In some cases, the harmonisation implies establishing a joint committee or a continuing shuttle between assemblies for a finite or even infinite number of rounds (as in Belgium and Italy). In other cases, the shuttle ends thanks to the principle that the second chamber can either fully accept or fully reject (as in the Netherlands). In cases of an absence of any harmonisation

---

[45] On congruence and symmetry, see Lijphart, A. (1984), *Democracies: Patterns of Majoritarian and Consensus Government in Twenty-One Countries*, New Haven, CT, Yale University Press, pp. 95–9; and Sartori, *Comparative Constitutional Engineering*, pp. 183–9.

[46] Russell adds the criteria of 'adequate perceived legitimacy'. Russell, M. (2001), 'What are second chambers for?', *Parliamentary Affairs*, 54, 3: 442–58, 456.

[47] On types of second chambers, see Traenhardt, D. (2010), 'Mehr Demokratie oder mehr Gewaltenteilung?', in Frantz, C. and K. Schubert (eds.), *Einführung in die Politikwissenschaft*, Hamburg, Lit, pp. 91–111.

mechanism, the power of each chamber may be constitutionally regulated in functional teems, depending on the nature of the issue debated.[48]

An example of the ambiguity that derives from a non-clear distinction between norms/rules of competence and the organisational bodies they apply to is the idea that parliamentary and presidential systems define 'two types of bicameralism' in which the difference is in the location of executive power: in the lower chamber in parliamentarism and outside both chambers in presidentialism.[49] The difference has nothing to do with uni- or bicameralism or with the location of the executive but instead with the presence or absence of competence to appoint and dismiss the top executive position; that is, with the political responsibility institute. It is much clearer to simply say that chambers (one, two or more does not matter) enjoy this competence in the first case and do not in the second.

A further example comes from the large literature that claims that multi-cameralism duplication offers stability in legislative decision-making: final decisions are harder to make and even harder to overturn.[50] To achieve this, the two houses must be differently composed and represent different interests, different parts of the electorate or different ways to represent the electorate.[51] However, the stability bias is better defined as the case in which both chambers have the competence to legislate and rules of harmonisation are absent. *From the institutional point of view*, the stability bias effect does not depend on different compositions or interests or representation principles but on the presence/absence of harmonisation rules/norms. Differences in composition and representation may increase the likelihood of

---

[48] Tsebelis, G. and B. E. Rasch (1995), 'Patterns of bicameralism', in Doering, H. (ed.), *Parliaments and Majority Rule in Western Europe*, New York, St Martin's Press, pp. 365–90, 371.

[49] Uhr, J. (2006), 'Bicameralism', in Rhodes, Binder and Rockman (eds.), *The Oxford Handbook of Political Institutions*, pp. 474–93, 480.

[50] Riker, W. H. (1992), 'The justification of bicameralism', *International Political Science Review*, 13: 101–16.

[51] Lijphart points out that the virtues of bicameralism emerge when the two chambers converge in competences but diverge in their systems of representation. Lijphart, *Democracies: Patterns of Majoritarian and Consensus Government in Twenty-One Countries*, p. 99. See also Tsebelis, G. (1995), 'Decision making in political systems: veto players in presidentialism, parliamentarism, multicameralism and multipartism', *British Journal of Political Science*, 25: 289–325, 310.

different majorities but they are neither a necessary nor a sufficient condition, as most depends on the distribution of competences and on harmonisation rules.[52] This same argument applies to the Madisonian idea that bicameralism diffuses power that would be too concentrated in a single assembly. This again is a valid argument if the harmonisation rules do not offer one of the two chambers primacy. Of course, without bicameralism, there cannot be duplication of competence powers, but mere multi-cameralism does not guarantee the effects of power dilution, while other norms/rules of competence apportionment may have those same effects (e.g. collegial leadership, dual executives, presidential vetoes).

Moreover, even among similar balances of political institutes, political norms drive the relationship between executive and legislative bodies in different directions. Sometimes the executive is a mere executor and so would properly be described as a committee of the legislative body.[53] In other instances, the executive is dominant and is in turn controlled by a powerful prime minister who can hire and fire individual ministers. In yet other cases, the members of the executive are subject to party discipline and their parties can effectively impose their preferred policies on them (here the distinction between a single-party government, a multi-party government and portfolio allocation becomes important).[54] The rotation norm in the Swiss collegial executive denies any special role to the chief executive. In government systems with top executive dualism (an elected head of state and a head of cabinet responsible to parliament), various competences are distributed between the president, the prime minister and the parliamentary majority because of norms that yield completely different outcomes. In every type of configuration, therefore, practices and norms may generate patterns of dominance of the executive and/or the assembly.[55]

---

[52] For a summary of normative arguments in favour of or against uni- and bicameralism, see Apahideanu, I. (2014), 'Unicameralism versus bicameralism revisited: the case of Romania', *Studia Politica. Romanian Political Science Review*, 14: 47–88.

[53] Bagehot, W. (1963 (1872)), *The English Constitution*, Glasgow, Collins, p. 67.

[54] See Laver, M. and K. A. Shepsle (eds.) (1994), *Cabinet Ministers and Parliamentary Government*, Cambridge, Cambridge University Press, pp. 3–12.

[55] Ieraci, G. (1994b), 'Forms of democratic government: a study of the impact of institutions on political competition', Oxford, Centre for European Studies, Discussion Paper no. 32, July.

The right of legislative initiative – that is, the proportion of bills passed on the initiative of private members (or parties) or governments – varies enormously from a virtual complete government monopoly (Netherlands) to substantial proportions of independent initiatives (Switzerland, Sweden). The strength of parliamentary committees also varies considerably, as do their relationships with ministers. In some countries, ministers control parliamentary committees; in others, they may be merely invited or not connected with them at all. The cabinet can more or less easily resist proposed amendments or can impose its original proposal ignoring them. Many of these variations relate to institutional norms that are fairly independent of institutional rules.

The variety of institutes and the even greater variety of single rules/ norms is such that an extensive analysis is impossible. To give an idea of this richness, Figure 6.2 summarises the main norms/rules linking the core political bodies of the presidency, the cabinet and the assembly/ies. Competence powers are listed in the figure for pure presidential, semi-presidential and parliamentary systems. Thus, under the label 'presidency', powers which belong to different kinds of presidencies can be found. Of course, some competences are not found in all types.[56] Here the aim is not to describe different types of institutional regimes but to clarify the extent to which all of them are characterised by inter-organisational norms and rules defining areas of exclusive/shared/overlapping competences.

The notes in this chapter concerning institutional regimes are meant to show that an institutional theory of regimes can be based on the core political institutes that characterise them, their relative balance and which institutes are dominant and which are subordinate. I suggest that in institutional analysis, political institutes should be discussed in general terms. We should not say that bicameralism or divided government increases policy stability. Institutional theory should take a different form, for example *if* two bodies, be they two chambers or a chamber and a cabinet or a cabinet and a president and so on, both share competencies X and Y *and* no institute of responsibility links the two *and* asymmetry harmonisation rules/norms are absent, *then* policy stability is more likely given the increase in the number of deciders and the forced negotiation system in which they operate. Hypotheses

---

[56] This is inspired by Ieraci, G. (1994a), 'Presidenzialismo e parlamentarismo nelle "Democrazie Difficili"', *Quaderni di scienza politica*, 1: 35–78.

Presidency intervenes in cabinet:

a) *on the formation of the cabinet by* choosing and dismissing the administration or the prime minister and ministers

b) *on the conduct of the cabinet by* intervening in the state administration, foreign policy, forcing minister to countersign acts

Cabinet intervenes in the presidency

a) *on the conduct of the president by* controlling the administrative acts of the president, intervening in the foreign policy acts of the president, refusing to countersign the acts of the president

b) *on the definition of the parliamentary agenda by* cooperating with declarations of urgency legislation; expressing itself on a call for extraordinary meetings, intervening in the powers of dissolution of the president

c) *on the legislative powers of the president by* intervening in the process of issuing legislation, authorising/ controlling the legislative interventions and initiatives of the president, jointly acting on declarations of state of urgency by the president

Presidency intervenes in parliament

a) *in the formation of the parliament by* dissolving the parliament

b) *on the parliamentary agenda by* declaring urgent legislative procedures, calling for extraordinary meetings

c) *on the legislative process by* vetoing parliamentary legislation, sending back legislation, starting new legislation, declaring a state of emergency

Parliament intervenes in the presidency

a) *on the formation of the cabinet by* co-acting in the selection of the administration or ministers

b) *on the conduct of the president by* controlling/authorising administrative and foreign policy acts of the president, refusing to countersign presidential acts

c) *on parliamentary agenda by* opposing urgency legislative procedure and the convening of extraordinary meetings, interfering in the procedures for dissolution of the chambers

d) *on the legislative powers of the president* opposing presidential vetoes, limiting presidential legislative interventions, co-acting in declarations of a state of emergency

e) *in the selection of the president by* electing/repealing the president

Cabinet intervenes in parliament

a) *on the formation of parliament* by asking for new elections

b) *on the conduct of parliament* by setting the legislative agenda, guillotining debates, asking for delegated legislation

Parliament intervenes in cabinet

a) *on its formation (support, investiture)*

b) *on survival (confidence and censure)*

c) *on the legislative process* advancing, discussing, approving, revising legislation, delegating legislation

Figure 6.2 Inter-institutional links.

expressed in this institute-based form may be more empirically accurate than those expressed in organisational terms referring to mono- or bicameralism, federalism, presidentialism or parliamentarism, and so on.

Institutional regimes are combinations of political institutes that need to be balanced without offending or sacrificing any of them beyond a certain point. Different regimes rest on the prominence of some institutes over others, but only to an extent that does not damage and offend them excessively. The points on indifference curves that indicate the absence, decay or obsolescence of institutes indicate transitions that lead from one type of institutional regime to another. The veto, regulative and legislative powers of many Latin American presidents may be so far reaching that they humiliate the decision institutes of the assembly/ies. Inclusion and representation institutes may be maximised to such an extent (proportionalism, coalition cabinets, permanent negotiation, etc.) that they may offend the institutes of responsibility and accountability. Representational manipulations may dramatically offend the authenticity of elective selection rules and the responsibility institute.

6.5 A Note on Political Regimes

Single norms/rules, institutes or institutional regimes can be studied in their own terms. However, if we focus on macro-outcomes, we need to include other factors and move from institutional regimes to the broader category of political regimes. *Political institutions* define the incentive system within which individual, collective, corporate or institutional actors, relating to each other within *political structures*, determine outcomes according to their *interests and values*. Therefore, theories that deal with final outcomes (policy quality, stability, regime survival, effective economic management, etc.) need to incorporate within the framework of institutes and rules/norms both actor preferences and actor configurations (political structures).

Political structures are neither norms/rules nor concrete physical objects nor supra-individual actors. Instead, they are properties of interactions among actors. Their attributes take the form of a relationship among the parts[57] and recurrent and stabilised patterns

---

[57] On political structure, see Easton, *The Analysis of Political Structures*, ch. 3.

of behaviour that do not have either an explicit normative content or an explicit organisational form. Violating recurrent patterns of inter-actions of this type may engender costs but not ex-ante known explicit sanctions, and no explicit rules of recognition exist to know whether one has violated or not. Political structures are *non-institutionally prescribed* recurrent interactions, stabilised practices and routine oper-ations among a set of actors. A political structure combines actors in a particular way.[58]

Individual actors may have a large variety of orientations that range from altruism to solidarity, from egoism to hostility, from self-sacrifice to mutual destruction or from masochism to indolence. However, collective, corporate and institutional actors usually relate to other similar actors with a much-reduced set of orientations. This is because certain types of actors' orientations are untenable at the supra-individual level. It is unlikely that a complex organisation can survive and prosper while entertaining self-sacrifice or indolent orientations, while individuals can do this more easily. Structures, therefore, emerge from recurring interaction patterns that have some special character which can be generalised to a set of actors, which, like institutions, limits the range of available alternatives and constrains the actors' options to a more limited set. However, political structures are deprived of any normative claim. *By adding political structures to institutional regimes, we move to political regimes.* Four types of political structures cover the core types of actor constellations in polit-ics: *political structures of competition, cooperation, negotiation* and *conflict.*

Although structures of political competition are crucial in most definitions of regimes, they are not institutional features of regimes. The level of competition among qualified political actors is governed by norms/rules of selection, inclusion, representation and responsibility as necessary conditions. Sacrificing these institutes makes political com-petition unviable. However, political competition is a behavioural fea-ture of actor interaction that is institutionally generated but not institutionally mandated. The presence and authenticity of the above-mentioned institutes, while making behavioural political competition

---

[58] Morlino uses the term 'anchoring' in a similar vein: Morlino, L. (1998), *Democracy between Consolidation and Crisis: Parties, Groups and Citizens in Southern Europe*, Oxford, Oxford University Press, pp. 338–45.

possible and even likely, are compatible with very different levels of competition. Competition as contestability is fostered by specific norms/rules of inclusion and representation, but it also largely depends on leadership and organisational mobilisation choices. Competition as electoral availability depends on political identities, cleavages and partisanship. Competition as differentiation and decidability of the political offer depends on the disposition of parties and elites not to collude. Competition as incumbent vulnerability depends largely on voters' psychological orientations towards the electoral choice.[59] In short, political actor interactions of a competitive nature can be studied from the institutional point of view by discussing political institutes that make them possible, but other factors pertain to behavioural orientations that cannot be reduced to them. The party system is a typical political competition structure. It is not an institution but a set of interactions among qualified actors. Multipartism and bipartism are configurations of actors that are in no way institutionally prescribed, although they may be institutionally assisted, such as when the literature suggests that a selection of representatives based on plurality voting in single-member districts favours a two-party structure of the party system. To be considered a political party, it is institutionally required to present signatures for candidacies, candidates, lists and programmes, but it is not prescribed whether you compete or collude, with which means or to what extent and so on.

Cooperation structures assume coordination among actors to achieve common goals that cannot be achieved without cooperation. Cooperative relationships assume that the prize or the goal to be achieved is neither in the hands of one actor nor can it be achieved through competition or exchanges: it can only be reached through a coordination of efforts and does not exist without them. Actors that actively cooperate tend to see their interests and values as complementary or identical. In cooperation structures actors share means, information, resources, personnel and so on in view of the common goal and with limited, but different, levels of fear of their misuse by other actors given the complementary nature of interests. This notwithstanding, cooperation requires punishment of opportunists who become

---

[59] On the dimensions of competition, see Bartolini, S. (1999–2000), 'Collusion, competition and democracy', Part I, *Journal of Theoretical Politics*, 11: 435–70; Part II, *Journal of Theoretical Politics*, 12: 33–65.

side-tracked by other goals during the cooperative interaction. Coalitions, alliances, clubs, associations and even movements are typical political cooperation structures.

Negotiation political structures are related to negotiations as a decisional norm/rule. They require interests and values to be perceived as diverging by actors, but not mutually exclusive. For negotiations to take place, each actor must control some prize or some share of the prize valued by its adversaries and must in principle be willing to share a part of it in exchange for something else. In negotiations, actors use promises concerning prospective advantages or disappearing disadvantages as means, and threats concerning prospective damages and disappearing advantages. These threats are usually only used to obtain the best terms of exchange in the negotiation. Special relationship patterns among interest groups are typically negotiation structures – structures of interest intermediation. Corporatist arrangements, for instance, constitute a special kind of negotiation structure that involves government representatives and requires the credibility of commitments by interest groups with respect to their constituencies.[60]

Threats to generate direct damages may make the competitive or negotiation relationship slide into a *conflict* structure. In conflict structures, actors inflict damages on each other.[61] Strength is directly or indirectly used against adversaries to test the force of actors and their reciprocal capacity to resist the withdrawal of advantages or the growth of damages deriving from the conflict. This often happens when some of the actors involved perceive the prize from the negotiation to be in the hands of adversaries and needing to be directly subtracted from them as they are unwilling to share it. Whether the aim is to obtain full victory in a zero-sum game or to reach the successive negotiation stage in a favourable position, the logic of means utilisation does not change.[62] In conflict situations, negative incentives have an advantage over positive ones: while a positive incentive in the form of a promise must be kept, threats do not need to be enforced if

---

[60] Streeck, W. and P. Schmitter (1985), 'Community, market, state – and associations? The prospective contribution of interest governance to social order', *European Sociological Review*, 1: 119–38.

[61] This is the formulation of Lasswell, H. and A. Kaplan (1950), *Power and Society: A Framework for Political Enquiry*, New Haven, CT, Yale University Press.

[62] Scharpf, *Games Real Actors Play*, pp. 152–3.

they are successful at influencing somebody's else behaviour. However, threats are problematic too. Severe deprivation threats and the actual implementation of them via an explicit creation of losses may generate strong reactions of hostility. Resistance and disobedience may be generated by the threat, even if it would be better for the actor to accept the imposition and give up. There might be a perception of risk of annihilation, which is likely to generate the most expensive resistance and to mobilise resources previously not available in the pre-threat situation.

There is no need here to go beyond these short notes on the main types of political structures, which are not objects of concern in this work. They suffice to make my point: *analysis of political regime outcomes results from the combination of institutional design features and political structures features*. If we argue that the combination of hyper-presidentialism with multi-party systems is especially unbalanced because it is likely to generate immobilising executive–legislative deadlock, produce ideological polarisation and a difficult interplay between coalition-building in presidential and legislative elections,[63] we advance a testable hypothesis combining a specific institutional design with a specific form of competition political structure. In an extensive discussion of the merits and vices of presidentialism, parliamentarism and semi-presidentialism, Linz reviews the implications of different types of regimes, discussing twenty-one topics/problems. Most of these topics/problems start with an institutional feature and extend to political structures and to how both have cultural conditions and implications.[64]

---

[63] Mainwaring, S. (1993), 'Presidentialism, multipartism, and democracy: the difficult combination', *Comparative Political Studies*, 26: 198–228.

[64] Linz, *Presidential and Parliamentary Democracy*, pp. 3–87. The topics/problems are: (1) dual democratic legitimacy in presidentialism; (2) the rigidity of the fixed term in presidentialism; (3) problems of identifiability and accountability of presidents in separation of powers versus parliamentarism and fusion of powers; (4) the winner-takes-all logic of presidential elections and the culture it induces; (5) the implication of the no re-election or no immediate re-election principle; (6) ambiguities of the presidential office: head of state and partisan leader; representative of the whole people and implicit plebiscitary risks; (7) the possible election of an outsider; (8) plebiscitary leadership and 'delegate democracy'; (9) presidential government stability versus parliamentary government instability; (10) presidents and vice-presidents; (11) presidentialism and the impact on the party system; (12) the strength of leadership in parliamentarism and presidentialism; (13) presidentialism, parliamentarism and multi-ethnic societies; (14) presidentialism and control of the military; (15) the head of state in parliamentary regimes; (16) semi-presidentialism or semi-parliamentarism of bipolar executives (Weimar and

Similarly, analyses that normatively discuss the capacity of different regimes to increase the legitimacy of political institutions and pacify societies highly divided along ethno-linguistic and racial divides necessarily merge institutional designs with specific political structures. Lijphart has consistently advanced an ideal of 'consensual democracy' articulated through a combination of eight power-sharing mechanisms.[65] His majoritarian versus consensual democracy scheme incorporates many institutional and political features (particularly in the party system and elite cooperation). Consensual democracy, constructed in opposition to the somewhat idealised Westminster model, requires that all the institutes that concentrate decisional power are disabled: majority voting, direct election of the chief executive, unicameralism or highly asymmetrical bicameralism, plurality electoral systems, centralisation and so on.[66] This sacrifice considerably affects the institutes of responsibility and accountability. At the same time, it requires specific political structures in which political competition is relatively mute, all relevant interests are involved and represented in the negotiations and the consensus is sensitive to the power resources of all the main actors. Multilateral bargaining has high transaction costs typical of all negotiation systems and the multiplication of players is normatively justified by the legitimacy of policy outputs without much regard to the efficiency of the process.[67]

Spanish Republics); (17) unstable or switching solutions; (18) the dual executive and the military; (19) presidentialism with a cover of prime minister; (20) presidentialism, parliamentarism and democratic stability: relationship with the party system; and (21) mechanisms to correct fractionalisation of the party system in parliamentary democracies.

[65] Lijphart, A. (2004), 'Constitutional design for divided societies', *Journal of Democracy*, 15: 96–109; Lijphart, *Democracies: Patterns of Majoritarian and Consensus Government in Twenty-One Countries*.

[66] Lijphart's prescriptions are even more specific: a ceremonial head of state; a collegial executive; a constitutional requirement that the executive be made of equal numbers of members of the main ethnolinguistic groups; representation of the main parties in cabinet; alternation between the presidency/prime ministership (as in Lebanon); a list proportional representation system; inclusion of all parties with at least 5 per cent of the vote in the executive (as in South Africa). These groups have the authority to run their own internal affairs dealing with identity issues, especially in the realm of education and culture, and extend power-sharing to civil society, the judiciary, the police and the military.

[67] Horowitz expresses doubts about the multiplication of power centres and proposes a more institutional model based on the electoral law and federalism incentives. Horowitz, *Constitutional Design*, pp. 15–36.

The most thorough attempt to go beyond the distinction between institutional design and political structures has been made by George Tsebelis. His framework incorporates institutional design and the actor configurations (and preferences) in a single concept, veto players and, in a single measure, the number of them. He therefore does not distinguish between presidentialism, parliamentarianism, uni- and bicameral systems, two- and multi-party systems, corporatist and pluralistic models of interest intermediation, and so on, but only among different configurations of veto players.[68] The argument is shaped with reference to policy stability (which is seen as causing 'government stability' and 'regime stability' rather than being caused by the latter) as a value to be achieved and that increases with the number of veto players and with the internal cohesion of each veto player, and decreases with their congruence; that is, similarity in political positions. The normative conclusion is that if policy stability is a value, the preference is for as many veto players as possible.[69]

This approach focusses on actors (players) and their preferences, with all the difficulties embedded in the attribution of preferences. Veto players are not only institutional but also partisan and socioeconomic. Veto players are 'actors' like organisations (such as chambers, courts, parties and interest groups) rather than norms/rules or institutes. Given that they must have policy preferences, this is unavoidable. The institutional configuration results, perhaps, in being too sacrificed by the multiplication of non-institutional veto players, but even in this case veto players result from a combination of institutional norms/rules with substantive organisational actors.

Theories of political regimes belong to two traditions: one which emphasises institutions as credible commitments and generally

---

[68] Tsebelis , 'Decision making in political systems' and (2002), *Veto Players: How Political Institutions Work*, Princeton, NJ, Princeton University Press.

[69] The assumption is that parties are unitary actors and only vote on policies and have no preferences about other issues. Even so, it is hard to measure the distance (incongruence) among institutional veto players independently of the distance among partisan veto players. In other words, the number applies to institutional veto players, but less so to their 'distance' or even cohesion. Other debated issues concern the problem of distinguishing real veto players from other 'relevant actors', the proliferation of veto player indices and classifications, and the equivalence between different types of veto players. For a review, see Ganghof, S. (2003), 'Premises and pitfalls of veto player analysis', *Swiss Political Science Review*, 9: 1–25.

concludes that a dispersal of powers and veto points helps the stability of commitments and the security of rights with a relatively weak central government; and one which emphasises the effectiveness of government and the decisiveness of policy direction, usually requiring a higher concentration of power.[70] Theories of regime outcomes have difficulty in focussing on institutional configurations alone, and no theory of normatively desired outcomes can do so. At the same time, focussing on macro-outcomes combining institutional design and political structures may blur their analytical distinction. This is an important loss because institutional design is subject to intentional reform and manipulation, while political structures of actor interactions are less prone to intentional changes. Distinguishing between the two, therefore, has some advantages and may increase our grip on regime political outcomes.

---

[70] Macintyre, A. (2003), *The Power of Institutions*, Ithaca, NY, Cornell University Press.

7 | Conclusion

Specificities of Political Institutions

This book advances a few core points. The first is that a coherent way to define political institutions is to see them as *norms and rules* at the micro level, *institutes* as a combination of related norms/rules at the meso level and *regimes* as combination of institutes and their relations at the macro level. There is no novelty in understanding institutions as norms/rules. The point is to draw all the logical and empirical consequences from this understanding, to distinguish clearly different types of norms/rules and to specify the particularities of the norms/rules that we define as 'political'.

I have argued that approaches that define political institutions as games, behavioural regularities, rules of conduct, organisations, practices and routines or cultural templates are likely to lead to incoherent and contradictory conclusions. At best, they identify only a subset of institutions and generalise their properties to the entire institutional phenomenology. In so doing, they stretch the concept of institution beyond the empirical referents implicit in their definition. Encompassing definitions that put together a large variety of phenomena – norms, rules, organisations, regular behaviours, practices, conventions, cultural templates and so on – are equally problematic because they extend almost indefinitely the institutional phenomenology to the point of making it unclear what is not institutional. Often, under the umbrella of wide definitions, one analyses only a type of institutions and leaves the others aside. In this case, the empirical referents are shrunken and unrepresentative of the broad definition.

If institutions are norms/rules, political institutions are a special kind of these norms/rules. Political institutions should not be confused with norms/rules of conduct or with norms/rules of recognition. Norms/rules of conduct impose duties; they either forbid or require certain actions. They lay down standards of behaviour and are constituted by the deontic modalities of obligation, prohibition and permission which are shared with moral and social language.

Rules of recognition define the procedural sources and steps and the sanctioning mechanisms for violations of the rules of conduct. They are mainly procedural and remedial. Of course, in politics, as in any other field, behaviour may follow conventions, social norms and role expectations or may violate them. Politicians and activists need not be unethical opportunists and disloyal cheaters, at least no more than any other category of individuals. But political institutions cannot be identified with the logic of normatively appropriate conduct. Political institutions are made up of norms/rules that 'confer' prerogatives and powers not in the form of guaranteed individual powers (the rights to …) but in the form of public powers. Political institutions do not prescribe interindividual behaviours but primarily confer powers and competencies. They consist of rules and norms of conferral.

I have also argued that political norms/rules are layered vertically to an extent that social and economic institutions are not. While sometimes social norms are horizontally interconnected, I am not aware of any special attention given to the vertical layering of social norms, conventions, role expectations and the like. In contrast, political norms/rules are layered. Vertically, 'institution' indicates anything that goes from a single norm/rule, the articles of a statute or a rule of procedure up to complex codes and interrelated set of institutional rules and norms, and finally to complex organisations with their dense institutional orderings. Therefore, a hierarchical layering of political institutions must distinguish atomistic accounts from molecular and holistic accounts.

Single norms/rules are highly specific and often contextual. Molecular institutions refer to a set of norms/rules that relate to the same functional problem and combine by addition to constitute the 'institute'. Institutes are more general than the single norm/rule and may include different application modalities. They are not necessarily characterised by the same single norms/rules in different times and places. The institute maintains itself and travels through time and space while being embodied in changing single norms/rules. Finally, higher-level institutions constitute an entity more complex than the sum of their parts. They show emerging properties that are not additive – that belong to none of the atomistic or molecular parts but emerge from the inter-institutional layering and interconnectedness. In this case, interactions among norms/rules and institutes are explicitly foreseen as new, emerging norms/rules and institutes. My proposal is to keep the term 'institution' as the general label and distinguish between *rules/norms* as single institutions, *institutes* as sets of related atomistic institutions and *institutional regimes* as sets of institutes and their interactions.

I have insisted that an effort must be made to separate organisations and institutions. Considerable theoretical and empirical confusions and contradictions derive from mixing these two concepts. A sacrifice must be accepted because no neat distinction between the two is fully satisfactory. Political institutions as norms/rules, institutes or regimes cannot be actors, while organisations are actors composed of people, common purposes, independent interests, historical legacies and so on. If institutions equal organisations, then institutions have structure and culture, intentionality and action. If we include organisations within the semantic space of the concept of institutions, we bring with them the many other things that organisations carry as defining properties. This generates unsolvable problems when dealing with institutions that show neither ends nor strategic action, differentiation or integration of preference mechanisms (such as constitutions, electoral systems, penal codes, property, marriage). If, on the contrary, we exclude organisa-tions from the semantic field of institutions, we de-vertebrate the holistic study of organisations of their embedded institutional struc-ture. In this second case, however, institutions can still be studied in isolation from other properties of organisations. It seems to me that the choice that engenders lower analytical costs is that of trying to keep institutions and organisations as separate as possible and to merge them only for the research agenda of organisational studies. The costs of neatly separating the two phenomena seem to be less than those of making them the same thing – or worse, of making organisations a type of institution.

The points made in the chapters in this work converge on the con-clusion that the nature of political institutions cannot be derived by extension from social and economic institutions and that it is mislead-ing to assimilate them to the latter. Political institutions are a very special kind of institution. Some of their most important features derive more from their being 'political' than from their being 'institutional'. To give substance to this final point, I close this work by discussing more precisely the particularities of political institutions that help to set them aside from other types of institutions.

7.1 Primordiality

A persistent vision of political institutions prevalent in sociological and economic thinking is that they derive from something else that pre-exists them. They emerge from the substratum of other socio-economic institutions at a certain stage when solving collective action problems requires them. The standard argument is a version of the following story.[1] In primitive societies, unwritten norms and conventions alone are capable of providing stable expectations and ensuring social order and they can do so without special (political) institutions that are tasked with enforcing them. When societies grow bigger in size, more impersonal relationships among individuals develop and customary institutions no longer suffice. Some creative individuals set up agencies to provide protection. Protective firms compete for customers, using violent means to oppress and attack other protective agencies. The emergence of a single protective agency (the ruler, the state) results from collective learning, division of labour, competition between entre-preneurs of violence and an evolutionary process of selection among competing agencies. More complex political institutions develop to deal with new functional requirements linked to the change in scale of interactions. At this stage, political institutions foster cooperation and solve collective action problems, facilitate exchange or comity, and enhance welfare in large-scale societies. All institutions, including pol-itical ones, are negotiated solutions to some problem of cooperation.[2] They are solutions to some dilemmatic situation in which individuals pursuing their own self-interests can evolve norms of cooperation and a cooperation strategy.[3]

In this work I have argued from many points of view that the claim that political institutions can be derived from pre-existing customary institutions and are generated by the same mechanisms is not

---

[1] Nozick, R. (1974), *Anarchy, State, and Utopia*, Oxford, Blackwell, must be credited with this account of the spontaneous emergence of the minimal state as a protective agency: 'Out of anarchy, pressed by spontaneous groupings, mutual protection associations, division of labor, market pressures, economies of scale, and rational self-interest there arise something very much resembling minimal state', pp. 16–17. Mantzavinos, *Individuals, Institutions, and Markets*, reviews the literature on this approach in a chapter on the origin of the state as a protective agency.

[2] Shepsle, 'Studying institutions: some lessons from the rational choice approach'.

[3] Axelrod, R. (1984), *The Evolution of Cooperation*, New York, Basic Books.

convincing. This perspective leaves unsolved the problem of the 'generalisation' of spontaneously generated orders and game outcomes to non-participating members and to new generations.[4] Aside from this problem, this version of the emergence of political institutions works poorly, even from a historical point of view. The state as the monopolistic protective agency is not the proper yardstick to identify the emergence of political institutions. That known states have political institutions does not mean that political institutions require a state to exist.[5] *The primordial political institution is not a complex protective agency but the norms of leadership/followership.* Focussing on this early and universal political institution makes it easier to realise that its origins are primordial and not derivative.

Primitive societies were probably not full of opportunists and free riders, but they were utterly unsafe, and the value at stake was the physical survival of the members. Even within groups of equals, rulership was made easier by the pressure of existential threats linked to growing interactions and conflicts among different species and among groups of the same species. In the organisation of defence and the extraction of resources necessary for it, the creation and acceptance of command was easier, if not inevitable. Primordial political institutions were rooted in the dimension of inter-group defence/offence, in the fear/opportunities of external aggression. Only ex post were they used to improve the enforcement of intra-group institutions.

In situations of extreme danger in which the survival of the group and the physical integrity of its members are at stake, the most pressing question is: who can best lead us? The definition of the character of the ideal leader is an early challenge for every group of both animals and humans, often to be solved under extreme pressure. Repeated assignments of value to certain characters may have generated the norms of selection of the best suited to lead the group. Several repeated choices

---

[4] Works that criticise the emergence of institutions as self-organising entities include Knight, *Institutions and Social Conflict*, pp. 171, 188 and 189; Hudgson, 'What are institutions?', pp. 13–15; Rothstein, *Political Institutions: An Overview*, pp. 133–66; and Moe, T. M. (2005), 'Power and political institutions', *Perspectives on Politics*, 3: 215–33.

[5] States are complex sets of organisations and elaborate infrastructural capacities: 'an articulated and differentiated bureaucratic organization, a hierarchy of offices, for infrastructural support to production and distribution'. Service, E. (1975), *Origins of the State and Civilization*, New York, Random House, pp. 71–102.

and appointments may differentiate the role definition from the person definition.

Studies of leadership roles in all sorts of animals and primarily in our closest mammal relatives, the primates,[6] reveal 'a universal feature of animal sociality that is often overlooked: leadership and followership, where one or a few individuals steer the behaviour of many'.[7] Leadership in animals is usually associated with key decisions concerning moving or staying, hunting choices, and fighting or escaping when faced with threats.[8] There are elaborate strategies to ascertain leadership and to impose it based on a variety of skills and capacities. Dominance hierarchies are best known in the class of social mammals.[9] At the same time, strategies develop to contain dominance and leadership. In chimpanzees, both wild and captive males are extremely ambitious politically and they invariably form political coalitions to try to unseat the alpha male. Females too can band together to partially control their alphas.[10] Because leadership roles and rebellious behaviour against leadership are found in all four primate species (gorillas, bonobos, chimpanzees and humans), their roots stretch over several million years, back to our common ancestors.[11] Paleoanthropological evidence indicates that leadership/followership roles existed among the hominids we can no longer observe. It existed in the nomadic hunter-gatherer human groups before the Neolithic revolution. A recent review provides a transdisciplinary synthesis of biological and social-science views of leadership from an evolutionary perspective and concludes that human leadership exhibits both commonalities with and differences from the broader mammalian

---

[6] On the evolutionary analysis of leadership, see van Vugt, M., R. Hogan and R. B. Kaiser (2008), 'Leadership, followership, and evolution: some lessons from the past', *American Psychologist*, 63: 182–96.

[7] King, A. J., D. P. Johnson and M. van Vugt (2009), 'The origins and evolution of leadership', *Current Biology*, 19: 11–16, 11.

[8] See Couzin, I. D., J. Krause, N. R. Franks and S. A. Levin (2005), 'Effective leadership and decision-making in animal groups on the move', *Nature*, 433, 7025: 513–16.

[9] And in the class of birds, notably chickens.

[10] I draw this information from de Wal, F. (1989), *Peace-Making among Primates*, Cambridge, MA: Harvard University Press.

[11] Gorillas, bonobos, chimpanzees and humans share a common ancestor and more than 98 per cent of its genes. According to Richard Wrangham (*The Goodness Paradox*), most behaviours these species exhibit today must have been present in their shared predecessor several million years ago.

pattern.[12] Since the invention of writing about 5,000 years ago, leadership roles have been properly documented.[13]

There are several strategies and means of leadership selection, some of which are quite soft and involve minor or limited conflict. The documented differences between humans and other primates in their attitudes to power and command strengthen the thesis that strong resistances to authority existed within the group that could only be overcome by the even stronger threats to physical integrity. Our daily life within the human group tends to be quiet and non-aggressive, while we can trigger extremely aggressive wars against other groups. From this point of view, we are different to other primates. We are a domesticated species; we are dogs, not wolfs. We have auto-domesticated in the sense that to live together we began to select traits (and people) of lower aggressiveness and to eliminate those who used violence to their advantage within the group and did not conform to the norms and rules of the group.[14] The question of the natural aggressiveness of humans remains controversial but the idea that intense violence and a high number of victims characterised the prehistoric period is widely shared: 'Most ethnographically reported chiefdoms seem to be involved in constant warfare.'[15] Anthropological and ethnographic research lends support to the role of warfare and physical insecurity in the development of early political institutions, although usually violent activities are less documented than other bureaucratic developments.

Rulers were under constant threat of being ousted by alternative rulers and subjects were under constant threat of being conquered, killed or dispossessed in a lost war. Groups without an efficient command would fail to deploy the defence/aggression mechanisms that could ensure their survival when facing groups that had them. The primordial development of a monopolistic provider of behavioural

---

[12] Smith, J. E. et al. (2016), 'Leadership in mammalian societies: emergence, distribution, power, and payoff', *Trends in Ecology & Evolution*, 31: 54–66.

[13] It seems that leadership institutions are more ancestral than the origin of the belief in supranatural realities. See Girotto, V., T. Pievani and G. Vallortigara (2008), *Nati per credere. Perché il nostro cervello sembra predisposto a fraintendere la teoria di Darwin*, Turin, Codice Edizioni, p. 163.

[14] The paradox lies in the fact that our present docile and cooperative nature has evolved thanks to our past capacity to be organised murderers; Wrangham, *The Goodness Paradox*.

[15] Wright, 'Recent research on the origin of the state', pp. 381–2.

compliance was likely to be a fitting solution for group survival, providing evolutionary advantage in a situation of inter-group violence.

Therefore, to interpret the roots of political institutions in exclusive connection with in-group enforcement of commitments is misguided. Customary institutions were likely to be enough for the problems of curbing and punishing in-group opportunism but not for the problem of surviving as a group in a violent world. This was particularly so after the Neolithic revolution, when agriculture and breeding made the groups less nomadic and the close connection with land and cattle made escaping more difficult and costly. Based on available information, I am inclined to believe that the fundamental political predicaments – who is a member of the group; which are the rules on setting rules; why should I abide by rules I have not contributed to devising – which are so theoretically unmanageable on a rationalistic basis could be more easily overcome in the face of the colossal stakes of inter-groups conflicts. Political institutions and the high level of coercion associated with them emerged very early and were not derivative from the customary social institutions serving the function of internal disciplining and punishment.

7.2 Scope

Every group, whether membership or territorial, has 'political institutions'; that is, norms/rules of conferral that set up authorities as more or less legitimate sources of new norms/rules. *Membership groups* such as political parties, trade unions, sports and recreational associations, bureaucratic organisations, and firms and companies are constituted by the will of their members and endowed with rules to make rules. Whether the voluntary membership is remunerated with salaries and material goods or with other forms of mobilisation of commitments (ideological, religious, etc.) is of no concern here. *Territorial groups* not based on voluntary adhesion and defined by the sheer territorial location of a population also have norms/rules to make rules. In short, both authority fields (membership groups in which membership is voluntary and not confined) and governmental fields (territorial groups with non-voluntary and highly confined membership) show the feature of a monopolisation of the function of behavioural compliance production. The difference is, of course, in the scope of the political production.

In membership groups, the statute is the regulation of the group, but also the pact that keeps together all the individuals belonging to it. It determines not only the compass of action but also the compass of individual consensus. Associations of this kind do not generate fundamental political predicaments and involve limited problems of power because they do not imply forced participation and the decisions they reach have no force outside the group. This associational phenomenology expresses an internal institutional ordering based on consensus and not on subjection. Any potential risk to the members (exploitation, subordination, harassment or physical threats) is contained by voluntary adhesion, particularly if alternative organisations exist that can offer functionally equivalent goods. For these reasons, their political institutions normally do not differentiate and complexify beyond a certain level.

In territorial groups (government fields), the pact is fictitious. It determines the scope of institutional action – the whole territory and whoever happens to be in it – but does not determine the compass of individual consensus. The essential precondition of the imaginary community is not voluntary adhesion but the territorial institution. Territorial political institutions originally had the main function of acquiring, keeping and defending the possession of a territory. For this reason, political institutions extend in principle their reach to all people and other institutions within the territory. The corresponding society is a 'territorial society'.

Dominant groups have long directly exercised their territorial possession with limited concern about consensus. The emergence of the principles of liberty, auto-determination and nationality fostered a levelling of the relationship between the territorial institution of government and those who are governed. The powers implied by territorial possession are structured by other apparently impartial institutions and spared by the implications of domination. Political institutions come to be regulated by a common statute and activated by a government constituted according to statutorily predefined rules. The result of this modification is the apparent disappearance of the territorial institution as the dominant one and the emergence of a government that 'represents' the entire community. However, the true nature of this process reveals itself when the territorial order is at stake or in the case of 'rights' – for example, property rights or liberty rights – which identify a way to enjoy the territory within which they are recognised and exercised. There is, in fact, no property of things belonging to others' territory or liberty of persons in the territory of others but concession or acceptance by others. The scope of the political production of territorial institutions is therefore inherently broader. They generate collectivised decisions valid for those who live in the territory. To portray the state as an 'association' rather than as a territorial institution is mythology.

In a concise formulation, the point is that both authority fields (membership groups) and government fields (territorial groups) have internal ordering institutions, but only territorial institutions have external ordering institutions. In a legislative assembly, there are norms/rules that concern its internal organisation of offices and people: selection rules; committee structure rules; agenda-setting rules; decision rules; procedure rules; and so on. These are *internal ordering* rules that apply to the membership group of the parliamentary assembly and resemble very much the internal ordering norms/rules of any kind of organisation (shareholder assemblies and political party conferences, for instance). However, shareholder assemblies and political party conferences have no capacity to extend the outcomes of their internal ordering outside the membership of the hemicycle. In contrast, legislative assemblies have the capacity to decide for non-members. They are endowed with an *external ordering* capacity that extends to the entire territorial group. In political organisations like legislative assemblies the rules for internal ordering (which are present in any organisation) translate into rules for external ordering (only typical of territorial political institutions).

The external ordering capacity deriving from conferral norms/rules usually engenders the presence of other norms/rules that specify the conditions under which it is valid and binding for the entire territorial group. These are norms/rules for *inter-institutional ordering* and they emerge in more complex differentiated institutional orders. An absolute monarch and a dictator are not subject to these inter-institutional norms/rules as their decisions and commands become effective for the subjects without a need for any further validation. This is the essence of monocratic rule. In more complex institutional systems, the competence of the president of the republic to dissolve parliament (in parliamentary systems) or to veto legislation (in presidential systems) is part of the conferred powers of the presidential institution but not the parliamentary one. The rules that pertain to the powers of a supreme

Table 7.1 *The ordering scope of membership and territorial groups*

Rules/norms for internal ordering	Institutes of membership, inclusion, selection, decision, etc.	Aggregation of members' preferences, typical of any organisation, social, economic or political
Rules/norms for external ordering	Institutes of conferral for the production of compliance over the territory	Only typical of top political organisations (executives, assemblies, courts)
Rules/norms for inter-institutional ordering	Institutes of balancing, recognition and redress that relate core political institutes to each other	Typical of more complex and differentiated institutional orders

or constitutional court to strike out as invalid a legislative or presidential decision (before or after its application) are not rules of the parliament or of the presidency. Every key political organisation has its own rules embedded in a wider framework of rules that bear on its activities. We say that a given decision will become valid *if* it is approved by the second chamber, *if* it is signed by the monarch or president, *if* it is endowed with appropriate financial coverage, *if* it is not repealed by a court or popular referendum. All these 'ifs' specify inter-institutional rules for the validity of the command in complex and articulated institutional orders (Table 7.1).

No other type of normative order has this complexity of interrelated systems of norms/rules. They do not exist for customs, conventions, social norms or rule expectations, which have few or no inter-institutional relationships. They do not exist or are elementary for all associational entities. The wide scope of territorial norms/rules of conferral can only be tamed by a complexification of inter-institutional orderings.

7.3 The Generative Nature of Institutions

Customs, conventions, social norms and role expectations cannot change intentionally but only slowly and marginally. A growing level of non-abidance may point to their obsolescence and decline, leaving the field open to a situation of non-normativity. The institution of contract has no capacity to modify itself, except in the marginal sense of interpretative change. The penal code has no capacity to generate a redefinition of the gravity of offences for individuals or society at large. It is a platitude worth remembering that political institutions are made up of norms/rules with which other institutions are deliberately created and modified. Norms/rules of conferral specify the rules for discussion, criticism and revision of any other institution, including themselves. They may engage in *contro-grade* transformation and change all types of other institutions. Therefore, new institutions are not necessarily generated by cooperation among a set of autonomous, independent and potentially unilateral actors that find an equilibrium in the form of an ex-ante agreement that is not to be regretted ex post. A considerable number of changes in norms/rules simply derive from decisions taken through political institutions and within the sphere of competence conferred on them, and they do not require very sophisticated efforts to explain them.

A special problem emerges when the institutions to be modified or changed are the political institutions themselves. In this case, the creative role of political institutions is not meant to achieve a specific outcome – a reform of pension entitlements or a fight against corrupt practices or dysfunctional conventions and norms, for instance – that can be evaluated ex post and can be further modified with the same procedure. The rules on how to make rules are more problematic to deal with than the rules that they produce. As political institutions are content-free, they open the way not to a specific outcome but to the whole set of unknown outcomes that could be achieved through them. Actors, even the small number of relevant actors, are forced to think not about specific outcomes but about the long-term implications of the conferral of new powers of competence and of exercise. The veil of ignorance is vast in this case.

7.4 Weak Normativity and Sanctionability

Norms of conduct that derive from customary or social institutions have poor or no rules of recognition. Their violation is accompanied by spontaneous and poorly defined social sanctions. These are valid to the extent that and as long as they are respected by enough people, and they lose their effectiveness when they no longer are. No action can be declared null or invalid because it violates a convention or a social norm. When social norms are written into rules, recognition rules are associated with them that more precisely define the nature of violation and the punishment for infringement.

Violation of norms/rules of conferral rarely results in direct sanctions. In circumstances in which the rules of conferral themselves establish a constitutional jurisdiction to evaluate their acts, this jurisdiction may declare the 'nullity' or 'invalidity' of the act but it can hardly generate sanctions on the acting agent. If this constitutional jurisdiction is absent or ephemeral, it makes little sense to ask about the validity of the norms/rules of conferral. There is no higher-level institution to provide us with criteria with which to judge this validity. In this case, rules/norms of conferral are presumed to exist if they are unchallenged, accepted and employed in general practice.

Consider the case of a given political order in which the most important political norm is that everything of importance must be referred to Stalin for a decision. This norm leaves much uncertainty as to what 'everything of importance' is and even more uncertainty about what might happen if an agent violates the vague norm. However, there is not much point in asking whether this political norm is valid, and the three codified Soviet constitutions of 1918, 1924 and 1936 specified no rules of recognition for such a norm of conferral. It simply determines how commands can be achieved and the existence of the norm of conferral is a statement of fact.

To a considerable extent, therefore, political institutions like norms/rules of conferral are not sustained by anything other than their factual likelihood of being obeyed, powerful mythologies (democracy, rule of law, goods, dictatorship of the proletariat, etc.), traditions or the vagaries of political strife. When challenged, reference to them takes the form of an attempt by one party to impose its preferred solution on the challengers. In other words, conferral norms/rules that constitute public authority can only solve problems that are framed within that political institution's framework. They cannot provide rules for conflict resolution in situations that are exceptionally new or radically antagonistic. If the conferral of public powers fails to generate enough consent to marginalise any radical opposition, then no rule of recognition can be effective.

Therefore, political institutions generate rules backed by sanctions, but they themselves are not norms/rules backed by sanctions. This directly derives from the fact that political institutions are not rules of conduct but rules of attribution, power conferring rules. The sanctioning element for violation of norms/rules of conferral is often non-immediate and left to uncertain political effects: unrest, loss of political grip, loss of support, non-re-election and so on.

A bill requires a legislative majority of votes to be duly passed. If this obtains, we cannot say that those voting in favour of the bill have obeyed the law requiring a majority decision, and neither can we say that those who voted against disobeyed it.[16] If the assembly fails to reach a majority decision, it is not a violation of the majority decision rule. The rules that confer on certain bodies (groups of legislators, subnational governments, courts, groups of citizens, etc.) the possibility of referring an act to a constitutional court for a constitutionality check do not prescribe such behaviour and, therefore, cannot sanction whether it is done or not done. Executives can or cannot present a given bill or issue application measures to make it effective. A president of a parliamentary republic can dissolve parliament under specific circumstances and a prime minister can ask (or not ask) a president to do so. However, the circumstances of both the request and the decision to dissolve or not are almost entirely left to evaluation by the incumbent and action or non-action can hardly be sanctioned. In fact, there are plenty of examples of parliamentary dissolutions that could have been avoided and plenty that could have been but were not. The norms that guide a leader in the selection of top collaborators, public offices under their control and advisors can only be sanctioned by making the act invalid, and only if political rules pertaining to inter-institutional relationships foresee that such nominations must be confirmed by other bodies. When in autumn 2019 Prime Minister Boris Johnson resorted to the old and archaic institution of parliamentary suspension to overcome the deadlock of a divided parliament over the Brexit option, the Queen signed the act without objecting. The British Supreme Court declared the act illegal, but no consequences followed or could follow from this except its nullity. I have taken the example from the contemporary world but conferral rules, the violation of which is not sanctioned, can concern 'god's will', the respect for an immutable tradition or the charismatic gifts of the leader.

In these examples and many similar ones, the final sanctioning is weak and limited to uncertain and long-term consequences in terms of

---

[16] Hart, *The Concept of Law*, pp. 31–2.

political and public support. Norms/rules of conferral inevitably leave a great margin of discretion in what they authorise or prohibit. Even when they must be issued following precise procedures that can be evaluated ex post in relation to other legal sources, their violation cannot be charged against those who have taken the decision. The obligation to respect ex-ante defined procedures is often a weak constraint as special circumstances may justify deviance from them. The responsibility principle in politics is unrelated to 'responsiveness'. Politicians cannot be obliged to respond sympathetically to certain requests and they are not necessarily evaluated on their responses. Accountability remains a soft principle. Politicians can hardly be asked to account for the reasons why a decision has been taken or not taken, and even if the decision or non-decision is perceived as violating some rule/norm, the sanction may be limited to future support.

Therefore, even when recognition rules include checks on acts by rulers, they do so not by imposing sanctions but by making the acts void. Limits on the legislative capacity of assemblies, governments, prime ministers, presidents and kings – when they exist – *do not consist of legal duties but of legal disabilities*. For political institutions, legal responsibility dissipates almost entirely. The constitution of public authority is the constitution of the power (or capacity) to confer rights or duties that will take the form of orders backed by the threat of sanctions. The rules that confer the power to confer these rights/duties do not belong to the same species as they cannot be sanctioned, given the indeterminacy of the conferring power function. The more one gets closer to the nucleus of norms/rules of conferral, the more their normative and sanctioning elements rarefy.[17]

7.5 Particular Enforcement

In politics, institutions are often seen in the light of the lives of organisations and therefore in close connection with organisations'

---

[17] It is noteworthy that what disconcerted contemporaries about the beheading of kings in the seventeenth and eighteenth centuries, and even today leaves us uneasy about the killing of Muammar Gaddafi or Saddam Hussein, is not their personal destinies but the disquieting principle that the conferring power rule was subject to sanctioning. We need to invoke crimes against humankind and similar shocking misdemeanours to justify the event.

membership, preferences, culture, practices and actions. I have extensively argued (see Chapters 2 and 3) that this combination of aspects of
behaviour with aspects of norms/rules confuses institutional analysis.
However, in politics a special connection exists between political institutions (norms/rules) and political organisations.

It is argued that in politics, institutions are seen first and foremost as
organisations: only in politics are organisations always on the front
line; rules and procedures, however important, have to be defended and
supported by organisations. In the political context, institutions are
therefore primarily organisations. In politics, the emphasis should be
on organisations rather than on procedures or rules: rules and procedures become applicable, in politics, through organisations. Only if rules
and procedures are legitimised by organisations, the authority of which
individuals recognise, can they also be recognised. The connection
between political organisations and political institutions is close
because much of politics concerns individuals not involved in the
decisions taken. It cannot be taken for granted that this external
constituency will abide by the rules political institutions have generated. Institutionalisation must be built and can decay. This underlines
the need in politics for organisational support for the fundamental
political institutions.[18]

As I see it, the point is that in politics recognition rules and
therefore normativity and sanctionability are few and weak.
Consequently, legitimation and enforcement largely depend on
organisational support. This is a fair point, which, however, does
not require political institutions to be equated with political organisations. It points to the particular problem of *enforcement* of political
institutions. It is unusual for political institutions to be self-enforcing
or enforced by peer pressure in the way social institutions are. The
political environment is so murky that relying too much on these
mechanisms exposes citizens and politicians alike to experiences of
deep disappointment. Relying on third-party enforcement, on an
authority that is separated from and above the parties and receives
from them the mandate to enforce the rules of the game, is foolhardy.
It is difficult to imagine that those on whom political powers and
competences have been conferred will agree to set an impartial referee
for their exercise. A fourth-party enforcer, a body that the rules of

---

[18]   Blondel, 'About institutions, mainly, but not exclusively, political', pp. 721–3.

conferral themselves set as controller of the rules of conferral, is the role reserved for constitutional courts. They are in fact empowered by the rules of conferral to establish the rules of recognition with which to evaluate the outcomes of political institutions and eventually enforce sanctioning by annulment. Leaving the enforcement of political norms/rules to constitutional jurisdictions presents the problems discussed in the previous section. The fact is that enforcement of norms/rules of conferral is indeed the core problematic aspect of the political.

Therefore, although elements of first-, second-, third- and fourth-party enforcement exist, enforcement in this delicate domain must rely on more substantive equilibria among a variety of social and political forces, without which no political norm/rule can effectively be sustained in the long run. Support is central for political institutions in a way that it is not for social and economic institutions. Political organisations are the source of this support/contestation and they provide the legitimation especially required for political decisions. Enforcement and legitimation of political institutions usually depends on the activities of organisations towards their rank and file or ordinary citizens. In politics – but not in the social and economic realms – the problem of legitimation is acute because decisions taken with the rules apply to the whole community and proceed from the few to the many. Political organisations are essential to establish the link between the few and the many and to legitimise the collectivised choices of the few in front of the many. Political norms/rules cannot be sustained without such support. Their nature is so indeterminate, controversial and contested, their normativity so weak and the sanctioning of violation so poor and unclear and subject to feeble and rather imprecise rules of recognition, that their survival and change is the result of fights, confrontations and alliances among political organisations.

Nevertheless, even if mass political organisations are crucial for the enforcement, legitimation and support of political norms/rules, the two should not be confused. It is not necessary to assimilate political institutions within political organisations to argue that, unlike other kinds of institutions, political norms/rules cannot be enforced among qualified actors and in front of the mass public without the active supporting, checking and contesting role of independent and lively mass organisations.

7.6 Instability and Contestedness

Even from the point of view of their stability, political institutions present some particularities that set them aside from most others. Theories of institutions underline their capacities to persist and endure and to de-institutionalise and change. Cognitive frames, social norms and conventions of all kinds are likely candidates for the stability and persistence view, given their widespread permeation of any social group.

Evolutionary theories of norm/rule development require variation in the options, a mechanism of selection of the best-fitted institution and cultural inheritance (as genes play no role, of course). The selection mechanism is usually driven by efficiency evaluations, which in turn result from competition between different institutions[19] depending on a group or multi-level selection approach to evolution.[20] The pace of change must be reduced to marginal adaptations over time. In the new institutional economy approach, institutional change is due either to change in preferences (new values, attitudes and ideas) or to change in the relative costs individuals face, which produces changes in incentives and more efficient institutions. Relative prices and costs reflect the relative scarcity of resources and alter power structures and the bargaining power of actors.[21] Norm changes emerge spontaneously and unintentionally and then are self-reinforcing. People are confronted with a new problem and face uncertainty about how to handle it. Actors resort to the legacy of the past to interpret the situation and engage in experiments to deal with the new problem. By trial and error and repeated success as the problem recurs, actors gradually learn how to handle it. Over time, a behavioural norm develops that offers a solution to the recurrent problem, which becomes the way people expect others to behave in certain situations. The way new norms/rules come into existence depends on the initial conditions of the context and the change is influence by inherited existing values and beliefs. Path

---

[19] This idea permeates North, D. C. (1981), *Structure and Change in Economic History*, New York, Norton.

[20] For this perspective, see Lewis, O. and S. Steinmo (2012), 'How institutions evolve: evolutionary theory and institutional change', *Polity*, 44: 314–39.

[21] North, *Institutions, Institutional Change and Economic Performance*, pp. 15–16, and North, D. C. (1995), 'Five propositions about institutional change', in Knight, J. and I. Send (eds.), *Explaining Social Institutions*, Ann Arbor, University of Michigan Press, pp. 15–26.

dependency and the related process of lock-in and embeddedness imply that institutional change tends to be gradual and incremental, although predicting the direction and pace of change is difficult.

Other theories unlike the evolutionary ones elucidate various modalities through which institutional change takes place and underline the plurality of the sources of these changes. Change logics include problem-solving, experimental learning and contagion, but also conflict among individuals and groups with diverging interests and the process of confrontation, bargaining and coalition resulting from initial preferences weighted by the power of actors. In this case, change can occur as a result of mobilisation and resource control.[22] Institutions do not persist or break down but often simply change over time in an incremental, gradual and partial way according to four modalities of institutional change: *layering* – introducing new rules on top of or alongside existing ones; *conversion* – a changed enactment of existing rules due to their strategic redeployment; *displacement* – the removal of existing rules and the introduction of new ones; and *drift* – a changing impact of existing rules due to shifts in the environment.[23]

These theories tend to agree that the rate of intentional change is optimistically overestimated. Changing complex institutions produces series of actions and reactions that need to be combined before the ultimate outcome can be understood; complexity obscures the causal structure of the system; changes that may appear to be locally adaptive may produce unanticipated or confusing consequences; concurrent intentional changes may produce outcomes that are not intended by anyone. Therefore, theories of institutional change in general (that is, not specifically political institutional change) tend to emphasise their unintentional, incremental, partial nature and their layering.

At first sight, the stability bias attributed to customs, social norms, role expectations and in general non-political norms/rules could be even stronger for political institutions. If we see political institutions as resulting from long-term unintended incremental adaptations rather than from intentional design, some bias towards stability is inevitable.[24] As I have argued, intentional redesign of the political

[22] March and Olsen, *Rediscovering Institutions*, pp. 59-60.
[23] Mahoney and Thelen, *A Theory of Gradual Institutional Change.*
[24] See Héritier, A. (1999), *Policy-Making and Diversity in Europe: Escape from Deadlock*, Cambridge, Cambridge University Press; Thelen, *How Institutions Evolve*, pp. 208–40; Mahoney and Thelen, *A Theory of Gradual Institutional*

order is difficult. Sunk costs seem to be higher, given that much has been invested in learning how to operate the norms/rules. An additional bias towards stability derives from the fact that political institutions must be intentionally changed by the same people meant to apply them. Politicians are the key actors in reforming the rules that will affect their future behaviour.[25] This means that their future interests are involved in the calculation. Whatever uncertainty exists about how the new rules will affect their status and position turns into complex negotiations and status quo biases among those who expect negative outcomes. Political institutions are not specific outcomes but they define the framework within which contending interests conflict, compete, bargain and cooperate to generate outcomes. The generating capacity of political institutions implies high stakes being involved in their change. There are more fears about the unintended consequences for the rules on making rules than those for the rules themselves. Ignorance concerning who will take advantage of changes happening now and in the long run generates more complex calculations than is the case for other types of institutional changes. In fact, none of this is the case when the question is of reforming social, economic or administrative institutions. In short, changing rules/norms of conferral is not the same thing as changing policies.

Notwithstanding these sound considerations, the evidence only partially supports a stability view. Political institutions are continually debated and fought over, deliberate reform of them is frequently on the agenda and they often change. A recent estimation suggests that the life-span of modern constitutions is about nineteen years.[26] Empirical research on about 180 political institution reforms in eighteen countries in the West after World War II suggests a high frequency and that such reforms often come in bundles in specific periods, often responding to declining public support, consensus and legitimacy concerns. Moreover, they are often characterised by short-termism, ad hocness and simple-mindedness.[27] This evidence only refers to relatively

Change; van der Heijden, J. (2011), 'A short history of studying incremental institutional change: does explaining institutional change provide any new explanations?', *Regulation and Governance*, 4: 230–43.

[25] Macintyre, *The Power of Institutions*, p. 107.

[26] Hirschl, R. (2013), 'From comparative constitutional law to comparative constitutional studies', *International Journal of Constitutional Law*, 11: 1–12, 2.

[27] Bedock, C. (2017), *Reforming Democracy: Institutional Engineering in Western Europe*, Oxford, Oxford University Press.

peaceful polities with 'proper' political institutions. Imagine what the rhythm of change would be if one were to include the sultanistic, oligarchic, caudillo, dictatorial, authoritarian, totalitarian, military and bureaucratic regimes of the world and of the past. The impression is that political rules/norms may be less stable than economic, administrative and social institutions and that the stability view derives from a few cases of considerable historical steadiness, examples that are often taken to be paradigmatic.

This puzzling evidence finds a partial explanation in the paradoxical nature of political institutions. On the one hand, they involve high stakes, considerable veils of ignorance, concerns about prudence and therefore a status quo bias. On the other hand, they offer big rewards, incomparable to those deriving from the reform of other kinds of institutions. The political institutions constitutive of a command make different groups clearly perceive the advantages of manipulating such rules and are more likely to generate strong interests and normative stands towards soliciting and practising different institutional solutions. Other kinds of institutions are not subject to the same strong interest orientation.

In the case of rules of conferral, problem-solving, evolutionary adaptations and price sensitiveness seem less suitable. Mechanisms of competitive selection among different institutions are absent. At any given time, there is only one type of rules of conferral that exercises monopolistic control over the territory. Competition in the real sense is simply impossible and, by comparison, imports and imitations can only concern examples from other times or places, with the associated uncertainties of any transposition. For political institutions there is always a formal supplier of change, government actors who, if unconstrained, have both incentives and competencies to change the rules to their advantage. Deciding on political institutions generates limited collective action problems by definition: conferral rules define the actors qualified to change decisions and the mechanisms of preference aggregation. The sunk costs argument is less relevant for those interested in imposing changes to their advantage. Almost everybody concerned is continually calculating the potential costs and gains of any marginal or big change. No other normative source has the specific feature of a mechanism to select among alternative proposals and make it binding for all members of the territorial group.

Finally, political institutions are often chosen at critical junctures, at constitutive moments of uncertain normativity. They may be modified via external imposition by other resourceful actors (e.g. the military, the monarchy, a revolutionary party, rebellious revolts) rather than by agreement. Radical shocks are likely to be more frequent and, above all, more important.[28] Forced major changes in existing rules/ norms of conferral affect and modify underlying interests and resources, and their capacity to stabilise depends on such changes in a lasting way. It is not infrequent to observe that radical changes in political institutions leave other types of socio-economic and even administrative norms and rules in various subsystems almost unaffected. Political revolutions are more frequent than socio-economic ones.

Social, economic and administrative institutions are more easily and less contentiously evaluated, discussed and changed following the modalities of problem-solving, competitive evaluation, contagion and imitation, and are more easily allowed to evolve unintentionally. For them, it is easier to separate problem-solving and performance evaluation from interest evaluation and lack of trust. For political institutions, attention, learning, technological innovation and so on are probably less important. Unintended consequences cannot be completely excluded but intentionality and close evaluation are always present. In discussions and changes of core political institutions, actors are not easily deflected from a careful evaluation of the risks and advantages from their specific points of view.

Institutional designers have very short time-horizons, while political institutions have longer-term effects: their interests may change and make institutions that they themselves have designed quite unappealing from their point of view; they may be prisoners of fads and fashion and mistakes in the evaluation of the implementation circumstances.[29] Nevertheless, this does not change the fact that no other type of institution is so carefully patrolled, scrutinised, evaluated and contested as the norms and rules of conferral. There are, therefore, ambiguities in the evaluation of the stability of political institutions, in the frequency of their change and in the radical or incremental nature of

---

[28] On radical shocks, see the very perceptive points in March and Olsen, *Rediscovering Institutions*, pp. 64–5.

[29] On these pitfalls, see Pierson, P. (2004), *Politics in Time: History, Institutions, and Social Analysis*, Princeton, NJ, Princeton University Press, pp. 208–12.

such changes. These ambiguities cannot be resolved by resorting to models that derive from the development of social, administrative and economic institutions.

7.7 Intentional 'Inefficiency'

What was said in the previous section about the ambivalent nature of the change processes of political institutions paves the way for a discussion of their *efficiency*. Economists judge institutions in terms of fostering economic growth and innovativeness, reducing transaction costs and so on. Social institutions can be judged from the point of view of the stability and predictability of social relations, solving social dilemmas and creating and transmitting social identities. Which is the normative standard for judging political institutions?

Given the considerations in the previous section, efficiency or problem-solving considerations do not loom large in the processes of devising or changing the rules of conferral. The interests and perceptions of the qualified actors tend to prevail with no guarantee that any coherent design may result. The concept of efficiency is a doubtful yardstick for politics in general and for political institutions in particular.[30] The evaluation criteria are simply too many to be reconciled in an efficiency function: in addition to the usual long-term economic performance,[31] speed of decision, inclusiveness, representation, accountability, legitimacy, consensus, peace and order could all be standards of efficiency, often conflicting with one another. In fact, it is often the case that the contrary prevails for political institutions: that is, changes make them inefficient, intentionally inefficient.

[30] Long-term and ex-post efficiency evaluations of social and economic institutions are particularly tricky. The theses that mercantilism 'has been proved bankrupt, and the institutions of liberal democracy have limited ... the success of rent seeking' (Keohane, R. (2001), 'Governance in a partially globalized world', *American Political Science Review* 95: 1–13, 9) and that the legal institutions of chattel slavery, slave codes and indentured servitude were eventually proven inefficient (Wright, G. (2006), *Slavery and American Economic Development*, Baton Rouge, Louisiana State University Press) make no reference to the perceptions and the advantages/costs of the actors of the time, but instead refer to mystical 'historical efficiency'.

[31] On the limits to rational institutional design, see the introduction to and the collection of contributions in Czada, R., A. Héritier and H. Keman (eds.) (1996), *Institutions and Political Choice: On the Limits of Rationality*, Amsterdam, VU University Press.

From the historical point of view, the problem is how it transpired that in some cases a specific set of political institutions developed introducing uncertainty, so that public authority holders were made unsafe about their future exercise of them. If the normative standard with which to evaluate the efficiency of political institutions is making authority holders constrained and unsafe, it is not surprising that cumbersome procedures, duplicated structures and not very effective organisations develop, undermining performance.

Citizens and groups fear both public authority gaining enough power and autonomy to pursue its own goals without consideration of their interests and preferences and other groups forcing sympathetic public authorities to go in the direction of harmful legislation. In short, the more concentrated the institutional power of public authorities, the higher the possibility of radical departures from the status quo but, at the same time, the higher the possibility for new authorities to completely reverse previous deals. If authority is supreme, unchecked and unbalanced, then each authority can unmake what was done before. On the contrary, in power-sharing institutional designs, new institutions, new policies and new deals can be introduced with greater difficulty to the advantage of groups or incumbent authorities. At the same time, this difficulty in changing the status quo is reflected in more stable deals over time. In other words, changes are more difficult, but once they are introduced they have stronger stability, are more difficult to modify and endure over time.

Political losers must give way, but they often participate in the design of new institutions in such a way as to make them ineffective in their performance. That is, political institutions may turn out to be inefficient because of the need to protect losers and indeed also winners that expect to soon be losers. In the end, their design is subject to discounting an efficiency cost in exchange for safety costs for all the actors involved.[32] This is why, when initial balances are available, political institutions tend to develop in the direction of inefficiency, of ever-growing specifications of control and monitoring mechanisms for many relevant political actors. This implies not only introducing uncertainty in the holding of public authority via political competition and

---

[32] The point of the excellent article by Moe, T. M. (1990), 'Political institutions: the neglected side of the story', *Journal of Law, Economics, and Organization*, 6: 213–53, 230.

introducing institutional forms of power-sharing – separation of powers, territorial federalism, bicameralism, constitutional review procedures, multi-partitism, proportionality principles and so on – but also protecting existing policies from future radical redefinitions. Further protection against bureaucratic encroachment is sought in accountability and oversight processes, reporting requirements, detailed definitions of the instruments and means of the bureaucratic structure, legislative vetoes, and growing possibilities to appeal to courts. And even further, specifying in a detailed way the mandate of the agency, leaving as little as possible to interpretation and leaving few discretionary powers to bureaucrats and therefore little possibility for future authorities to gain control. 'Agency goals, decision criteria, timetables, internal procedures, personnel rules and virtually anything affecting the agency can be effectively and minutely specified in the original legislation.'[33]

In historical cases of dynastic executives and bureaucracies pre-existing democratisation (Europe), and therefore of high previous concentrations of power, groups may request to be involved not only in the decisional processes but also in the implementation processes. To increase security about the direction and quantity of policy change, resourceful groups may demand to be given a share in the implementation of the policy (or to be incorporated somehow in the public bureaucracy meant to implement the policy). Political winners may also want to include losers in the agreement to give them a stake in the change, retaining control but accommodating some of their crucial interests.

This incorporation can be achieved with the development of political norms – rather than codified rules – of ex-ante consultation and necessary negotiations. Even powerful clienteles can be organised around a specific structure or policy. Repeated deals, reputational mechanisms and public commitments may increase the cost of changes in policy direction. Strong norms of reciprocity may be generated among political players engaging repeatedly in the same competitive game in full knowledge that their tenure of public authority is likely to be short and unsafe. In this sense, any government may refrain from subverting an existing deal in the knowledge that a future government could do the

---

[33] Moe, 'Political institutions', pp. 228 and 247.

same. Of course, these mechanisms are more widespread in fully mobilised and democratised polities.

These rules, procedures and controls, while they offer guarantees to
potential and actual losers, affect the effectiveness of policy change.
Therefore, the inefficiency of political institutions does not only come
from the uncertainty, lack of information, limitations of rationality,
incrementalism, short-termism and so on of actors. It is also a specific
property that cannot be judged by any other standard than the mutual
guarantee it offers with respect to the dangerous monopolisation of
behavioural compliance production. The inefficiency of political institutions is inbuilt in the protection of citizens and groups and from the
autonomy of their agents, politicians and bureaucrats, whom they both
fear. This may contribute to making democratic institutions rather
ineffective in performance terms but it clarifies how inappropriate
and misleading it is to judge political institutions by the normative
standards of economic efficiency.[34]

---

[34] Miller and Hammond argue that political limitations to economic efficiency are
a 'logical inevitability'. Miller, G. and T. Hammond (1994), 'Why politics is
more fundamental than economics: incentive-compatible mechanisms are not
credible', *Journal of Theoretical Politics*, 6: 5–26, 8.

References

Abbo, S. et al. (2006), 'The ripples of "The Big (Agricultural) Bang": the spread of the early wheat cultivation', *Genome*, 49: 861–3.

Agranolf, R. M. and M. McGuire (2001), 'American federalism and the search for models of management', *Public Administration Review*, 61: 671–81.

Albert, R. (2015), 'How unwritten constitutional norms change written constitutions', *Dublin University Law Journal*, 38: 387–418.

Alexander, D. R. (1974), 'The evolution of social behavior', *Annual Review of Ecology and Systematics*, 5: 325–83.

Alexy, R. (2002), *A Theory of Constitutional Rights*, Oxford, Oxford University Press.

Alford, J. R. and J. R. Hibbing (2004) 'The origin of politics: an evolutionary theory of political behavior', *Perspectives on Politics*, 2: 707–23.

Alford, J. R., C. L. Funk and J. R. Hibbing (2005), 'Are political orientations genetically transmitted?', *American Political Science Review*, 99: 153–67.

Altman, D. (2008), 'Collegiate executives and direct democracy in Switzerland and Uruguay: similar institutions, opposite political goals, distinct results', *Swiss Political Science Review*, 14: 483–520.

Anderson, E. N. and P. R. Anderson (1967), *Political Institutions and Social Change in Continental Europe in the Nineteenth Century*, Berkeley, University of California Press.

Aoki, M. (1996), 'Towards a comparative institutional analysis: motivations and some tentative theorizing', *The Japanese Economic Review*, 47: 1–19.

Aoki, M. (2000), 'Institutional evolution as punctuated equilibria', in Ménard, C. (ed.), *Institutions, Contracts and Organizations*, Cheltenham, Edward Elgar, pp. 11–33.

Aoki, M. (2001), *Comparative Institutional Analysis*, Cambridge, MA, The MIT Press.

Apahideanu, I. (2014), 'Unicameralism versus bicameralism revisited: the case of Romania', *Studia Politica. Romanian Political Science Review*, 14: 47–88.

Aranda Jimenez, G., S. Monton-Subias and M. Sanchez Romero (eds.) (2011), *Guess Who's Coming to Dinner: Feasting Rituals in Prehistoric Societies of Europe and the Near East*, Oxford, Oxbow Books.

Ardrey, R. (1976), *The Hunting Hypothesis*, London, William Collins Sons & Co.

Arrow, K. J. (1951), *Social Choice and Individual Values*, New York, Wiley.

Atenza, M. and J. Ruitz-Manero (1993), 'Tre approcci ai principi di diritto', in *Analisi e diritto*, Torino, Giappichelli, pp. 13–16.

Aureli, F. et al. (2008), 'Fission-fusion dynamic', *Current Anthropology*, 49: 627–54.

Axelrod, R. (1984), *The Evolution of Cooperation*, New York, Basic Books.

Bagehot, W. (1963 (1872)), *The English Constitution*, Glasgow, Collins.

Bahro, H., B. Bayerlein and E. Veser (1998), 'Duverger's concept: semi-presidential government revisited', *European Journal of Political Research*, 34: 201–24.

Bar, Y. O. (2002), 'The Natufian culture and the early Neolithic: social and economic trends in Southwest Asia', in Bellwood, P. and C. Renfrew (eds.), *Examining the Farming/Language Dispersal Hypothesis*, Cambridge, McDonald Institute for Archaeological Research, pp. 113–26.

Bartolini, S. (1988), 'Principio di maggioranza, regola di maggioranza e decisione di maggioranza', introduction to Favre, P., *La Decisione di Maggioranza*, Milan, Giuffré, pp. 2–27.

Bartolini S. (1999–2000), 'Collusion, competition and democracy', part I, *Journal of Theoretical Politics*, 11: 435–70; part II, *Journal of Theoretical Politics*, 12: 33–65.

Bartolini, S. (2000), *The Electoral Mobilisation of the European Left: The Class Cleavage 1880–1980*, Cambridge, Cambridge University Press.

Bartolini, S. (2018), *The Political*, Colchester, ECPR Press.

Battegazzorre, F. (2012), *Saggi sopra la teoria delle istituzioni politiche*, Genoa, Coedit.

Baylis, H. T. (1980), 'Collegial leadership in advanced industrial societies: the relevance of the Swiss experience', *Polity*, 13: 33–56.

Bedock, C. (2017), *Reforming Democracy: Institutional Engineering in Western Europe*, Oxford, Oxford University Press.

Beger, P. L. and T. Luckmann (1967), *The Social Construction of Reality*, New York, Doubleday Anchor.

Bellwood, P. and C. Renfrew (eds.) (2002), *Examining the Farming/Language Dispersal Hypothesis*, Cambridge, McDonald Institute for Archaeological Research.

Bendix, R. (1973), *State and Society*, Berkeley, University of California Press.

Berger, J. and M. Zelditch Jr (eds.) (2000), *New Directions in Sociological Theory: The Growth of Contemporary Theories*, Lanham, MD, Rowman & Littlefield.

Bingham Powell, G. (1989), 'Constitutional design and citizen electoral control', *Journal of Theoretical Politics*, 1: 107–30.

Birnbaum, P. (1988), *State and Collective Action: The European Experience*, Cambridge, Cambridge University Press.

Black, D. (1958), *The Theory of Committees and Elections*, Cambridge, Cambridge University Press.

Blau, P. M. (ed.) (1975), *Approaches to the Study of Social Structure*, New York, Free Press.

Blau, P. M. and R. W. Scott (1962), *Formal Organizations*, San Francisco, CA, Chandler.

Blockmans, W. P. (1978), 'A typology of representative institutions in late medieval Europe', *Journal of Medieval History*, 4: 189–215.

Blondel, J. (2006), 'About institutions, mainly, but not exclusively, political', in Rhodes, R. A. W., S. A. Binder and B. A. Rockman (eds.), *The Oxford Handbook of Political Institutions*, Oxford, Oxford University Press, pp. 716–30.

Blossfled H.-P. (1996), 'Macro-sociology, rational choice theory and time: a theoretical perspective on the empirical analysis of social processes', *European Sociological Review*, 12: 181–206.

Bobbio, N. (1981), 'La regola di maggioranza: limiti e aporie', in Bobbio, N., C. Offe and S. Lombardini (eds.), *Democrazia, maggioranza e minoranze*, Bologna, Il Mulino, pp. 33–72.

Bobbio, N., C. Offe and S. Lombardini (eds.) (1981), *Democrazia, maggioranza e minoranze*, Bologna, Il Mulino.

Börzel, T. A. and T. Risse (2015), 'Dysfunctional institutions, social trust, and governance in areas of limited statehood', Berlin, SFB-Governance Working Paper Series, No. 67, Collaborative Research Center (SFB) 700.

Bovens, M. (2007), 'Analysing and assessing accountability: a conceptual framework', *European Law Journal*, 13: 447–68.

Braun, D. (2004), 'Intergovernmental relationships and fiscal policymaking in federal countries', in Imbeau, L. M. and F. Petry (eds.), *Politics, Institutions, and Fiscal Policy: Deficits and Surpluses in Federated States*, London, Lexington Books, pp. 21–48.

Brunner, O. (1984 (1898)), *Land und Herrschaft: Grundfragen der territorialen Verfassungsgeschichte Österreichs im Mittelalter*, Darmstadt, Wissenschaftliche Buchgesellschaft.

Buchanan, J. M. and G. Tullock (1962), *The Calculus of Consent: Logical Foundations of Constitutional Democracy*, Ann Arbor, The University of Michigan Press.

Bueno de Mesquita, B., A. Smith, R. M. Siverson and J. D. Morrow (2003), *The Logic of Political Survival*, Boston, MA, The MIT Press.

Bunn, H. T. and A. N. Gurtov (2014), 'Prey mortality profiles indicate that early Pleistocene Homo at Olduvai was an ambush predator', *Quaternary International*, 322/323, 16 February.

Burbank, J. and F. Cooper (2011), *Empires in World History: Power and the Politics of Difference*, Princeton, NJ, Princeton University Press.

Capoccia, G. (2015), 'Critical juncture and institutional change', in Mahoney J. and K. Thelen (eds.), *Advances in Comparative Historical Analysis*, Cambridge, Cambridge University Press, pp. 147–79.

Caravale, M. (1994), *Ordinamenti giuridici dell'Europa Medioevale*, Bologna, Il Mulino.

Carbon, J.-M., S. Peels and V. Pirenne-Delforge (2018), *Collection of Greek Ritual Norms*, 2 vols., Paris, Editions de Boccard.

Casella, A. and B. R. Weingast (1995), 'Elements of a theory of jurisdictional change', in Eichengreen, B., J. Frieden and J. von Hagen (eds.), *Politics and Institutions in an Integrated Europe*, New York, Springer, pp. 11–41.

Casey, G. (2009), 'The indefensibility of political representation', talk given at the Austrian Scholars Conference, 13 March.

Chapais, B. (2013), 'Monogamy, strongly bonded groups and the evolution of human social structure', *Evolutionary Anthropology*, 22: 52–65.

Chehabi, H. E. and A. Stephan (eds.) (1995), *Politics, Society, and Democracy: Comparative Studies*, Boulder, CO, Westview Press.

Cheibub, J. A. and F. Limogi (2002), 'Democratic institutions and regime survival: parliamentary and presidential democracies reconsidered', *Annual Review of Political Science*, 5: 151–79.

Cheibub, J. A., J. Elkins and T. Ginsburg (2010), 'Latin American presidentialism in comparative and historical perspective', *Texas Law Review*, 89: 170–3.

Chomsky, N. (1965), *Aspects of the Theory of Syntax*, Boston, MA, MIT Press.

Cole, S. (1970), *The Neolithic Revolution*, London, Trustees of the British Museum.

Congleton, R. D. and B. Swedenborg (eds.) (2006), *Democratic Constitutional Design and Public Policy*, Boston, MA, MIT Press.

Cook, K. S. and M. Levi (eds.) (1990), *The Limits of Rationality*, Chicago, IL, University of Chicago Press.

Couzin, I. D., J. Krause, N. R. Franks and S. A. Levin (2005), 'Effective leadership and decision-making in animal groups on the move', *Nature*, 433, 7025: 513–16.

Coyne, J. A. (2011), 'Can Darwinism improve Binghamton?', *New York Review of Books*, 9 September.

Crawford, S. E. S. and E. Ostrom (1995), 'A grammar of institutions', *American Political Science Review*, 89: 582–600.

Croce, M. (2014), 'Is law a special domain? On the boundary between the legal and the social', in Donlan, S. P. and L. Heckendorn Urscheler (eds.), *Concepts of Law: Comparative, Jurisprudential, and Social Science Perspectives*, Burlington, VT, Ashgate, pp. 153–67.

Czada, R., A. Héritier and H. Keman (1996), 'Introduction', in Czada, R., A. Héritier and H. Keman (eds.), *Institutions and Political Choice: On the Limits of Rationality*, Amsterdam, VU University Press, pp. 11–24.

Czada, R., A. Héritier and H. Keman (eds.) (1996), *Institutions and Political Choice: On the Limits of Rationality*, Amsterdam, VU University Press.

Daalder, H. (1971), 'On building consociational nations: the case of the Netherlands and Switzerland', *International Social Science Journal*, 23: 355–70.

Daalder, H. (1984), 'On the origins of the consociational model', *Acta Politica*, 19: 97–116.

Daalder, H. (1995), 'Paths towards state formation in Europe: democratization, bureaucratization and politicization', in Chehabi, H. E. and A. Stephan (eds.), *Politics, Society, and Democracy: Comparative Studies*, Boulder, CO, Westview Press, pp. 113–30.

Dahl, R. (1956), *A Preface to Democratic Theory*, Chicago, IL, The University of Chicago Press.

Dahl, R. A. (1971), *Poliarchy, Participation and Opposition*, New Haven, CT, Yale University Press.

Darwin C. (1868), *The Variation of Animals and Plants under Domestication*, vol. 1, London, John Murray.

Darwin, C. (1871), *The Descent of Man, and Selection in Relation to Sex*, London, John Murray.

Dawes, C. T. and J. H. Fawler (2009), 'Partisanship, voting, and the dopamine D receptor gene', *Journal of Politics*, 71: 1157–71.

Dawkins, R. (1976), *The Selfish Gene*, Oxford, Oxford University Press.

Deacon, T. W. (2012), *Incomplete Nature: How Mind Emerged from Matter*, New York, W. W. Norton & Company Inc.

de Fina, S. (1974), *Diritto e società*, Milan, Giuffré.

de Jouvenel, B. (1963), *The Pure Theory of Politics*, Cambridge, Cambridge University Press.

de Jouvenel, B. (1992 (1959)), 'Authority: the efficient imperative', in Hale, D. and M. Landy (eds.), *The Nature of Politics: Selected Essays of Bertrand de Jouvenel*, New Brunswick, NJ, Transaction, pp. 84–93.

del Mar, M. (2014), 'Beyond the state in and of legal theory', in Donlan, S. P. and L. Heckendorn Urscheler (eds.), *Concepts of Law: Comparative, Jurisprudential, and Social Science Perspectives*, Burlington, VT, Ashgate, pp. 19–42.

del Mar, M. and Z. Bankowski (eds.) (2009), *Law as Institutional Normative Order*, Farnham, Ashgate.

de Waal, F. (1989), *Peace-Making among Primates*, Cambridge, MA, Harvard University Press.

de Waal, F. (2005), *Our Inner Ape*, New York, Penguin Books.

de Waal, F. (2010), *The Age of Empathy: Nature's Lessons for a Kinder Society*, Portland, OR, Broadway Books.

di Carlo, L. (2017), *Teoria istituzionale e ragionamento giuridico*, Turin, Giappichelli.

di Maggio, P. J. and W. W. Powell (1991), 'The iron cage revisited: institutional isomorphism and collective rationality in organizational fields', in Powell, W. W. and P. J. Di Maggio (eds.), *The New Institutionalism in Organizational Analysis*, Chicago, IL, University of Chicago Press, pp. 41–62.

Doering, H. (ed.) (12995), *Parliaments and Majority Rule in Western Europe*, New York, St Martin's Press.

Donlan, S. P. and L. Heckendorn Urscheler (eds.) (2014), *Concepts of Law: Comparative, Jurisprudential, and Social Science Perspectives*, Burlington, VT, Ashgate.

Drewry, G. (1998), 'Political institutions: legal perspectives', in Goodin, R. E. and H. D. Klingemann (eds.), *A New Handbook of Political Science*, Oxford, Oxford University Press, pp. 191–204.

Dubreuil, B. (2008), 'Strong reciprocity and the emergence of large-scale societies', *Philosophy of the Social Sciences*, 38: 192–210.

Durkheim E. (1919) *Les règles de la méthode sociologique*, Paris, Librairie Félix Alcan.

Duverger, M. (1960, 5th ed.), *Institutions Politiques et Droit Constitutionnel*, Paris, Presses Universitaires de France.

Duverger, M. (1980), 'A new political system model: semi-presidential government', *European Journal of Political Research*, 8: 165–87.

Dworkin, R. (2004), 'Hart's postscript and the character of political philosophy', *Oxford Journal of Legal Studies*, 37: 119–37.

Earle, T. K. (1997), *How Chiefs Came to Power: The Political Economy of Prehistory*, Stanford, CA, Stanford University Press.

Easton, D. (1990), *The Analysis of Political Structures*, London, Routledge.

Ehrlich, E. (1936), *Foundational Principles of the Sociology of Law*, New York, Russel and Russel.

Eichengreen, B., J. Frieden and J. von Hagen (eds.) (1995), *Politics and Institutions in an Integrated Europe*, New York, Springer.

Eisenstadt, S. (1963), *The Political Systems of Empires: The Rise and Fall of the Historical Bureaucratic Societies*, New York, The Free Press.

Eisenstadt, S. N. (1968), 'Social institutions: the concept', in *International Encyclopaedia of the Social Sciences*, London, The Macmillan Company, vol. 14, pp. 409–29.

Eisenstadt, S. N. and B. Giesen (1995), 'The construction of collective identity', *Archives Européennes de Sociologie*, 36: 72–104.

Eisenstadt, S. N. and S. Rokkan (eds.) (1973), *Building States and Nations*, 2 vols., New York, Sage.

Elazar, D. E. (1987), *Exploring Federalism*, Tuscaloosa, University of Alabama Press.

Elgie, R. (ed.) (2001), *Divided Government in Comparative Perspective*, Oxford, Oxford University Press.

Ellickson, R. (1991), *Order without Law: How Neighbours Settle Disputes*, Cambridge, MA, Harvard University Press.

Elster, J. (2007), *Explaining Social Behavior: More Nuts and Bolts for the Social Sciences*, Cambridge, Cambridge University Press.

Etzioni, A (1961), *Modern Organizations*, Hempstead, Prentice Hall.

Etzioni, A. (1975), *A Comparative Analysis of Complex Organizations*, New York, Free Press.

Fabbrini, S. (2010), *Compound Democracies: Why the United States and Europe Are Becoming Similar*, Oxford, Oxford University Press.

Favre, P. (1976), *La décision de majorité*, Paris, Presses de la Fondation Nationale des Sciences Politiques.

Favre, P. (1988), *La Decisione di Maggioranza*, Milan, Giuffré.

Fawler, J. H. and C. T. Dawes (2008), 'Two genes predict voter turnout', *Journal of Politics* 70: 579–94.

Fawler, J. H., L. A. Baker and C. T. Dawes (2008), 'Genetic variation in political participation', *American Political Science Review*, 102: 233–48.

Ferguson, B. (2018), 'Perché combattiamo?', *Le Scienze*, no. 603, November, pp. 72–7.

Ferrante, M. and S. Zan (1994), *Il fenomeno organizzativo*, Rome, La Nuova Italia Scientifica.

Ferraro, J. V. et al. (2013), 'Earliest archaeological evidence of persistent hominin carnivory', *PLoS ONE*, 8, 4, article N.162164.

Finer, S. E. (1979), *Five Constitutions*, London, Penguin.

Finer, S. E. (1997), *The History of Government*, 3 vols., Oxford, Oxford University Press.

Foley, A. R. (2001), 'Evolutionary perspectives on the origins of human social institutions', in Runciman, W. G. (ed.), *The Origins of Human Social Institutions*, Proceedings of The British Academy, New York, Oxford University Press, pp. 192–3.

Frantz, C. and K. Schubert (eds.) (2010), *Einführung in die Politikwissenschaft*, Hamburg, Lit.

Frey, B. S. (1990), 'Institutions matter: the comparative analysis of institutions', *European Economic Review*, 34: 443–9.

Galligan, B. (2006), 'Comparative federalism', in Rhodes, R. A. W., S. A. Binder and B. A. Rockman (eds.), *The Oxford Handbook of Political Institutions*, Oxford, Oxford University Press, pp. 261–80.

Gandhi, J. and A. Przeworski (2007), 'Authoritarian institutions and the survival of autocrats', *Comparative Political Studies*, 40: 1279–1301.

Ganghof, S. (2003), 'Premises and pitfalls of veto player analysis', *Swiss Political Science Review*, 9: 1–25.

Garrett, E., E. Graddy and H. Jackson (eds.) (2008), *Fiscal Challenges: An Interdisciplinary Approach to Budget Policy*, Cambridge, Cambridge University Press.

Gaudemet, L. (1993), *Les Sources du droit canonique (VIIIe–XXe siècles)*, Paris, Cerf.

Geddes, B., J. Wright and E. Frantz (2014), 'Autocratic breakdown and regime transitions: a new data set', *Perspectives on Politics*, 12: 313–31.

Giglioli, P. P. (1989), 'Teorie dell'azione', in Panebianco, A. (ed.), *L' analisi della politica. Tradizioni di ricerca, modelli, teorie*, Bologna, Il Mulino, pp. 107–33.

Gilison, J. (1967), 'New factors of stability in Soviet collective leadership', *World Politics*, 19: 563–58.

Ginsburg, T. (ed.) (2012), *Comparative Constitutional Design*, Cambridge, Cambridge University Press.

Ginsburg, T., Z. Elkins and J. Blount (2009), 'Does the process of constitution making matter?', *Annual Review of Law and Social Science*, 5: 201–29.

Ginsburg, T., Z. Elkins and J. Melton (2012), 'Do executive term limits cause constitutional crises?', in Ginsburg, T. (ed.), *Comparative Constitutional Design*, Cambridge, Cambridge University Press, pp. 350–79.

Gintis, H. (2000), 'Strong reciprocity and human sociability', *Journal of Theoretical Biology*, 43: 169–79.

Girard, R. (1972), *La Violence et le Sacré*, Paris, Grassett (English translation: (1977), *Violence and the Sacred*, Baltimore, MD, Johns Hopkins University Press).

Girotto, V., T. Pievani and G. Vallortigara (2008), *Nati per credere. Perché il nostro cervello sembra predisposto a fraintendere la teoria di Darwin*, Turin, Codice Edizioni.

Goodin, R. E. (1966), *The Theory of Institutional Design*, Cambridge, Cambridge University Press.

Goodin, R. E. and H. D. Klingemann (eds.) (1998), *A New Handbook of Political Science*, Oxford, Oxford University Press.

Graham, B. A. T., M. K. Miller and K. W. Strøm (2017) 'Safeguarding democracy: power sharing and democratic survival', *American Political Science Review*, 111: 686–704.

Granovetter, M. (1985), 'Economic action and social structure: the problem of embeddedness', *American Journal of Sociology*, 91: 481–510.

Green, R. E., J. Krause, A. W. Briggs et al. (2010), 'A draft sequence of the Neandertal genome', *Science*, 328, 5979: 710–22.

Greenstein, F. I. and N. W. Polsby (eds.) (1975), *The Handbook of Political Science*, 8 vols, Reading, MA, Addison-Wesley Pub. Co.

Greenwood, R., C. Oliver, K. Sahlin and R. Suddaby (2008), 'Introduction', in Greenwood, R., C. Oliver, K. Sahlin and R. Suddaby (eds.), *The Sage Handbook of Organizational Institutionalism*, London, Sage, pp. 1–46.

Greenwood, R., C. Oliver, K. Sahlin and R. Suddaby (eds.) (2008), *The Sage Handbook of Organizational Institutionalism*, London, Sage.

Greif, A. and C. Kingston (2011), 'Institutions: rules or equilibria', in Schofield, N. and G. Caballero (eds.), *Political Economy of Institutions, Democracy and Voting*, Berlin, Springer-Verlag, pp. 13–43.

Greif, A. and D. Laitin (2004), 'A theory of endogenous institutional change', *American Political Science Review*, 98: 633–52.

Gretchen, H. and S. Levitsky (2004), 'Informal institutions and comparative politics: a research agenda', *Perspectives on Politics*, 2: 725–40.

Grimm, D. (1993), *Diritto e politica, in Enciclopedia delle Scienze Sociali*, Turin, Istituto dell'Enciclopedia Italiana Treccani, vol. 3, pp. 113–19.

Gross, E. and A. Etzioni (1985), *Organizations in Society*, Englewood Cliffs, NJ, Prentice-Hall.

Habermas, J. (1996), *Between Facts and Norms: Contributions to a Discursive Theory of Law and Democracy*, Boston, MA, Polity Press.

Hage, J. (2009), 'What is a legal transaction?', in del Mar, M. and Z. Bankowski (eds.), *Law as Institutional Normative Order*, Farnham, Ashgate, pp. 104–21.

Hale, D. and M. Landy (eds.) (1992), *The Nature of Politics: Selected Essays of Bertrand de Jouvenel*, New Brunswick, NJ, Transaction.

Hall, P. A. and R. C. R. Taylor (1996), 'Political science and the three new institutionalisms', *Political Studies*, 44: 936–57.

Hamilton, W. D. (1964a), 'The genetical evolution of social behaviour', I, *Journal of Theoretical Biology*, 7: 1–16.

Hamilton, W. D. (1964b), 'Genetic evolution of social behaviour', II, *Journal of Theoretical Biology*, 7: 17–52.

Harris, J. (2006), 'Development of civil society', in Rhodes, R. A. W., S. A. Binder and B. A. Rockman (eds.), *The Oxford Handbook of Political Institutions*, Oxford, Oxford University Press, pp. 131–43.

Hart, H. L. A. (1961 (1994)), *The Concept of Law*, Oxford, Oxford University Press.

Hart, H. L. A. (1961), *The Law as a Union of Primary and Secondary Rule*, Oxford, Oxford University Press.

Hawkins, D., D. A. Lake, D. Nielson and M. J. Tierney (2006), *Delegation under Anarchy: Principals, Agents, and International Organizations*, Cambridge, Cambridge University Press.

Hayden, B. (2011), 'Feasting and social dynamics in the Epipaleolithic of the Fertile Crescent', in Aranda Jimenez, G., S. Monton-Subias and M. Sanchez Romero (eds.), *Guess Who's Coming to Dinner: Feasting Rituals in Prehistoric Societies of Europe and the Near East*, Oxford, Oxbow Books, pp. 30–63.

Héritier, A. (1999), *Policy-Making and Diversity in Europe: Escape from Deadlock*, Cambridge, Cambridge University Press.

Héritier, A. (2007), *Explaining Institutional Change in Europe*, Oxford, Oxford University Press.

Hirschl, R. (2013), 'From comparative constitutional law to comparative constitutional studies', *International Journal of Constitutional Law*, 11: 1–12.

Hobbes, T. (2012 (1651)), *Leviathan or The Matter, Forme and Power of a Commonwealth Ecclesiastical and Civil*, Oxford, Oxford University Press.

Hohfeld, W. N. (1913), 'Some fundamental legal conceptions as applied in judicial reasoning', in Patterson, D. (ed.), *Philosophy of Law and Legal Theory: An Anthology*, Oxford, Blackwell, pp. 295–321.

Holden, M. (2006), 'Exclusion, inclusion and political institutions', in Rhodes, R. A. W., S. A. Binder and B. A. Rockman (eds.), *The Oxford Handbook of Political Institutions*, Oxford, Oxford University Press, pp. 163–90.

Hollingsworth, R. J. (2000), 'Doing institutional analysis: implications for the study of innovations', *Review of International Political Economy*, 7: 595–644.

Hooghe, L. and G. Marks (2003), 'Unraveling the central state but how? Types of multi-level governance', *American Political Science Review*, 97: 223–43.

Horowitz, D. (2002), 'Constitutional design: proposals versus processes', in Reynolds, A. (ed.), *The Architecture of Democracy: Constitutional Design, Conflict Management, and Democracy*, Oxford, Oxford University Press, pp. 15–36.

Huber, J. D. and C. R. Shipan (2009), 'Politics, delegation, and bureaucracy', in Goodin, R. E. (ed.), *The Oxford Handbook of Political Science*, Oxford, Oxford University Press, pp. 849–65.

Hudgson, G. M. (2006), 'What are institutions?', *Journal of Economic Issues*, 40: 1–25.

Huntington, S. (1968), *Political Order in Changing Societies*, New Haven, CT, Yale University Press.

Ieraci, G. (1994a), 'Presidenzialismo e parlamentarismo nelle "Democrazie Difficili"', *Quaderni di scienza politica*, I: 35–78.

Ieraci, G. (1994b), 'Forms of democratic government: a study of the impact of institutions on political competition', Oxford, Centre for European Studies, Discussion Paper no. 32, July.

Imbeau, L. M. and F. Petry (eds.) (2004), *Politics, Institutions, and Fiscal Policy: Deficits and Surpluses in Federated States*, London, Lexington Books.

Immergut, E. (1998), 'The theoretical core of the New Institutionalism', *Politics and Society*, 26, 1: 5–34.

Jacoby, S. (1985), *Wild Justice: The Evolution of Revenge*, London, William Collins.

Jepperson, R. L. (2000), 'The development and application of sociological institutionalism', in Berger, J. and M. Zelditch Jr (eds.), *New Directions in Sociological Theory: The Growth of Contemporary Theories*, Lanham, MD, Rowman & Littlefield, pp. 229–66.

Jones, T. (2006), 'We always have a beer after the meeting: how norms, customs, conventions, and the like explain behavior', *Philosophy of the Social Sciences*, 36: 251–75.

Kant, I. (1958 (1797)), *Groundwork of the Methaphisic of Morals*, New York, Harper Torchbooks.

Kappeler, P. M. and J. Silk (eds.) (2010), *Mind the Gap: Tracing the Origins of Human Universals*, Frankfurt, Springer.

Kassim, H. and A. Menon (2003), 'The principal-agent approach and the study of European Union: promise unfulfilled?', *Journal of European Public Policy*, 10: 121–39.

Katnelson, I. and A. R. Zolberg (eds.) (1986), *Working Class Formation in Western Europe and the United States*, Princeton, NJ, Princeton University Press.

Katoh, S. et al. (2016), 'New geological and paleontological age constraint for the gorilla-human lineage split', *Nature*, 530, 35: 215–18, doi: 10.1038/nature16510.

Kelsen, H. (1934), *Reine Rechtslehre: Einleitung in die rechtswissenschaftliche Problematik*, Leipzig, Deuticke (English version: (1967), *The Pure Theory of Law*, Berkeley, University of California Press).

Kelsen, H. (1945), *General Theory of Law and the State*, Cambridge, MA, Harvard University Press.

Keohane, R. (2001), 'Governance in a partially globalized world', *American Political Science Review*, 95: 1–13.

Khalil, E. (1995), 'Organizations versus Institutions', *Journal of Institutional and Theoretical Economics/Zeitscrift fur die gesamte Staatswissenschaft*, 151: 445–66.

King, A. J., D. P. Johnson and M. Van Vugt (2009), 'The origins and evolution of leadership', *Current Biology*, 19: 11–16.

Kingston, C. G. and R. E. Wright (2010), 'The deadliest of games: the institution of duelling', *Southern Economic Journal*, 76: 1094–1106.

Kiser, E. (1999), 'Comparing varieties of agency theory in economics, political science, and sociology: an illustration from state policy implementation', *Sociological Theory*, 17: 146–70.

Knight, J. (1992), *Institutions and Social Conflict*, Cambridge, Cambridge University Press.

Knight, J. and I. Send (eds.) (1995), *Explaining Social Institutions*, Ann Arbor, University of Michigan Press.

Kourikoski, J. and A. Lehtinen (2010), 'Economic imperialism and solution concepts in political science', *Philosophy of the Social Sciences*, 4: 347–70.

Kramer, J. and J. Meunier (2016), 'Kin and multilevel selection in social evolution: a never-ending controversy', *F1000Research*, 5: 776.

Krasner, D. (1999), *Sovereignty: Organized Hypocrisy*, Princeton, NJ, Princeton University Press.

Krol, G. (2020), 'Legislating parliaments in authoritarian regimes: Eurasian legislatures and presidents compared', Florence, European University Institute, PhD dissertation.

Lane, J.-E. and S. Ersson (2000), *The New Institutional Politics: Performance and Outcomes*, New York, Routledge.

Lasswell, H. and A. Kaplan (1950), *Power and Society: A Framework for Political Enquiry*, New Haven, CT, Yale University Press.

Laver, M. and K. A. Shepsle (eds.) (1994), *Cabinet Ministers and Parliamentary Government*, Cambridge, Cambridge University Press.

Lawrence, T. B. (2008), 'Power, institutions and organizations', in Greenwood, R., C. Oliver, K. Sahlin and R. Suddaby (eds.), *The Sage Handbook of Organizational Institutionalism*, London, Sage, pp. 170–97.

LeBlanc, S. A. with K. E. Register (2003), *Constant Battles: The Myth of the Peaceful, Noble Savage*, London, St Martin's Press.

Lee, R. B. and I. DeVore (eds.) (1968), *Man the Hunter*, New York, Aldine Publishing Company.

Leoni, B. (1961), *Freedom and the Law*, Indianapolis, IN, Liberty Fund (Italian version: (1994), *La libertà e la legge*, Liberilibri di AMA, Macerata).

Levi, M. (1990), *A Logic of Institutional Change*, in Cook, K. S. and M. Levi (eds.), *The Limits of Rationality*, Chicago, IL, University of Chicago Press, pp. 402–19.

Lewis, D. K. (1969), *Convention*, Cambridge, MA, Harvard University Press.

Lewis, O. and S. Steinmo (2012), 'How institutions evolve: evolutionary theory and institutional change', *Polity*, 44: 314–39.

Lieberman, D. E. (2014), *The Story of the Human Body: Evolution, Health and Diseases*, London, Penguin Books.

Lijphart, A. (1968), *The Politics of Accommodation: Pluralism and Democracy in the Netherlands*, Berkeley, University of California Press.

Lijphart, A. (1984), *Democracies: Patterns of Majoritarian and Consensus Government in Twenty-one Countries*, New Haven, CT, Yale University Press.

Lijphart, A. (2004), 'Constitutional design for divided societies', *Journal of Democracy*, 15: 96–109.

Linz, J. J. (1994), 'Presidential and parliamentary democracy: does it make a difference?', in Linz, J. J. and A. Valenzuela (eds.), *The Failure of Presidential Democracy*, Baltimore, MD, Johns Hopkins University Press, pp. 34–9.

Linz, J. J. and A. Valenzuela (eds.) (1994), *The Failure of Presidential Democracy*, Baltimore, MD, Johns Hopkins University Press.

Locke, J. (1988 (1689)), *Two Treaties of Government*, Cambridge, Cambridge University Press.

Loewenstein, K. (1965), *Political Power and the Governmental Process*, Chicago, IL, University of Chicago Press.

Lord, R. H. (1930), 'The parliaments of the Middle Ages and the early modern period', *Catholic Historical Review*, 16: 125–8.

Lorini, G. (2014), 'Meta-institutional concepts: a new category for social ontology', *Rivista di Estetica*, 56: 127–39.

Lovejoy, C. O. (2009), 'Reexamining human origins in light of Ardipithecus Ramidus', *Science*, 326: 74–8.

Low, A. J. (2003), *Manhood and the Duel: Masculinity in Early Modern Drama and Culture*, New York, Palgrave Macmillan.

MacCormick, N. (2007), *Institutions of Law: An Essay in Legal Theory*, Oxford, Oxford University Press.

Macintyre, A. (2003), *The Power of Institutions*, Ithaca, NY, Cornell University Press.

Mahoney, J. and D. Rueschemeyer (eds.) (2003), *Comparative Historical Analysis in the Social Sciences*, Cambridge, Cambridge University Press.

Mahoney, J. and K. Thelen (2010), 'A theory of gradual institutional change', in Mahoney, J. and K. Thelen (eds.), *Explaining Institutional Change: Ambiguity, Agency and Power*, New York, Cambridge University Press, pp. 1–37.

Mahoney, J. and K. Thelen (eds.) (2010), *Explaining Institutional Change: Ambiguity, Agency and Power*, New York, Cambridge University Press.

Mahoney J. and K. Thelen (eds.) (2015), *Advances in Comparative Historical Analysis*, Cambridge, Cambridge University Press.

Mainwaring, S. (1993), 'Presidentialism, multipartism, and democracy: the difficult combination', *Comparative Political Studies*, 26: 198–228.

Mann, M. (1993), *The Sources of Social Power, vol. 2: The Rise of Classes and Nation-States, 1760–1914*, Cambridge, Cambridge University Press.

Mantzavinos, C., D. C. North and S. Shariq (2004), 'Learning, institutions, and economic performance', *Perspectives on Politics*, 2: 75–84.

Manzanilla, L. R. (2009), 'Corporate life in apartment and barrio compounds at Teotihuacan Central Mexico', in Manzanilla L. R. and C. Chapdelaine (eds.), *Domestic Life in Prehispanic Capitals: A Study of Specialization, Hierarchy, and Ethnicity*, Ann Arbor, University of Michigan Museum of Anthropology, pp. 21–42.

Manzanilla L. R. and C. Chapdelaine (eds.) (2009), *Domestic Life in Prehispanic Capitals: A Study of Specialization, Hierarchy, and Ethnicity*, Ann Arbor, University of Michigan Museum of Anthropology,

March, J. G. and J. P. Olsen (1989), *Rediscovering Institutions: The Organizational Basis of Politics*, New York, The Free Press.

March, J. G. and J. P. Olsen (2006), 'Elaborating the "New Institutionalism"', in Rhodes, R. A. W., S. A. Binder and B. A. Rockman (eds.), *The Oxford Handbook of Political Institutions*, Oxford, Oxford University Press, pp. 3-20.

March, J. G. and H. A. Simon (1959), *Organizations*, New York, Wiley.

March, J. G., M. Schulz and X. Zhou (2000), *The Dynamics of Rules: Changes in Written Organizational Codes*, Stanford, CA, Stanford University Press.

Margalit, E. U. (1977), *The Emergence of Norms*, Oxford, Oxford University Press.

Margalit, E. U. (1978), 'Invisible-hand explanations', *Synthèse*, 39: 263–91.

Marshall, G. (1984), *Constitutional Conventions: The Rules and Forms of Political Accountability*, Oxford, Oxford University Press.

Marshall, G. (ed.) (1989), *Ministerial Responsibility*, Oxford, Oxford University Press.

Martin, T. W. (1968), 'Social institutions: a reformulation of the concept', *Pacific Sociological Review*, 11: 100–10.

Maryland v. Louisiana, 451 U.S. 725, 746 (1981).

Mattei, U. (1997), 'Three patterns of law: taxonomy and change in the world's legal systems', *American Journal of Comparative Law*, 45: 5–44.

May, K. (1952), 'A set of independent necessary and sufficient conditions for simple majority decisions', *Econometrica*, October, pp. 680–4.

Mayer, W. and B. Rowan (1977), 'Institutionalized organizations: formal structure as myth and ceremony', *American Journal of Sociology*, 83: 340–63.

McCubbins, M. D., R. Noll and B. Weingast (1998), 'Political control of the bureaucracy', in Newman, P. (ed.), *The New Palgrave Dictionary of Economics and Law*, London, Palgrave, pp. 50–5.

Mead, M. (1990 (1940)), 'War is only an invention – not a biological necessity', in *The Dolphin Reader*, 2nd ed., Boston, MA, Houghton Mifflin Company, pp. 415–21.

Ménard, C. (ed.) (2000), *Institutions, Contracts and Organizations*, Cheltenham, Edward Elgar.

Merton, R. K. (1940), 'Bureaucratic structure and personality', *Social Forces*, 18: 560–8.

Meyer, J. W. and B. Rowen (1991), 'Institutionalized organizations: formal structures as myth and ceremony', in Powell, W. W. and P. J. Di Maggio (eds.), *The New Institutionalism in Organizational Analysis*, Chicago, IL, University of Chicago Press, pp. 63–82.

Mille, P. D. (2011, reprint), *Deuteronomy*, Westminster, John Knox Press.

Miller, G. and T. Hammond (1994), 'Why politics is more fundamental than economics: incentive-compatible mechanisms are not credible', *Journal of Theoretical Politics*, 6: 5–26.

Miller, M. K. (2015), 'Democratic pieces: autocratic elections and democratic development since 1815', *British Journal of Political Science*, 45: 501–30.

Mitchell, L. E. (1999), 'Understanding norms', *University of Toronto Law Review*, 49: 177–258.

Moe, T. M. (1984), 'The new economics of organization', *American Journal of Political Science*, 28: 739–77.

Moe, T. M. (1990), 'Political institutions: the neglected side of the story', *Journal of Law, Economics, and Organization*, 6: 213–53.

Moe, T. M. (2005), 'Power and political institutions', *Perspectives on Politics*, 3: 215–33.

Monod, J. (1971), *Chance and Necessity: An Essay on the Natural Philosophy of Modern Biology*, New York, Alfred A. Knopf.

Monroe, K. R., A. Martin and P. Ghosh (2009), 'Politics and an innate moral sense: scientific evidence for an old theory?', *Political Research Quarterly*, 62: 614–34.

Moore, B. (1966), *Social Origins of Democracy and Dictatorship: Lord and Peasant in the Making of the Modern World*, Boston, MA, Beacon Press.

Moreno, E. (2011), 'The society of our "Out of Africa Ancestors" (I): the migrant warriors that colonized the world', *Communicative and Integrative Biology*, 4: 1–9.

Morlino, L. (1998), *Democracy between Consolidation and Crisis: Parties, Groups and Citizens in Southern Europe*, Oxford, Oxford University Press.

Nelken, D. (2014), 'Legal sociology and the sociology of norms', in Donlan, S. P. and L. Heckendorn Urscheler (eds.), *Concepts of Law: Comparative, Jurisprudential, and Social Science Perspectives*, Burlington, VT, Ashgate, pp. 138–51.

Nettl, P. J. (1968), 'The state as a conceptual variable', *World Politics*, 20: 560–92.

Newman, P. (ed.) (1998), *The New Palgrave Dictionary of Economics and Law*, London, Palgrave.

Nocilla, D. and L. Ciaurro (1987), 'Rappresentanza politica', in *Enciclopedia del diritto*, vol. 38, Milan, Giuffré, pp. 543–609.

Nordlinger, A. (1972), *Conflict Regulation in Divided Societies*, Cambridge, MA, Harvard University Press.

North, D. C. (1981), *Structure and Change in Economic History*, New York, Norton.

North, D. C. (1990), *Institutions, Institutional Change and Economic Performance*, Cambridge, Cambridge University Press.

North, D. C. (1994), 'Economic performance through time', *The American Economic Review*, 84: 359–68.

North, D. C. (1995), 'Five propositions about institutional change', in Knight, J. and I. Send (eds.), *Explaining Social Institutions*, Ann Arbor, University of Michigan Press, pp. 15–26.

Nowak, M. A., C. E. Tarnita and H. E. O. Wilson (2010), 'The evolution of eusociality', *Nature*, 466, 7310: 1057–62.

Nozick, R. (1974), *Anarchy, State, and Utopia*, Oxford, Blackwell.

Offe, C. (2006), 'Political institutions and social power: conceptual explorations', in Shapiro, I. et al. (eds.), *Rethinking Political Institutions: The Art of the State*, New York, New York University Press, pp. 9–31.

Olsen, J. (2013), 'The institutional basis of democratic accountability', *West European Politics*, 36: 447–73.

Oppenheimer, S. (2003), *The Real Eve*, New York, Carroll & Graft.

Ostrom, E. (1986), 'An agenda for the study of institutions', *Public Choice*, 48: 3–25.

Ostrom, E. (2010), 'Beyond markets and states: polycentric governance and complex economic systems', *American Economic Review*, 100: 1–33.

Panebianco, A. (ed.) (1989), *L' analisi della politica. Tradizioni di ricerca, modelli, teorie*, Bologna, Il Mulino.

Parsons, T. (1937), *The Structure of Social Action*, New York, McGraw Hill.

Parsons, T. (1954), *Essays in Sociological Theory*, Glencoe, IL, Free Press.

Parsons, T. (1975), 'Social structure and the symbolic media of exchange', in Blau, P. M. (ed.), *Approaches to the Study of Social Structure*, New York, Free Press, pp. 94–120.

Parto, S. (2003), 'Economic activity and institutions: taking stock', *Infonomics Research Memorandum Series*, Maastricht.

Patterson, D. (ed.) (2003), *Philosophy of Law and Legal Theory: An Anthology*, Oxford, Blackwell.

Pejovich, S. (1999), 'The effect of the interaction of formal and informal institutions on social stability and economic development', *Journal of Markets and Morality*, 2: 164–81.

Peters, B. G. (1998), 'Political institutions, old and new', in Goodin, R. E. and H. D. Klingemann (eds.), *A New Handbook of Political Science*, Oxford, Oxford University Press, pp. 205–20.

Peters, B. G. (1999), *Institutional Theory in Political Science: The 'New Institutionalism'*, London, Pinter.

Phillips, N., T. B. Lawrence and C. Hardy (2004), 'Discourse and institutions', *Academy of Management Review*, 29: 635–52.

Pierson, P. (2000), 'The limits of design: explaining institutional origins and change', *Governance: An International Journal of Policy and Administration*, 13: 475–99.

Pierson, P. (2004), *Politics in Time: History, Institutions, and Social Analysis*, Princeton, NJ, Princeton University Press.

Pinker, S. (2011), *The Better Angels of Our Nature*, New York, Viking.

Pitkin, H. (1967), *The Concept of Representation*, Berkeley, The University of California Press.

Poggi, G. (2000), *Durkheim*, Oxford, Oxford University Press.

Pollac, M. (1997), 'Delegation, agency and agenda-setting in the European community', *International Organization* 51: 99–134.

Polsby, N. W. (1975), 'Legislatures', in Greenstein, F. I. and N. W. Polsby (eds.), *The Handbook of Political Science*, Reading, MA, Addison-Wesley Pub. Co., vol. 5, pp. 277–91.

Popitz, H. (1992), *Phaenomene der Macht*, Tübingen, Mohr-Siebeck.

Popper, K. (1963, 5th revised ed.), *Conjectures and Refutations: The Growth of Scientific Knowledge*, London, Routledge.

Powell, W. W. and P. J. Di Maggio (eds.) (1991), *The New Institutionalism in Organizational Analysis*, Chicago, IL, University of Chicago Press.

Przeworski, A. (2004), 'Institutions matter?', *Government and Opposition*, 39: 527–40.

Rakoczy, H. and M. F. H. Schmidt (2013), 'The early ontogeny of social norms', *Child Development Perspectives*, 7: 17–21.

Rasch, B. E. and R. D. Congleton (2006), 'Amendment procedures and constitutional stability', in Congleton, R. D. and B. Swedenborg (eds.), *Democratic Constitutional Design and Public Policy*, Boston, MA, MIT Press, pp. 319–42.

Rawls, J. (2005), *Political Liberalism*, New York, Columbia University Press.

Raz, J. (1970), *The Concept of a Legal System*, Oxford, Clarendon Press.

Raz, J. (1999), *Practical Reason and Norms*, Oxford, Oxford University Press.

Raz, J. (2009), *The Authority of Law: Essays on Law and Morality*, Oxford, Oxford University Press.

Reckwitz, A. (2002), 'Toward a theory of social practices: a development in culturalist theorizing', *European Journal of Social Theory*, 5: 243–63.

Reynolds, A. (ed.) (2002), *The Architecture of Democracy: Constitutional Design, Conflict Management, and Democracy*, Oxford, Oxford University Press.

Rhodes, R. A. W., S. A. Binder and B. A. Rockman (eds.) (2006), *The Oxford Handbook of Political Institutions*, Oxford, Oxford University Press.

Richieston, P. J. and R. Boyd (2001), 'Institutional evolution in the Holocene: the rise of complex societies', in Runciman, W. G. (ed.), *The Origins of Human Social Institutions*, Proceedings of The British Academy, New York, Oxford University Press, pp. 198–234.

Ridley, F. F. (1975), 'Political Institutions: the script not the play', *Political Studies*, 23: 365–80.

Riker, W. H. (1975), 'Federalism', in Greenstein, F. I. and N. W. Polsby (eds.), *The Handbook of Political Science*, Reading, MA, Addison-Wesley Pub. Co., vol. 5, pp. 93–172.

Riker, W. H. (1980), 'Implications from the disequilibrium of majority rule for the study of institutions', *American Political Science Review*, 74: 432–44.

Riker, W. H. (1992), 'The justification of bicameralism', *International Political Science Review*, 13: 101–16.

Rokkan, S. (1970), 'Nation building, cleavage formation and the structuring of mass politics', in *Citizens, Elections, Parties: Approaches to the*

Comparative Study of the Process of Development, Oslo, Universitetsforlaget, pp. 79–82.

Rokkan, S. (1973), 'Cities, states, and nations: a dimensional model for the history of contrasts in development', in Eisenstadt, S. N. and S. Rokkan (eds.), *Building States and Nations*, New York, Sage, vol. 2, pp. 73–97.

Rokkan, S. (1999), *State Formation, Nation Building, and Mass Politics in Europe: The Theory of Stein Rokkan*, edited by P. Flora with S. Kuhnle and D. Urwin, Oxford, Oxford University Press.

Romer, T. and H. Rosenthal (1978), 'Political resource allocation, controlled agendas, and the status quo', *Public Choice*, 33: 27–43.

Roth, M. T. (1995), *Law Collection from Mesopotamia and Asia Minor*, Atlanta, GA, Scholar Press.

Rothstein, B. (1998), 'Political institutions: an overview', in Goodin, R. E. and H. D. Klingemann (eds.), *A New Handbook of Political Science*, Oxford, Oxford University Press, pp. 104–25.

Rousseau, J. J. (2012 (1762)), *The Social Contract*, London, Penguin.

Ruffini, A. (1976 (1927)), *Il principio maggioritario: profilo storico*, Milan, Adelphi.

Ruggie, J. G. (1993), 'Territoriality and beyond: problematising modernity in international relations', *International Organization*, 47: 138–74.

Runciman, W. G. (ed.) (2001), *The Origins of Human Social Institutions*, Proceedings of The British Academy, New York, Oxford University Press.

Russell, M. (2001), 'What are second chambers for?', *Parliamentary Affairs*, 54, 3: 442–58.

Salamini, F. et al. (2002), 'Genetics and geography of wild cereals domestication in the Near East', *Nature Reviews Genetics*, 3: 429–41.

Sartori, G. (1963), *Democrazia e definizioni*, Bologna, Il Mulino.

Sartori, G. (1974), 'Tecniche decisionali e sistema dei comitati', *Rivista Italiana di Scienza Politica*, 4: 5–42.

Sartori, G. (1987), *The Theory of Democracy Revisited Part One: The Contemporary Debate*, Chatham, Chatham House Publishers.

Sartori G. (1991), 'Comparing and Miscomparing', *Journal of Theoretical Politics*, 3: 243–57.

Sartori, G. (1997), *Comparative Constitutional Engineering*, New York, New York University Press.

Scharpf, F. (1995), 'Essai sur la démocratie dans les systèmes de négotiation', in Telò, M. (ed.), *Démocratie et construction européenne*, Brussels, Editions de L'université de Bruxelles, pp. 145–69.

Scharpf, F. (1997), *Games Real Actors Play: Actor-Centered Institutionalism in Policy Research*, New York, Westview Press.

Scharpf, F. W. (2000), 'Institutions in comparative policy research', *Comparative Political Studies*, 33: 762–90.

Schedler, A. (1994), *Taking Electoral Promises Seriously: Reflections on the Content of Procedural Democracy*, IPSA, Berlin, August.

Schipman, P. (2014), 'How do you kill 86 mammoths?', *Quaternary International*, 30: 1–9.

Schmidt, K. (2006), *Sie bauten die ersten Tempel. Das rätselhafte Heiligtum der Steinzeitjäger*, Munich, C. H. Beck.

Schmidt, M. F. H. et al. (2012), 'Young children enforce social norms', *Current Directions in Psychological Science*, 21: 232–36.

Schmitt, C. (2004), *On the Three Types of Juristic Thought*, Westport, CT, Praeger.

Schofield, N. and G. Caballero (eds.) (2011), *Political Economy of Institutions, Democracy and Voting*, Berlin, Springer-Verlag.

Schotter, A. (1981), *The Economic Theory of Social Institutions*, Cambridge, Cambridge University Press.

Scott, R. W. (2008, 3rd ed., first 1995), *Institutions and Organizations: Ideas and Interests*, Thousand Oaks, CA, Sage Publications.

Searle, J. R. (2005), 'What is an institution?', *Journal of Institutional Economics*, 1: 1–22.

Searle, J. R. (2010), *Making the Social World: The Structure of Human Civilization*, Oxford, Oxford University Press.

Searle, J. R. (2012), *Speech Acts*, Cambridge, Cambridge University Press.

Selznick, P. (1957), *Leadership in Organization*, London, Harper and Row.

Sen, A. (1964), 'Preferences, votes and the transitivity of majority decisions', *Review of Economic Studies*, 31: 163–5.

Service, E. (1975), *Origins of the State and Civilization*, New York, Random House.

Shapiro, I. et al. (eds.) (2006), *Rethinking Political Institutions: The Art of the State*, New York, New York University Press.

Shapiro, L. (1969), 'Collective leadership as lack of leadership', *Survey*, Winter/Spring, pp. 193–200.

Shapiro, S. P. (2005), 'Agency theory', *Annual Review of Sociology*, 31 (August): 263–84.

Shepsle, K. A. (1986), 'Institutional equilibrium and equilibrium institutions', in Weisberg, H. (ed.), *The Science of Politics*, New York, Agathon, pp. 51–82.

Shepsle, K. A. (1989), 'Studying institutions: some lessons from the rational choice approach', *Journal of Theoretical Politics*, 1: 131–47.

Shepsle, K. A. (2006), 'Rational choice institutionalism', in Rhodes, R. A. W., S. A. Binder and B. A. Rockman (eds.), *The Oxford Handbook of Political Institutions*, Oxford, Oxford University Press, pp. 23–38.

Shepsle, K. A. and B. R. Weingast (2010), 'Why so much stability? Majority voting, legislative institutions, and Gordon Tullock'. Paper, March.

Shugart, M. S. and J. M. Carey (1992), *Presidents and Assemblies: Constitutional Design and Electoral Dynamics*, Cambridge, Cambridge University Press.

Simon, H. A. (1957), *Administrative Behavior*, London, Macmillan.

Sjoblom, G. (1993), 'Some critical remarks on March and Olsen's "Rediscovering Institutions"', *Journal of Theoretical Politics*, 5: 397–40.

Sjoblom, G. (1994), 'Notes on the Concept of "Institution"', paper presented at the XVI World Congress of the International Political Science Association, 21–25 August, Berlin.

Skocpol, T. (1979), *States and Social Revolutions: A Comparative Analysis of France, Russia and China*, Cambridge, Cambridge University Press.

Smith, H. J. (2005), *Parenting for Primates*, Cambridge, MA, Harvard University Press.

Smith, J. E. et al. (2016), 'Leadership in mammalian societies: emergence, distribution, power, and payoff', *Trends in Ecology & Evolution*, 31: 54–66.

Spinoza, B. (1991 (1670)), *Theologico-Political Treatise*, Indianapolis, IN, Hackett Publishing Company.

Spitzer, S. (1975), 'Punishment and social organization: a study of Durkheim's theory of penal evolution', *Law & Society Review*, 9: 613–38.

Steinmo, S., K. Thelen and F. Longstreth (eds.) (1992), *Structuring Politics: Historical Institutionalism in Comparative Analysis*, Cambridge, Cambridge University Press.

Stiglitz, J. (1987), 'Principal and agent', in *The New Palgrave: A Dictionary of Economics*, vol. 3, pp. 966–71.

Stiner, M. C. et al. (2009), 'Cooperative hunting and meat sharing 400–200 kya at Qesem Cave, Israel', *Proceedings of the Natural Academy of Sciences*, 32, 106: 13207–12.

Stoppino, M. (2001, 3rd ed.), *Potere e teoria politica*, Milan: Giuffré.

Streeck, W. and P. Schmitter (1985), 'Community, market, state – and associations? The prospective contribution of interest governance to social order', *European Sociological Review*, 1: 119–38.

Strøm, K. (2000), 'Delegation and accountability in parliamentary democracies', *European Journal of Political Research*, 37: 261–89.

Strøm, K., W. C. Müller and T. Bergman (eds.) (2006), *Delegation and Accountability in Parliamentary Democracies*, Oxford, Oxford University Press.

Stueber, K. R. (2005), 'How to think about rules and rule following', *Philosophy of the Social Sciences*, 35: 307–23.

Styron, W. (1976), *Sophie's Choice*, New York, Random House.

Suarez-Rodriguez, J. J. (2016), 'Le fondement des principes juridiques: une question problématique', *Civilizar*, 16: 51–62.

Sugiyama, S. (2005), *Human Sacrifice, Militarism and Rulership: Materialization of State Ideology at the Feathered Serpent Pyramid, Teotihuacan*, Cambridge, Cambridge University Press.

Symons, D. (1989), 'A critique of Darwinian anthropology', *Ethology and Sociobiology*, 10: 131–44.

Taylor, M. (1976), *Anarchy or Cooperation*, London, Wiley (revised as: (1987), *The Possibility of Cooperation*, New York, Cambridge University Press).

Telò, M. (ed.) (1995), *Démocratie et construction européenne*, Brussels, Editions de L'université de Bruxelles.

Tharakan, G. (2007), 'The Maduga and Kurumba of Kerala, South India, and the social organisation of the hunting and gathering', *Journal of Ecological Anthropology*, 11: 12–13.

Thelen, K. (2003), 'How institutions evolve: insights from comparative historical analysis', in Mahoney, J. and D. Rueschemeyer (eds.), *Comparative Historical Analysis in the Social Sciences*, Cambridge, Cambridge University Press, pp. 208–40.

Thelen, K. and S. Steinmo (1992), 'Historical institutionalism in comparative politics', in Steinmo, S., K. Thelen and F. Longstreth (eds.), *Structuring Politics: Historical Institutionalism in Comparative Analysis*, Cambridge, Cambridge University Press, pp. 1–31.

The New Palgrave: A Dictionary of Economics (1987), 6 vols., London, Palgrave Macmillan.

Tilly, C. (ed.) (1975), *The Formation of National States in Western Europe*, Princeton, NJ, Princeton University Press.

Tomain, J. P. (1973), 'Executive agreements and the bypassing of congress', *The Journal of International Law and Economics*, 8: 129–32.

Tomasello, M. (2003), *Constructing a Language: A Usage-Based Theory of Language Acquisition*, Cambridge, MA, Harvard University Press.

Tomasello, M. (2014), *A Natural History of Human Thinking*, Cambridge, MA, Harvard University Press.

Tomasello, M. (2016), *A Natural History of Human Morality*, Cambridge, MA, Harvard University Press.

Tomasello, M. (2018), 'L'origine della moralità', *Le Scienze*, November, pp. 66–71.

Traenhardt, D. (2010), 'Mehr Demokratie oder mehr Gewaltenteilung?', in Frantz, C. and K. Schubert (eds.), *Einführung in die Politikwissenschaft*, Hamburg, Lit, pp. 91–111.

Trivers, R. L. (1971), 'The evolution of reciprocal altruism', *Quarterly Review of Biology*, 46: 35–57.

Tsebelis, G. (1990), *Nested Games: Rational Choice in Comparative Politics*, Berkeley, University of California Press.

Tsebelis, G. (1995), 'Decision making in political systems: veto players in presidentialism, parliamentarism, multicameralism and multipartism', *British Journal of Political Science*, 25: 289–325.

Tsebelis, G. (2002), *Veto Players: How Political Institutions Work*, Princeton, NJ, Princeton University Press.

Tsebelis, G. and B. E. Rasch (1995), 'Patterns of bicameralism', in Doering, H. (ed.), *Parliaments and Majority Rule in Western Europe*, New York, St Martin's Press, pp. 365–90.

Tuomela, R. (1995), *The Importance of Us: A Philosophical Study of Basic Social Notions*, Stanford, CA, Stanford University Press.

Tuomela, R. (2007), *The Philosophy of Sociality: The Shared Point of View*, Oxford, Oxford University Press.

Tuschhoff, C. (1999), 'The compounding effect: the impact of federalism on the concept of representation', *West European Politics*, 22: 16–33.

Uhr, J. (2006), 'Bicameralism', in Rhodes, R. A. W., S. A. Binder and B. A. Rockman (eds.), *The Oxford Handbook of Political Institutions*, Oxford, Oxford University Press, pp. 474–93.

Urpelainen, U. (2011), 'The origins of social institutions', *Journal of Theoretical Politics*, 23: 215–40.

van der Heijden, J. (2011), 'A short history of studying incremental institutional change: does explaining institutional change provide any new explanations?', *Regulation and Governance*, 4: 230–43.

van Hees, M. (1997), 'Explaining institutions: a defense of reductionism', *European Journal of Political Research*, 32: 51–69.

van Vugt, M., R. Hogan and R. B. Kaiser (2008), 'Leadership, followership, and evolution: some lessons from the past', *American Psychologist*, 63: 182–96.

Vinogradoff, P. (ed.) (2004), *Essays in Legal History*, Oxford, Oxford University Press.

Volpi, E. (2019), 'The politics of turning coat: a comparative and historical analysis of party switching'. Florence, European University Institute, PhD dissertation.

von Gierke, O. (2004 (1913)), 'Uber die Geschichte des Majoritatsprinzips', in Vinogradoff, P. (ed.), *Essays in Legal History*, Oxford, Oxford University Press, pp. 312–35.

Wallis, J. and B. Weingast (2008), 'Dysfunctional or optimal institutions? State debt limitations, the structure of state and local governments, and the finance of American infrastructure', in Garrett, E., E. Graddy and H. Jackson (eds.), *Fiscal Challenges: An Interdisciplinary Approach to Budget Policy*, Cambridge, Cambridge University Press, pp. 331–65.

Walsh, A. (2000), 'Evolutionary psychology and the origins of justice', *Justice Quarterly*, 17: 841–64.

Washburn, S. L. and C. S. Lancaster (1968), 'The evolution of hunting', in Lee, R. B. and I. DeVore (eds.), *Man the Hunter*, New York, Aldine Publishing Company, chapter 32.

Weber, M. (1978 (1922)), *Economy and Society*, edited by G. Roth and C. Wittich, Berkeley, University of California Press.

Weisberg, H. (ed.) (1986), *The Science of Politics*, New York, Agathon.

Williams, G. C. (1966), *Adaptation and Natural Selection*, Princeton, NJ, Princeton University Press.

Williamson, O. E. (1990), *Organization Theory: From Chester Barnard to the Present and Beyond*, New York, Oxford University Press.

Williamson, O. E. (2002), 'The theory of the firm as governance structure: from choice to contract', *Journal of Economic Perspectives*, 16: 171–95.

Wilson, D. S. (2015), *Does Altruism Exist? Culture, Genes, and the Welfare of Others*, New Haven, CT, Yale University Press.

Wilson, D. S. and H. E. O. Wilson (2007), 'Rethinking the theoretical foundation of sociobiology', *The Quarterly Review of Biology*, 82: 327–48.

Wilson, H. E. O. (1975), *Sociobiology*, Cambridge, MA, Harvard University Press.

Wong, K. (2014), 'L'ascesa del predatore umano', *Le Scienze*, 554: 54–9.

Woodhouse, D. (1994), *Ministers and Parliament: Accountability in Theory and Practice*, Oxford, Clarendon Press.

Woodman, G. (2009), 'Ideological combs and social observations: recent debates about legal pluralism', *Journal of Law and Society*, 42: 21–59.

Wrangham, R. (2019), *The Goodness Paradox: The Strange Relationship between Virtue and Violence in Human Evolution*, New York, Pantheon Books.

Wright, G. (2006), *Slavery and American Economic Development*, Baton Rouge, Louisiana State University Press.

Wright, H. (1977), 'Recent research on the origin of the state', *Annual Review of Anthropology*, 6: 379–97.

Xenophon (317 BCE (1914)), *Cyropaedia*, 7 vols, translated by W. Miller, Cambridge, MA, Harvard University Press.

Zeder, M. A. (2007), 'The neolithic macro (re)evolution: macroevolutionary theory and the study of culture change', *Journal of Archaeological Research*, 17: 611–63.

Index